CROSSING THE RIVER

Creating a Conceptual Revolution in Community & Disability

DAVID B. SCHWARTZ

BROOKLINE BOOKS

Copyright © 1992 Brookline Books

Library of Congress Cataloging-in-Publication Data

Schwartz, David B., 1948 -
    Crossing the river : creating a conceptual revolution in
community and disability / David B. Schwartz.
        p.   cm.
    Includes bibliographical references and index.
    ISBN 0-914797-54-9 (hardback): $34.95. — ISBN 0-914797-82-4
(paper) : $24.95
        1. Developmentally disabled — Social conditions.
    2. Developmentally disabled — Services for. 3. Social integration.
    4. Developmentally disabled — United States. I. Title.
    HV1570.S345 1992
    362.1'968 — dc20   91-43833
                                                                        CIP

An excerpt from The Psychological Sense of Community by Seymour B. Sarason (1974) is reprinted with permission of Jossey-Bass, San Francisco, California.

The author has dedicated all royalties to be donated to efforts to assist individuals with disabilities in Pennsylvania.

To Beth,
Who knows her communities;
and to
Dr. Carl Berger,
Who knows his profession.

"I am done with great things and big things, great institutions and big successes, and I am for those tiny invisible molecular moral forces that work from individual to individual, creeping through the crannies of the world like so many rootlets, or like the capillary oozing of water, yet which, if you give them time, will rend the hardest monuments of man's pride."

William James

Contents

Series Editor's Preface

In the post World War II era there have been several revolutions in how people with developmental disabilities have been regarded and treated. The first was initiated by parents who sought to obtain recognition and improved services for their children. Heretofore these children had no nonprofessional advocacy groups, one result of which was that programs and institutions for these children were second-class citizens at budget time. Those who oversaw programs and services were relatively powerless individuals in state departments of mental health. The rise of a militant parent organization heralded a realignment of power.

The second revolution was, in part, a consequence of the 1954 desegregation decision in that advocacy for handicapped individuals became powered by consideration of *rights*. Here nothing is more revelatory of what was in the air than the change in title of the National Association for Retarded Children to the National Association for Retarded *Citizens*. Citizens have rights no less than anyone else. To call these handicapped individuals children was to entrust their welfare and future to the goodness of others, and that was far less dependable than protection by constitutional rights.

A third revolution is wrapped up in the term deinstitutionalization, a set of values and rights that gave power to the simple idea that where a person could live and work should be determined by where a person could *learn to live and work*. Labels were not grounds for segregation. Segregation was a last, not first, resort.

All of these changes — remarkable for the relative speed with which they had impact — coalesced, so to speak, in federal law 94-142, the Education for All Handicapped Children Act of 1975.

Entering the field as I did in 1942, I have lived through these dramatic changes. That they have brought improvements in the lives of people goes without saying. But it is also the case that each of these changes promised more than was realistically possible and was sobered by obstacles that implementation inevitably encounters, especially when a change requires attitude change in the society in general.

David Schwartz has had the courage to look sympathetically, critically, and analytically at the discrepancy between how far we have come and how far we wanted to go. He is no Johnny-come-lately to the substantive and administrative issues under the umbrella of developmental disabilities. What he conveys to us so clearly, concretely, and skillfully is how dangerous it is not to face squarely the inadequacies of ways of thinking that earlier had been productive but are now a source of obstacles to creativity.

Although this book will be of obvious interest to those in one way or other in the sprawling field of developmental disabilities, its virtues go far beyond any one field. Mr. Schwartz is a thinker, a cool observer of the social scene, an illuminator of axioms underlying its conventional wisdom, axioms which, because they are unverbalized and silent, wield tremendous power. Mr. Schwartz takes seriously that the unexamined life — whether it be our work, family, or personal life — can be our greatest folly.

Fortunately, his style of writing is as refreshing as the issues are important. Of all the books I have read in the area, none comes close to this one. It is interesting, important, and thought provoking. Mr. Schwartz is not up in the clouds. He is down here on earth, directing our attention to issues that if we do not confront *now* will mean that complacency is preferred to change.

Seymour B. Sarason
Yale University

Foreword

Those who, like me, are privileged to count David B. Schwartz as one of our friends and colleagues know that he has wit, wisdom, and willingness. (How else could he have endured and succeeded in a bureaucracy and brought such change to his adopted state, Pennsylvania?) This book adds to his reputation by being an ambitious and friendly critique of the ways that services are delivered to people with developmental disabilities.

I say so because few texts in the field of mental retardation and developmental disabilities have attempted so much as this one. For starters, Schwartz takes the best thoughts of some truly pioneering intellectuals in the field of developmental disabilities and shows how they can be put into effect under present circumstances — circumstances that challenge the very heart of those ideas and present formidable obstacles to living them out. The reader will learn early on that Schwartz's professional genealogy ties him directly to Seymour Sarason, Burton Blatt, Wolf Wolfensberger, John McKnight, John O'Brien, Karl Koenig (founder of the Camphill movement), and Jean Vanier (founder of the L'Arche movement).

This book reveals the impact of those extraordinary individuals on the field of developmental disabilities. More than that, however, this book extends their work by showing how its visions can be put into effect through, not in spite of, the aid of government. At the risk of being thought nihilistic, Schwartz inveighs against much of what the field has created, including in particular the "community-based care" movement. Yet, like his intellectual forebears, he does not seek to jettison the progress, only to ensure that, by constructive critique, it is not perverted and rendered dangerous to those very individuals whom it seeks to help.

Nihilism and reformism are heavy concepts, even in a book dedicated to concepts. What makes Schwartz's treatise particularly appealing, and ambitious, is that it is explicitly existential. One can make a convincing argument that Schwartz's intellectual predecessors also include Sartre and Camus. It was they, after all, who asked about the meaning of life in an age of scientific rationalism.

These questions take somewhat different forms in this book, yet only in degree, not in kind: Once one knows about the nature of a developmental disability and about how the norms and forms of society affect people with disability and indeed all of us (adversely, Schwartz argues), one also must ask, "so what?" That is the critical and fundamentally existential question: so one knows something, so what? What difference does it make? Schwartz argues, and I agree, that it makes all the difference in the world: It is not enough to know, unless one also acts. Schwartz tells us what some of us already know and what many of us may not want to know: we have not been human enough, we have been too mechanistic in our approaches to people with disabilities and to ourselves, and we have relied too much and too exclusively on professionalism and advocacy. Yet we have not "cured" people with disabilities or ourselves by our presence with them. What we must do, he says, is to be less the scientific rationalist (less Cartesian and Newtonian) and more the poet, more the caring, open, vulnerable, risk-taking person; less the technological society, more the affective one.

This book is ambitious in still a third sense, for it is remarkably catholic, that is, inclusive. In an era that preaches inclusion and participation by people with disabilities, it is rare to find a text within the field of disabilities that itself is inclusive in its conceptual reach. The "paradigm shifts" made known to us by Kuhn's critique of the laws of physics and epistemology are for Schwartz only partial examples of how scientific conceptions are progressively discredited and replaced by new ones. Changes in how medicine is practiced and agriculture is husbanded are analogies for his message. His documentation of the Hegelian construct (thesis, antithesis, and synthesis) in those disciplines, and most usefully in the field of developmental disabilities, captures our attention and persuades us to listen carefully for his message. His message is that the human ecology is out of whack, that reliance on professionalism and advocacy is necessary, yes, but not sufficient; that policy reform and technology are necessary, yes, but not sufficient; that our being helpers and healers is necessary, yes, but not sufficient. Time and again, one finds the word and the message: get our lives into balance. That is what is both necessary and will be sufficient.

To rebalance our lives, Schwartz says, requires us to look at ourselves and people with disabilities in a different perspective. What is necessary is to see people with disabilities as making positive — indeed, essential — contributions to all of us. This is their instrumental value to us individually; it is their ultimate value to us as a society. As individuals, we are leavened by their presence in our lives; as a society, we are enriched and bonded to each other by their presence in and participation in our lives. After all, it is one thing to be "in" the community; it is quite another to be "of" it.

Professionalism, advocacy, policy reform, and technology can achieve the "in" but not, alone, the "of". To achieve the "of" — Sarason's psychological sense of community — one needs to recognize not only that individuals with disabilities make positive contributions to us individually and collectively (a theme developed and articulated by the students of theology and disability, such as Gaventa, Palmer, and Nouwen), but also that the prevailing political philosophy and policies founded on it are blockades to this new self-view and world view.

One thinks not only about the communal ideal, but also about John Donne's famous poem: No man is an island, we are all part of the main; therefore, never seek to know for whom the bell tolls, it tolls for us all. What we lose, Schwartz argues, when we lose our present self-view and world view is our isolation and, arguably, our anomie, our sense of desperation. Most men may live lives of quiet desperation, and most professionals, family members, and people with disabilities may be part of that main, in Donne's analogy. But that need not be so, as Schwartz, like his intellectual precursors, argues. Indeed, in the Camphill villages, in L'Arche communities, and indeed in large cities and small hamlets of Pennsylvania, "in" and "of" (attachment to the main — a rebalancing of our human ecology) is taking place. There is a not so quiet revolution under way, and Schwartz not only has been part of it, he tells about it here. It is a revolution not limited to the disability field but of general import and impact.

The course of my own efforts in the field has added to my appreciation of this attempt to reformulate its premises. I mentioned the positive contributions theme in my essays in Parents Speak Out (1976, 1985) and in addresses to the AAMR annual meetings in 1985 and 1986; I have critiqued the mechanistic paradigms in my essays on aversive interventions; I have helped create a L'Arche community in Kansas City and served on the national board of advisors for the Camphill communities of North America; I have begun a "community participation/partners" effort in my hometown of Lawrence, Kansas; I have written about the political philosophy of civic republicanism and urged that it take the place of individualistic liberalism; and I have written true stories and imaginary fables about disability because rationalism and data fail too often to tell the story, to reveal a truth.

I wondered as I read this fine book what I might have done to be part of that revolution, part of the rebalancing of the human ecology, part of the rejoining that puts "of" in place of "in". That is not a question I will answer in full here: suffice to say that I am satisfied to be part of the cadre that is crossing the river, that is making an incursion on the past so that we might assure our collective futures.

The question for you, reader, is the same: what have you done, what will you do, to consider crossing the river and then to get into the lifeboats that head from one shore to another? Ask that of yourself as you read this book. If you will, and if you will answer the questions, you will be doubly enriched by Schwartz: you will learn, and you will act accordingly.

Thank you, David, for writing to all of us and about some of us.

H. RUTHERFORD TURNBULL III
Professor of Special Education and Law
    Co-director, Beach Center on Families and Disability
The University of Kansas, Lawrence, Kansas.

Author's Preface

One of my earliest memories of my father is of him sitting in his study writing a book. It took him twenty years. He would come home from his demanding days at office, clinic, and university, and he would· write. He wrote, I believe, for a number of reasons. He wanted to think through and make sense of all that he was seeing during the day; all of the many patients, all of the diverse clinical problems. He wanted to share the new approaches that he and his colleagues were developing, in the hope that they might alleviate others' suffering. And he wished to try to offer some contribution to his chosen field.

I say all of this to answer the question that an author traditionally addresses in a preface: Why did you write this book? I wrote it, I believe, for the same reasons. I also have demanding days. But the process of trying to think through the daily experience in which I have been engaged is certainly worth the evenings involved. I, too, hope that in some modest ways the lives of some people may be influenced for the better by this volume. And I also wish to offer something to the ongoing thinking of my field, a field which has offered me such rich opportunities for challenge, growth, and service.

This book grew out of my experience serving as Executive Director of the Pennsylvania Developmental Disabilities Planning Council. Although I have written much of this in the first person, it should be understood that it reflects the thinking and work of a good many people with whom it has been my good fortune to be associated. It is from the community of Council members, committee members, and friends that everything attempted and reported in various parts of this book flowed.

This group, over the years, developed into an energetic community devoted to both inquiry and action. What might have been merely another board arguing over the politics of allocations became over time a fellowship of members committed, in the phrase of Chairperson Joe Leonard, to "reasoned discourse." Members tried to strive for a forum which encouraged spirited debate, but in which there was room for sharp disagreement without rancor. It was not uncommon to see people who had been in passionate disagreement over some proposed action at a late night committee meeting later sharing a drink and warm conversation in the hotel bar.

Through countless meetings, retreats, trips, shared meals, arguments, and the meeting of shared dangers, we eventually discovered that we were living out the bustling and bumpy reality of participatory democracy. Like all democratic processes, it has been a hard one. There have always been diverse points of view about how the situation of people with developmental disabilities should best be addressed. I would not want to give the impression that consensus was achieved by the full community on the validity of the approach which I outline here. Other different approaches were always actively pursued, although I do not specifically talk about them here. The environment of such diverse opinion served to test and challenge everything that was proposed or done. Everything had to be hammered out in a difficult process. That has been all to the good.

It goes without saying that while this book arose out of our thinking and work together, it represents solely my own perspective on and interpretation of that experience. It would not surprise me if no one involved agreed with me completely, and I am sure that some people may very much disagree with me. I speak then only for myself; this in no way represents the opinions or official policies of the Pennsylvania Developmental Disabilities Planning Council or the Commonwealth of Pennsylvania.

Acknowledgements

I can only acknowledge in the briefest fashion the contributions of a few of the many people to whom I owe gratitude for the work leading up to this book and to the book itself. Chief among these are the two exceptional individuals who have served as chairpersons of the Council during my tenure and to whom I owe so much: Lucy D. Hackney and Joe H. Leonard. They served as inspired leaders, offered me encouragement, guidance and caution, and were always there when I needed them. Mark Friedman also served in a key role in the development of the group and in the approach which we attempted; I can only offer my thanks for the countless hours of work together. Joan Goodman, Robert Garrett, Leslie Mathis, and Joanna Johnson chaired important committees, and Bill Gannon made important contributions as vice-chairperson. There have been so many other important contributors to the Council's work that I wish that it were possible to thank each of them individually.

The extraordinarily talented staff members of the Council deserve a special mention: Harry Guise, Don Hahn, Rosemary Barrett, Mary Kent, Joan Ober, Bonnie Snyder, and Sandra Dusek have triumphed over bureaucracy, misunderstanding, and the occasional personalized displeasure of disappointed funding applicants with perpetual good humor and efficiency despite any and all obstacles. I also owe a particular debt to two friends and advisors. Mel Knowlton served as a seasoned guide to the treacherous terrain of government and of public position when I first arrived, and helped me to think through most of the initial directions. Bill Madeira offered counsel and diplomatic abilities when they were most needed. Appreciation is due as well to the key state officials who afforded us the freedom to pursue the unconventional.

In the writing of this book itself I owe my thanks to a few other people for encouragement and help. Bob Perske reintroduced me to the work of Thomas Kuhn and offered useful advice about how to go about the business of writing. Helen and Hubert Zipperlen and John O'Brien read this manuscript and offered useful suggestions. Ronald House offered me much appreciated hospitality and access to materials when I most needed it. Above all, I owe thanks to Dr. Seymour Sarason, who suggested that I undertake this project and who as series editor helped with its organization and with other specific guidance. Having an opportunity to work with someone whose writings have been so influential in most of my professional work has been a rare and wonderful privilege. Finally, I want to thank my wife Beth; no greater love has any writer than to edit another's work.

I hope that in some small way this volume is some justification for the faith of so many people in me and in our efforts together.

DAVID B. SCHWARTZ
Harrisburg
September, 1990

"The term 'developmental disability' means a severe, chronic disability of a person which —

(A) is attributed to a mental or physical impairment or combination of mental or physical impairments;

(B) is manifested before the person attains age twenty-two;

(C) is likely to continue indefinitely;

(D) results in substantial functional limitations in three or more of the following areas of major life activity: (i) self-care, (ii) receptive and expressive language, (iii) learning, (iv) mobility, (v) self-direction, (vi) capacity for independent living, and (vii) economic self-sufficiency; and

(E) reflects the person's need for a combination and sequence of special, interdisciplinary, or generic care, treatment, or other services which are of livelong or extended duration and are individually planned and coordinated."

Public Law 100-146, The Developmental Disabilities Assistance and Bill of Rights Amendments of 1987.

CHAPTER 1

Introduction and Plan of the Book

There is some evidence that a sea change is taking place in the field of developmental disabilities. What do I mean by a sea change? In one sense, things tossed under the vast influence of the oceans can undergo marked transformations. Pearls can form in oysters from the irritation of sand. The term, similarly, can describe the transformation which can affect a voyager by ship. Sea change can produce a subtle alteration in the way the world appears to us, in the way we think and feel. Such a change comes upon the traveler after one has pulled away from the familiar shore of ordinary life and sees it receding in the distance, with the destination yet far from sight. One is afloat between points of solid earth, off in the space between two places. During a sea change, experienced cruise passengers will tell you, the world one has left behind seems strangely distant and suspended. One may think unusual thoughts or do unusual things while the world is in transition upon the seas.

The journey that a field like developmental disabilities takes in the unfolding of its history is a voyage not between places or worlds, but between views of the world: *Weltanschauung*, as the Germans call it. Such changes have to do with the way we view the situation of people with these disabilities in society. From that viewpoint or conception we derive our many undertakings. Every law, every policy, every social program of an age can be understood as expressing, usually unconsciously, the reigning world view of the time.

Less than eighty years ago, for example, people with mental retardation were considered by informed professional opinion to constitute a collective genetic reservoir of social evil and corruption in the body of humankind. That conception of disability led dedicated professionals of the time to build institutions to segregate or even sterilize such people.

Less than forty years ago that world view began to be displaced by the parent advocacy movement and, later, by a new generation of professionals of which I am a member. My generation, led by a new conception of the work to be done, struggled to overcome public fear of people with developmental disabilities in order to establish group homes in neighborhoods. What we struggled against was fear promoted in large part by our predecessors' conception of things.

Our conception of mental retardation or any other developmental disability, our view of these persons and their capabilities, determines what we do as individuals and as groups, and what the public policy of each historical age will be.

This is a time of great change, of rapid and complex movement within the field of developmental disabilities. Beneath all of this movement, beneath the new inventions and practices and newly debunked myths and newly proclaimed truths must lie changes in the conception of developmental disability itself. Is a significant change occurring? Are we in fact on the sea between two countries of belief? It is the purpose of this book to explore and address that question. If another conceptual change is taking place, understanding it may lead us to know what actions we will find ourselves taking next.

Our collective conception of developmental disabilities is inextricably intertwined with the larger collective world view of our culture. Such fields as this one, in fact, can be said to mirror values and beliefs in the larger culture. One may learn much about the world view of the culture by examining the views in a particular field of endeavor. Just as a small fossil may, to the practiced eye, help one to extrapolate the climate of the earth during a certain period of historical time, so may changes in the theory and practice of developmental disabilities reveal subtle shifts in the larger cultural climate of belief. "Mental retardation," Seymour Sarason once noted, "is a good window through which to look at our society."

When I started in this field in 1970, there was a clear note of optimism in the fledgling movement to build a community services system for people with disabilities. All of the elements necessary for such optimism were there. One was the particular time in national history. Many of us involved in the work were children of the sixties, shaped in one of those periods of national history in which we believed that the world might be made anew. A new order of peace and of love seemed at hand. It was, admittedly, up against great odds, but is not opposition an essential element for any movement? One could go to the rain and music of Woodstock and find social harmony without institutionalized overbearing authority. One could even stop a government's senseless war.

The "deinstitutionalization" movement of persons with developmental disabilities, like the anti war movement, was a movement against a current mode of social and cultural belief and practice. It was a reaction against the evil, soul-killing institutions in which so many people were incarcerated, as revealed by Burton Blatt's 1966 *Christmas in Purgatory*. It was a reform movement, and bureaucratic institutions were the necessary malevolent opponent in need of reform, or, in this case, replacement. We advocated not reform but revolution. Our institutions became our "Johnson's [Vietnam] War" against which we could define ourselves, archetypal young heroes against the old kings of the institutional superintendents. Like Pinel in 18th century France, we led the shackled and chained to liberty, out of the dark stone walls of the state institutions and into the light of the sun.

This new social movement involved by design the creation of thousands of new settings.[1] These settings, the group homes and fledgling agencies, formed the seeds of communities called together by vision and opposition. They were, like most new settings from marriage to nations, forges of growth and personal transformation for all involved in them. It was a heady time in social reform.

That heady time is now undeniably past. The new settings and the new "alternative" community system they collectively formed are now riddled with seemingly intractable problems. Task forces on finance, on abuse, on staff recruitment and retention meet urgently. Remedial actions are proposed. Yet underneath such actions lies a sense that the breakdown of our precious new settings is proceeding so rapidly that our efforts, redoubled though they might be, are insufficient and in vain.

This half-spoken disillusionment, this gnawing sense of crisis that we feel powerless to control, is evident not only in our own field. It is apparent in society as a whole. As a culture we feel adrift. The temper of the country today is not that of the Peace Corps and Vista and a War on Poverty when we "knew" what was to be done (whether or not this turns out to be true is another matter) and we set out to do it. Although we in social services are extremely, even frenetically, active, we are not really sure what we should do. We confess privately that we lack faith that our social programs, any social programs at all, can be made to work anymore. Crime, education, children's welfare, disability; all seem out of control. We retreat into cultural pessimism, "blaming the victim," and a generalized xenophobia. Prisons expand, drug abusers assume their place as the newest corrupt seed within society, mental hospital commitment laws are loosened.

Yet against this anomie, this sinking sense of loss of direction, some indication of a new direction seems to be forming. As always happens at such times, a new light begins to emerge around which people, although only a few at first, begin to gather. The light is a new conception. It is light needed to fill the void of our disillusionment with the increasing failure of the community system that we have built.

This conception has to do with rediscovering the importance for all people of being and feeling embedded in a web of personal relationships, an essential element we somehow neglected in our enthusiasm to build what we conceived to be caring systems. It has to do with that essential sense of having a "sense of place" in the world which Seymour Sarason termed "the psychological sense of community." This sense, Sarason pointed out, is the key element without which no caring can arise from a human service setting.

This new direction in thinking, predictably, is forming the germ of a fledgling movement within the field. Again, all of the preconditions for such a movement exist: enthusiasm, contrast, and resistance. As usual, it mirrors similar changes stirring in the world view of society at large. Against the established belief system supporting chemical agriculture and agribusiness a small organic gardening movement increasingly thrives. Against the prevailing belief in the necessity of nuclear power (I write this a few miles upriver from Three Mile Island) a small movement proposing solar energy, conservation, and other local approaches holds on despite enormous opposition by power companies. Small, as we remember E.F. Schumacher said, is beautiful.

This book is about this issue — a change in world view — as seen in the field of developmental disabilities. Specifically, it has to do with the experience of one small governmental and advocacy organization, the Pennsylvania Developmental Disabilities Planning Council, which found itself in the flux of unfolding history where forces of change could be observed, engaged, and learned from. This book is an attempt to discover and reason out what this change in conceptions may be about.

Developmental Disabilities Planning Councils, or Governors' Councils on Developmental Disabilities, as they are sometimes called, are an unusual type of setting. While located in government, they have memberships and constituencies more typical of voluntary associations, and grant-making roles similar to foundations. They exist in the midst of the tumult of government, service providers, and advocacy but at a remove from ongoing operational responsibilities. They are thus in a good place to observe developing trends in the field.

Their charge to spend federal funds imaginatively to improve the situation of people with developmental disabilities in their states, however, is their primary advantage in learning. Being ambiguously and indirectly in the midst of everything and blessed with rare opportunities to experiment with new ideas, they provide an unequaled platform from which to engage trends, try out new concepts and theories, and test them against the hard rock of reality.

The academic always runs the risk of developing theory untested in action, while the social activist runs the opposite risk of pursuing action unguided by theory. Both extremes are insufficient for trying to understand and act effectively in the world. I am reminded of Sir William Osler, who said that while practice without theory was like sailing into an uncharted sea, theory without practice was like not going to sea at all. The curious makeup of these organizations affords them rare opportunities to chart seas from a vessel immediately afloat upon them. They can be places in which theory and practice in public policy can be woven together in the deep and rapidly evolving currents, weather and even storms, one eye always fixed upon the guiding stars. This experience is important. Yet it is not through experience alone, as Myles Horton cautioned, that one learns. It is only through analyzed and reflected experience that learning takes place. If one learned through experience alone there would be no market for psychotherapy.

Problems Encountered in Organizing the Book

Conceiving and organizing this book presented various conceptual and practical problems. For one, it was to attempt to tease out and order subtle trends from a bubbling cauldron of activity of an extremely complex field in which a thousand activities are actually happening all at once. There would be a temptation to simplify too much. Or it might be eventually read as a simple solution to a problem for which there can realistically be no simple solutions. Care had to be taken in this regard.

Second, my work is squarely in the middle of this activity. Although this provides lots of data, it tends to so overwhelm one that order can be lost in the sea of crisis and incessant demand. It is for this reason that the famous community organizer Saul Alinsky pithily recommended an occasional incarceration in jail as one of the only ways to free oneself from "the tyranny of action." Fortunately, vigorous social organizing in my own field rarely offers such enforced opportunities for reflection, but the essential insight remains true. Suffice it to say that the development of a plan for a book always represents a challenge of organizational abilities against data. The temptation to include too much experience here constituted a problem to be overcome if the book was to effectively communicate just a few important issues, problems and trends.

Third, I was convinced it would be necessary to place the current developments in the field I planned to describe in an historical context. Our field, like many, tends to be ahistorical. A minimally adequate tracing of the evolution of ideas leading to the current situation would, clearly, be essential. Yet an intellectual history of this field could quickly become a book in itself, even were I qualified to write one. Ultimately, I had to make the decision to comment only on trends in recent history which set the stage for current developments.

This does inadequate justice to the subject, but most readers will know recent historical trends, and several excellent books exist which cover the history of all or various parts of the field in detail.

It was necessary to simplify the work of the Pennsylvania Developmental Disabilities Planning Council to cover just those areas of effort which particularly pertain to the topic at hand. The Council has been and is active in many areas, of which only a portion explicitly derive from the emerging conception which I am discussing. But I had to tell the reader enough about Developmental Disabilities Planning Councils for him to understand the setting in which these observations and experiments took place. This book is not about that organization, but about an emerging theme in which that organization has been engaged. While it had also been my original intention to use a number of pertinent grant projects as detailed examples, it quickly became clear that, because of space limitations, two projects and a brief overview of others would have to serve to illustrate theory in practice. Since underlying conceptions such as this one can find expression in practice in diverse ways, a few different examples should serve to show the range of possibility and the underlying theme.

Finally, I had to consider the hazard that the conceptual change I am describing might be seized upon as the new "solution" to the situation of people with disabilities. Some people might see the ideas presented as a new panacea, failing to realize it is merely the most recent unfolding of the historical process and is as subject to deterioration, perversion, and failure as all of its many predecessors. Although I have addressed this in a specific concluding chapter, some hazard must uncomfortably remain.

Overview of the Book

To understand what this proposed conceptual revolution would mean in practice, I begin by sharing the experience of two leaders of projects commissioned to explore this idea in Pennsylvania communities. In Chapter 2, Sharon Gretz shares her experiences in starting an effort to connect isolated people with disabilities into the associational life of a small city, an approach derived primarily from the thinking of John McKnight. A. J. Hildebrand follows in Chapter 3 by describing the creation of a citizen advocacy project, the most seminal and consciously planned approach to this type of work, which follows a concept originated by Wolf Wolfensberger.

Chapter 4 steps back from these two projects to look at the organization that called for the creation of these social experiments and funded them, the state developmental disabilities planning council. How was this organization equipped to foster a conceptual revolution, and why?

Chapter 5 examines developmental disabilities practice as it currently exists. Particular attention is given to emerging problems and difficulties in the community service system. A case is made that a wide variety of systemic problems have a common theme, and can be interpreted symptomatically as signs of breakdown in the currently dominant approach we have been using. This may mean that the theory or conception underlying the current approach has been exhausted, and that the stage is now set for its replacement by a new world view. Such successions are often experienced as "conceptual revolutions."

Chapter 6 explores the process through which such conceptual revolutions take place, as described by Thomas Kuhn in *The Structure of Scientific Revolutions*. Through the examination of such revolutions in the fields of winemaking and of medicine, I suggest that the process of conceptual change as described by Kuhn in scientific thinking applies to other fields of human endeavor as well. The understanding of conceptions of the world as "paradigms" is introduced. Chapter 7 turns its attention to the process of conceptual change in the history of developmental disabilities, and examines currently dominant "professional/bureaucratic" conceptions governing practices affecting people with disabilities.

A contrasting "associational" world view is the topic of Chapter 8. Is "the psychological sense of community" truly the key characteristic which must be present for any helping to be useful? Of what importance are such ideas as social inclusion, connectedness, and one's sense of "place" in society? Will ordinary people care for and about people of devalued social status if asked to do so? If the psychological sense of community is paramount, how did we as a field come to lose perception of its validity? The conception around which a new revolution may be taking place is explored in some detail from a theoretical point of view.

Chapter 9 moves the questions raised in this theoretical discussion to the level of practice. If you entered an arena of public policy with the charge to help improve practice in a state just as such a transition in world views was beginning, what would you do to try to promote this development and to test its validity? This brings us to the actions and social experiments conducted by the Pennsylvania Council. An understanding of the basis of actions taken by this organization is covered in two parts. The first considers the theoretical basis of the social change which was attempted through government. The second describes a variety of other approaches commissioned by the Council in more condensed form.

Since all settings, even those inspired by a new vision of the world, are subject to decay and failure of responsibility to those whom they serve, Chapter 10 considers the question: "What really keeps people with disabilities safe in society?" The influences of the two world views introduced in Chapters 7 and 8 are explored through the question of safety for vulnerable people. The focus of an additional project aimed at developing an alternative to regulatory safeguards is briefly discussed.

In two final chapters I consider a number of important questions raised by the preceding theoretical and practical work. If this kind of vision were to be more widely adopted, what might the larger implications of such a step be? Chapter 11 asks the important questions: "What could go wrong? What hazards might attend the adoption of the new approach as a basis for public policy and professional action? Does this promise a new solution to the essential situation of people with disabilities in the world? If deterioration of all social programs is inevitable, why is it important to understand and plan for deterioration in this new approach, too?"

In the final chapter I speculate on some deeper reflective issues. Why does work like this seem worth doing? What might be the relevance of the situation of people with disabilities and work on their behalf for society? What might be its greater meaning? Is there anything contained within the drama of people with disabilities in the world which might have relevance for the larger world drama unfolding so quickly before us these days? While it is risky to speculate publicly upon such issues within the professional field, it is here that I take this risk. A concluding section appends some final reflections on the meaning of the work undertaken.

Following the last chapter is an appendix listing a number of "Rules for Funding Social Change" which may be of practical use to funders and others wishing to experiment with the kinds of social change actions described here, and which I judged, frankly, too irreverent for the main text.

From this brief overview of the contents of the book, the reader will see that I have undertaken the rather ambitious project of trying to weave the complex strands of current crises in practice and policy, experience in new and untested areas, and historical and reflective understanding into a web of meaning. While pressing issues affecting the immediate welfare of people with disabilities always tend to compel our immediate attention, it is my belief that it is important to try to comprehend the meaning of these complex and emotional events in which we daily find ourselves. Whether I have discerned that meaning correctly or incorrectly will be judged by the reader. That there are considerable undercurrents of change taking place in society and in our field seems a fact beyond dispute. Society and its institutions are always undergoing complex change, although this probably proceeds at greatly varying rates at different times. The present time seems to be one poised on the edge of potential great change, if both the storms affecting our current practice and the appearance of seeds of new conceptions can be assumed to have their usual significance in history. If this flux is indeed a process of transformation, then it is important to know in what direction destiny may be sweeping us. Is the seeming collapse of our current community service system really a signal that our old way of thinking is fading and that a new way is about to arise?

We are on the seas, of that I am sure. Whether the sea change I seem to read in the skies, the currents and the stars will come to pass we will know only later. That *caveat* made, Chapter 2 begins, as noted, with a glimpse of the possibilities of a land which might lie at the end of a voyage to a new and different way of approaching our work.

Endnotes

1.   The creation of settings, as defined by Sarason, is "any instance in which two or more people come together in new relationships over a sustained period of time in order to achieve certain goals." (1972) This term can encompass the establishment of marriages, agencies, or nations.

CHAPTER 2

Citizen Participation:
Connecting People to Associational Life

Sharon Gretz

Not too far from Pittsburgh, there is a tiny little town with a funny name which no one ever seems to have heard of. The heart of the town, on the main street, is a delicatessen. At the deli, a steady trickle of townspeople come in in the morning and again at lunch for fresh-brewed coffee, enticing food and friendly conversation. Several years back I found myself there. This little town with the funny name held a special interest for me. Soon the deli would hold a special significance as well.

Stunned and knocked to its knees in the early '80s by the collapse of the steel and manufacturing industries, the town was now fighting to come back. Recovery and rebirth were in progress. However, many people were forced to leave to find work and provide for their families. Those who remained in the community were put in the position of needing to pull together if there were going to be any community at all.

In the midst of this process, eight new people had moved into town. These individuals had no ties to the community whatsoever. They had no roots, no history there. In fact, community, any community, was hardly contained in their histories at all. The eight people had severe disabilities. Between them, their histories held over 145 years of life within the walls of institutions.

In 1985 the agency for which I worked led a complex effort to "spring" these eight people from institutions to life in a community. The community picked was the little town with the funny name.

December 23rd, 1985 was liberation day. The whole thing took a tremendous amount of energy, persistence, and probably audacity. Oh, it was a great feeling to see them leave. Exhilarating, in fact — for the people who moved and for the people who played a part in making it happen. One of the public entities that had made it possible was the state Developmental Disabilities Planning Council. They had initiated a project to get people with disabilities out of nursing homes. They had provided money for people to set up their households.

Sharon Gretz has worked in human services for people with severe disabilities since 1979. In her citizen life she is a cub scout den mother, on the board of a parent-teacher organization, and a citizen advisor to her local school board.

After several years it was clear that those who had believed that these eight people were not capable of living in the community had been wrong. They were still there. They were making it. They had staff support. They were involved in day training programs to learn skills. There were staff available to attend to their personal care needs. There were staff to take them shopping, banking and out to dinner. Yet something began to gnaw at those of us at my agency who were intimately involved in this whole thing. The feeling was inarticulate at first, but the gnawing arose with the question "Is just being there enough?" Was life in the community about simply being present, or did it have to do with having a presence? Tom Kohler, who is involved in citizen advocacy in Georgia, cut through everything. For me he posed the question, "If you imagined two worlds, the client world and the citizen's world, where would you say most people spend the bulk of their time?" I remember feeling like my heart stopped. There was no need to think about the answer. Our people were clients all of the time. In this little town where they lived, the people I knew, the liberated eight, were virtually invisible. Although they were there, they were not seen and certainly not known. Few, if any, relationships had developed outside of "the program." Belonging had not come by simply being there.

With this reality in our minds, we again looked for a way to help these eight people "live in the community." We wanted to find ways of helping people belong — to be full-fledged citizens.

About this time the state Developmental Disabilities Planning Council made funding available for a new kind of project called "Citizen Participation." We wrote a proposal, and were awarded a grant. It was just a small grant in terms of money. With this tiny little grant we began. I was hired to figure out what this new approach would be. As it turned out, I didn't know what I was getting myself into. I was used to things like developing policies, designing programs, making assessments, writing reports, supervising staff, counting units of service, coming up with "forms" for this or that, and generally "putting out fires." With this, I couldn't just call someone else in my field and ask for the "how-to's." At the time, I knew no one in my professional world who was doing this kind of work. And so this tiny little town and this small grant held a certain intimidation for me. My own struggle began with the question, "How can I get in touch with the real life of the community?"

We started with the idea of finding a community member who would be a "bridge builder" between the eight people we supported in apartments and the town itself. The "bridge builder" would need to be someone who was well known and respected in the community,

who belonged to many associations and groups, and who was inno-
cent of involvement in our human service world.

When the time came to look for our first "bridge builder," I started
to become uncomfortable and actually afraid about how to do it. I
guess in my mind I knew that putting an ad in the Sunday classified
would not do it. But what would? I started by asking people from
work if they knew anybody who might know someone else who was
very involved in the community. After a few tries, someone told me
that his aunt had lived there all of her life and maybe she could help.
He called his aunt and she said that the person we should talk to was
Sophie.

I found out that Sophie was a hairdresser who had run a shop in
town for many years. She was also the mayor. Would she be well
known? If you think about a small-town beauty shop, chances were
high she would know just about everybody and everything in town.
Would she be well-respected? Well, after all, someone had elected her
mayor and trusted her enough to be the top-ranking leader of the
community. And finally, she had no ties to the human service world.
Perhaps she could help. I needed to call her and ask.

I was given Sophie's telephone number. I want to be perfectly
honest here and tell you that I looked at Sophie's telephone number
on my bulletin board for many days. As I struggle now to understand
my hesitancy to call her, several things come to mind. How could I ask
a perfect stranger to get involved? What if she just said no? Would her
"attitude" be right? Finally I called.

I went to meet Sophie one day to get to know her. We met at her
office as mayor because it was Monday. On Mondays, Wednesdays
and Thursdays, Sophie works as mayor. On Tuesdays, Fridays and
Saturdays, she cuts hair at the beauty shop. As we began to talk,
Sophie's phone rang constantly. No, she hadn't heard about any jobs
lately; yes, the town council would meet Monday night; etc. During
some of her phone calls I started wondering what I would say. I didn't
want to interview her. How would I know if she was the one?

I can't remember now exactly what I said but somehow I told her
why I was there. Sophie immediately started to tell a story about a
woman she knew who had cerebral palsy and went to live in an
institution. Some years later the woman wanted to move out of the
institution and back to an apartment high-rise in her town. She kept
calling Sophie and asking her to help her come home. Eventually,
Sophie was able to help arrange it. Sophie said everyone in the
building was nervous and upset when it came time for the woman to
move in. Sophie thought that was silly and made it her business to talk
to everyone in the building about her friend's abilities, nice personal-

ity, and desire to come back home. When her friend finally moved in, the people in the building had a welcoming party.

Sophie went on to tell me about some other people with handicaps who had moved into a new special "independent living" building in town. She was worried they might become isolated. So she had invited them to come to a tea party on community day and had made special arrangements so they could get into the building. No one came. She didn't understand why they didn't come. She thought maybe I knew why. Sophie wanted to know if she did something wrong.

Sophie went on to say that if we were going to be working at getting people involved in the community we needed to talk to Frank. She said Frank knew everybody in a thirty-mile radius and belonged to every association, group, and club. In fact, Frank had probably started most of them. I made arrangements to come back again to meet Frank. On the way out, Sophie asked me again if she had done something wrong when the new people in the special building didn't come to the tea. As I looked into her questioning face I felt compelled to supply an answer. As I searched my mind looking for words or theories to provide some type of professional explanation, I realized that there were none — none that could or should negate her kind and open gesture. I just quietly said no.

I went back to Sophie's office on a later day to meet Frank. Frank is technically retired from work in a local factory. His handshake and smile are warm and welcoming. We all decided to walk to the deli down the street to have coffee and talk. As we walked I noticed how different my pace was from theirs. Frank and Sophie slowly sauntered; Frank with his hands loosely in his pockets, Sophie casually swinging her purse. Me — I was fighting to slow my typical fast and long strides, carrying my purse and my overloaded briefcase.

As we walked I felt in good company. Everyone we passed said hello to Sophie and Frank — a lady carrying shopping bags; people driving by; men gathered on a bench on the corner outside the post office. In the deli, everyone who worked there knew them too. A small group of people were gathered just inside the door. Some were young and some were old. All had a kind word and a comment on the day. I was introduced to all of them. Sophie sold some raffle tickets as we waited for coffee.

Sophie and I talked with Frank about what we wanted to do about getting people whom I supported in their apartments more involved in community life. Frank said he thought it was a good idea, but didn't want to commit himself right that minute. He said he had so many activities that he didn't want to say he could help until he had thought about it. Frank pulled out a folded piece of paper from his breast pocket and showed it to me. On the paper were notes of meetings and times — Lions Club, Festival Committee, Food Pantry and so on. I thought it was interesting that he didn't have an appointment book.

Frank started to tell me a story about when he ran a band group of kids that marched in area parades. Frank is very involved in parades. A girl who couldn't use her right arm wanted to be on the flag team. Some parents of other kids began to complain because she was the only one who carried a flag in her left hand and it messed up the flag formation. The parents said the group wouldn't be judged well in parades. Frank told them he didn't care; the girl was marching and she would carry her flag in her left hand. He said the girl is about thirty now and when they run into each other in town he feels good because she always talks about the band group, and how happy she was carrying the flag. Something inside me felt good, too. Then Frank said he didn't care who a person was, what problems they had, or what people couldn't do. What was important was, if someone wanted to be included then there was something important that he could find for them to do. Frank told Sophie he could help if we wanted him to.

Meeting Frank and Sophie and spending time with them sensitized me in an unexpected way, as a person as well as a human service worker. They taught me in small ways, never intending to change me as I may have initially meant to change them. Although I didn't realize it at first, I came to them expecting that I would be the teacher, the educator, the expert who would instill in them and their community how to go about "community integration." While I was busy explaining about people's physical limitations, they were already brainstorming about what people could do. I sensed in Sophie and Frank this enormous capacity for caring. It didn't have anything to do with "disability." It had to do with how they felt about all people. They sensed utility and worth in everyone. They wanted their community to be a good place to live. Over the years they had been willing to invest in making it that way.

I initially worried because Sophie and Frank didn't know about word usage and terms I used. "Social Role Valorization," goal plans and units of service meant nothing to them. Someone at my agency asked me if they were really qualified to do what we wanted them to do. I labored over that thought for a great while. Eventually I came to just know that their "professional" qualifications were not an issue. The only way I can describe having come to this conclusion is that my heart told me. Inviting people into community life was already their life's passion. They had shown me their capacity to welcome and embrace people. I didn't worry any longer about what words they knew. And finally when I went to the deli to talk and have coffee with

Sophie and Frank, I no longer carried my briefcase. Once we agreed upon what we wanted to do together, we arranged for Frank to receive a small "retainer" to help defray some of his expenses. The first person he started to connect with the community was Albert.

Albert

Albert is a rather heavyset man in his early sixties who spent the bulk of his years living in a nursing home. Albert is a tremendously likable guy who talks and laughs loudly. He frequently dons a strawbrimmed hat and wears suspenders and large boots that are seen by some as his trademark. Albert's labels include cerebral palsy and mental retardation. He uses a wheelchair to get around. It almost always takes him a long time to complete a thought out loud as he stutters quite severely. Albert is also quite notorious for being as stubborn as a mule.

Frank arranged for Albert to help out once a week at a local free food pantry for the many unemployed people in town. Frank organized, started and runs the food pantry. Each week Albert joins the other volunteers who give out food. Albert is responsible for handing out tickets to families as they come in. Each ticket is numbered. But since Albert didn't know his numbers, they had to figure out a way to keep them in order. Since Albert started at the food pantry they tried several systems so that he could do his part. Frank and another person also began helping Albert learn numbers in quiet moments at the pantry. Frank told me that Albert has come to recognize more and more of the numbers. The funny thing is that it never happened in ten years of instruction at special day programs.

The people at the food pantry really like Albert. Frank says they kid and joke with him all the time and help him out when he needs it. Albert, originally rather subdued, has warmed up to them as well. Even the families who come in look forward to seeing him there.

When Albert lived in the nursing home, he got in the habit of securing his most prized possessions by wrapping them in many layers of handkerchiefs, socks and bags and keeping them close to his body. Each week at the food pantry, someone asks Albert if he'd like to put on his name badge, at which time he gets out one of his bags and proceeds to unwrap the many layers to reveal his prized badge. In social service circles this is known as "institutional behavior" that needs to be corrected. At the pantry this is just known as Albert's ritual. One of the workers there told me that the ritual means that Albert feels proud to be a part of their group. It never occurred to them that there was anything wrong with it.

It's important to understand that everything has not been perfect either. I remember the time after Albert had been at the pantry several months when Frank called me to say that there was a problem. Albert wasn't making it to the bathroom in time and was wetting himself. My reaction was one of horror and fear; fear that they were going to suggest he not come anymore. Sure that I was going to beat Frank to the punch, I suggested perhaps someone else could or should take Albert's place. Frank was shocked. "Absolutely not!" he replied. Albert belonged with them. They just wanted to solve the problem. As it turned out, arrangements were made for Albert's attendant to meet him at the food pantry and help him get to the bathroom. When things are quieter, Frank helps him, too.

Sometimes Albert dozes off and someone slips by without their ticket, which messes up the system. Frank comes by and pokes Albert when this happens. Now he has a sign at Albert's table that says, "Please stop here and get a ticket." Sometimes Albert would mix up the tickets and give out the wrong ones. They fixed that by making a stick post and putting the tickets on it. Albert just has to pick the one on top. Occasionally there are people who don't want to deal with Albert. When this happens, Frank's response is "If you want food, you have to see the man."

Two years have passed and Albert is still there. Everyone associated with the food pantry has accepted Albert just as he is. I'm sure many professionally experienced persons would look at Albert's deficits and deem him unready. At the food pantry Albert's disabilities aren't denied, yet his unique contribution is accepted and welcomed. Nobody tries to change him. He has a place.

Pete

Pete is a gregarious guy in his fifties. Pete gets immense satisfaction in telling off-color jokes to unsuspecting parties. His laugh afterwards is probably the most infectious I've ever heard. Pete also is devoted to his faith. He loves to read the Bible, talk about Scriptures, and talk about God's presence in his life. Pete fell off a truck when he was a young man. His fall resulted in serious head injury. Pete lived at home with his mom until she could no longer take care of him. He spent many years in a nursing home before moving to his own apartment two years ago. Sometimes Pete gets very agitated, aggressive, and hard to reckon with.

I asked Frank if he might get to know Pete and his interests, and Frank decided to take him along to his weekly community Bible study group. The first week people listened silently as Pete told his story and shared his faith. I am told that Pete's presence is appreciated and his remarks respected within the group. Never at a loss for words, Pete at times monopolizes the conversation and interrupts people who are talking. From what I understand, people in the group handle this by lightly squeezing Pete's arm when he starts to take over. Pete has come to understand that in this group when that happens he needs to give someone else a turn.

Frank told me after one Bible study meeting, Pete blew up at a man when he suggested to Pete that it was cold and he might want to put his coat on before he left. That old apprehension still dwelled in me somewhere. I asked Frank what he told the man. Frank told him "Pete doesn't mean anything bad by it. He just does that once in a while." They still wanted Pete to come. I was also surprised to find out sometime after the fact that the people in the Bible study built a ramp for Pete so that he could enter the church with more ease.

Sometime after Pete had become a regular member of the Bible study his day program came to a halt. The agency that had been funding his program had decided he was not capable of working, so they gave up trying to prepare him. Now Pete had absolutely nothing to do with his days. He came down to our agency building and tried to help out but usually ended up just sitting around. By this time I had met Gene, who was a good friend of Frank's. Gene was a helper at the food pantry and had taken a liking to Albert. Gene told Frank and me that he wanted to get involved in helping our citizen participation efforts. Gene was a lifelong resident who had been an executive in the sales field. When I met Gene he was between jobs and had pretty much given up on wanting to be a part of the sales field any more. He was looking for something different in his life — a way to be of real help to the people in his community. This was what led him to the food pantry, and Frank in particular. As he expressed it to me, he saw in Frank what lived and breathed in his own heart. Frank was a symbol of pure love—an example of how human beings could interact in their world. He started spending time with Frank and learning from him.

Gene already knew Pete. I asked Gene if he thought there might be something for Pete to do in the community that would have some real meaning. Gene contacted his friend named Lynn Ann. Lynn Ann had several years earlier begun, as she put it, "to try and get neighbors helping neighbors. There were many problems facing our community." Her network grew through voluntary efforts of people. She works full time without pay. She and others try to help the situations of single-parent poor families and homeless families. One effort is to help people find affordable housing.

Gene asked Lynn Ann if there might be something in her office that Pete could do. Lynn asked her other volunteers and together they came up with a job for Pete. Now several times a week, Pete's job is to go through apartment rental ads in local newspapers. When he finds an ad below a certain dollar amount, Pete cuts it out. After going through all the ads, Pete organizes the ads by location and price and puts them into a 3-ring binder. When someone calls in need of housing, everyone uses Pete's book. As Lynn Ann says, "Pete is making a real difference in people's lives." She is planning to invite a family who finds a home through the book to come in and meet Pete. Lynn Ann feels that it is important for Pete to see his value to others.

When showing people Pete's book Lynn Ann, with pride, shows how he is getting better and better with organizing it. They saw at first that he was having trouble knowing where to paste the ads in. Their solution was to draw a grid on notebook paper and make lots of copies. Having the lines on the paper has helped Pete to do his job better.

Life in Lynn Ann's office has changed significantly since Pete arrived. There is a new spirit in the office. Lynn Ann says the best thing about having Pete there is simply him being himself. Pete's gift of gab is revered here, especially the jokes. Lynn Ann and Pete have a deal — Pete has to keep telling her jokes because she often gets too serious. In return Lynn Ann's promise is to be a good boss. When Pete yells over "Hey Lynn, I have a joke," the entire office comes to a hush. The punchline is delivered, everyone either laughs or moans — and then they get back to work.

Bonnie

Bonnie is a young black woman who is somewhat shy and timid. When she smiles it seems to cover her whole face. Bonnie spent about 24 of her 28 years in a state school and hospital. Bonnie needs a lot of assistance for most physical tasks except driving her electric wheelchair. I asked Sophie if she would spend time getting to know Bonnie and to think of how she could get involved in their community. Sophie invited Bonnie to be a member of a committee that was organizing a community festival. Bonnie was delighted. The one thing she couldn't believe is that none of the other residents living at our residential apartment program were doing it too. I remember her saying, "You mean it's just me, mine alone, no other clients?" Bonnie's jobs for the day were to greet people at the tea, hand out art awards at the children's art contest, and review the parade on the reviewing stand.

Let me insert here that all along I have tried to stay physically away from these community groups and events so as not to impose or intrude on the community's natural way of doing things. I decided in this case I would go to the celebration and imagined all these scenarios of Bonnie's Triumphant Day. The morning of the celebrations I grabbed my daughter and off we went to blend into the crowd.

Well, my expectations differed a lot from what happened for Bonnie that day. She was physically present in all these activities but didn't really seem involved. She was introduced over the microphone at the art awards. People in the auditorium clapped but then she was just sort of ignored as things went on around her. I remember looking down at the ground and feeling embarrassed for her. Sophie wasn't there. I scanned everywhere for her but she was busy preparing for something else. Soon it was over.

The next day, I asked Bonnie how she felt. She told me she felt funny, like everyone was staring at her, and that she felt left out. She told me she didn't want to do anything like that again. I know Sophie felt bad that others hadn't really included Bonnie that day. She told Bonnie that she was glad she came and hoped next year Bonnie would help on the committee again. Bonnie smiled her immense smile and said she really wanted to try it again.

Some of the people in charge that day told Sophie they were surprised at how the children responded to Bonnie. They weren't afraid of her and gave her a big hand. They thought the kids would be afraid. Perhaps they didn't realize that it was they themselves who were afraid. There are several things that I make of this. Again I say it is not for me to judge — it is not my expectations that are important here. It is clear that individuals with severe disabilities will need to be supported in different ways as they come to be involved in communities. Why did we expect this woman who had lived in an institution for twenty-four years to feel self-assured on a stage alone in front of strangers? Now instead of being horrified I can compare it to my own feelings at walking into my first PTA meeting and not knowing a soul.

Bonnie also had this real desire to sing. Although her voice was quiet, it was a beautiful voice. Where might Bonnie find a place to sing? By now Gene was totally involved in our efforts. He thought that perhaps a church choir might be a place. Bonnie was definitely interested. Gene knew a woman named Gloria who is the matriarch of a large Baptist church. At eighty years old, Gloria has had a rather rough life. One of twenty-five children born to her parents in Alabama, Gloria had struck out on her own at thirteen. After moving to our area, marrying and having six children, she became very ill. She entered a hospital and stayed for five years. In the meantime her family got split up into foster homes and her husband took sick and died. All Gloria could think about in these years was getting well and reuniting her family. She says everyone pretty much decided she would die soon. Her response was to pray. She says it's hard to express how it felt to walk out of the hospital, find her children and bring them home. She decided at that time that she was blessed and from then on decided to make it her business to "do right by people."

Gene asked Gloria, "Might your church be a place for Bonnie?" Gloria's response was that at her church the doors were open. Gloria asked the church elders, the pastor, and the deacons who all in turn asked the congregation to welcome Bonnie. And this they did.

Bonnie originally went to church with her attendant. But after a while the ushers and some others told the attendant that she needn't stay anymore. Bonnie could rely on them to help with anything she needed.

After a little while, Bonnie ran into some financial problems and also stopped going to church because her attendants had become unreliable. Gene told Gloria what was going on and again Gloria went to the deacons and congregation and asked, "What can we do?"

One day the deacons went to Bonnie's apartment and presented her with three hundred dollars. They had asked the church members if they would consider giving a dollar or two to help Bonnie pay her rent. They also said they had volunteers lined up to come and get Bonnie ready for church if it were necessary.

I heard that the day of Bonnie's baptism into the church was quite an event to see. It was different from any other baptism ever performed there. Faced with the problem of taking her wheelchair into the baptismal pool, the deacons conferred and decided on another way. There was some concern about the response of the church elders since they would be breaking down deeply rooted tradition. However, on the day of her baptism, Bonnie, draped in cloaks and doused with water, was met with a resounding eruption of applause.

Other Communities

After many of these experiences one automatically begins to ask, "Is this community a 'typical community'?" Maybe it was just some kind of fluke. Maybe I had just gotten lucky and stumbled into it by sheer chance. Or maybe not. Maybe, just maybe, it was an example of what one might find in other communities. Just walking through this tiny community you wouldn't immediately notice the climate of hospitality. It was there, but needed to be found. The finding part, tapping into the network that brought life, this was the most important thing. I went to another community to see what I could find there. One of the first persons I found was Eddie.

Eddie

Eddie is an energetic and loving nine-year-old boy. He loves to run and play as other children do. Eddie also has Down Syndrome. When I first met Eddie's mother, Melanie, she was at a particularly low point. She and her husband had been embattled with our local school district over Eddie's right to go to his neighborhood school, rather than being bused out of the school district to a segregated classroom.

Melanie and her husband Ed had dreams for Eddie. They wanted him to grow up to be a contributing member of society. They wanted him to go out in the world with the support of family and friends — to be accepted — to feel love. They had fought his entire life to realize their dreams. Melanie and Ed tried to surround Eddie with activities that involved other typical kids. However, these activities usually involved children who were peers of Eddie's younger brother. Melanie wondered if kids his own age would accept him. Could he ever be invited to a birthday party, not because of his younger brother, but in his own right? The past summer had started with plans for Eddie to go to a special day camp for children with disabilities. But Melanie wondered if Eddie could "make it" at a regular day camp.

Rob is an enthusiastic young minister at a local church whom I had met at a friend's house. We discussed promoting the involvement of people with disabilities in their communities. Rob told me it was easier said than done. At the church, he is involved with children's activities. One year he had tried to get several children from a nearby home for children to come to the day camp he directs, and to make whatever accommodations were necessary for them to participate fully and equally. Yet the staff at the Children's Home threw out one roadblock after another. The same thing had happened with a local rehabilitation hospital. He had extended an open invitation for any patient at the hospital to come to services at their beautifully accessible church. No one has ever come. As we were departing, Rob said if there were anything he could ever do, to let him know.

After knowing Eddie for a while, I called Rob and asked if there might be a place for him at Rob's day camp. They had one spot left. After Melanie registered Eddie she called me and said, "It's all so strange. It was too easy! No one's ever just said 'yes' to Eddie." Before camp started Melanie discussed Eddie's abilities and style with Rob. Melanie was concerned that Eddie would get too tired going the full eight hours. Maybe she should pick him up early, she thought. Rob's response was "No problem. If he gets tired he can lie down in the nurse's office for a while and then rejoin us. Don't worry."

As camp proceeded I was struck by how nervous Eddie's mom was. Would he be kicked out because he's not a good swimmer? What if he wandered off? It was as if she were expecting a call any day to say that Eddie wasn't good enough. The call never came.

Eddie's behavior was not perfect, as no child's is. He did wander off sometimes. He didn't always listen to his camp counselor. One day, while painting, his particular painting extended to the floor of the church building. Still no call came. On the final day of camp, parents were invited to attend an awards ceremony and final celebration. Eddie received several awards for art and nature study. He also received the "non-swimmers free-style award." It wasn't the awards that struck Eddie's mom, however; it was the feeling in being there that day. Other children hugged Eddie and said they would miss him. A parent of one of the other children in Eddie's group came up to Melanie and said that Eddie's presence was the best thing about camp this year and thanked her for sending him. I mean, imagine it — being thanked for Eddie's presence. This was a new experience! Another parent said that she too was thankful for Eddie. She said that he brought out the best in her own child. Everyone said their good-byes. They also added, "Please come to camp next summer."

After camp was over, Eddie and his family were at a community festival. During the course of the evening several children came up to Eddie to talk. They were children who had met him at camp.

My own participation in Eddie's camp experience was minimal. I knew Eddie and I knew Rob. It was only a matter of connecting them. Together Rob, the camp counselors, the children and Eddie came to their own solutions. They did it their way — as it should be done. For me it meant trusting them and resisting the impulse to interfere and give professional advice. They felt no need to call on me. My involvement took the form of supporting Eddie's mom and helping her get through her underlying fear that Eddie "wouldn't be good enough" and would be rejected.

In a postscript to Eddie's story, word has come to his family that Eddie will be finally going to his neighborhood school this fall. Although his family knows that not all children will welcome him, it is the experience at camp that renews their faith that their son will find people in his life who will accept him as he is.

Shelly

Shelly is described by those who know her as a "doll." She's very friendly and very talkative. She lives in a residential program in a large suburb. Shelly has cerebral palsy and mental retardation. She uses a wheelchair and pretty much has to rely on other people for her physical care. Shelly wanted to be involved in something but her staff described her also as being terrified — she always backed out of everything.

Knowing that Gene knew some people in Shelly's community, I

decided to use this "trust network" again to find people there who would say "yes" to Shelly. After Gene had spent some time with Shelly, he found that the thing that she wanted more than anything was to find a way to help other people who had someone they loved die. About six months previously, Shelly had lost her boyfriend to cancer. She felt she knew something about what it feels like and could offer help to someone else who had those feelings.

Gene knew of several groups that met in her community which had as their focus supporting each other after this kind of experience. One met in a hospital, and one met in a church. Gene asked the leaders of both groups, and each said that Shelly would be welcome. Gene decided to take her the first time. When he called to tell her staff person at the residence, the meeting happened to fall on the same night Shelly was to see her psychologist. The staff person said they'd have to see if her psychologist would change her night. A return phone call indicated that no, the psychologist would not change and furthermore she felt that it was entirely inappropriate for Shelly to go. After all, Shelly couldn't even help herself. How could she help anyone else? She herself was in a "grief denial stage" and "inappropriately displayed her grief." On the basis of the psychologist's advice, the staff said that Shelly couldn't go. When Gene went to explain it to Shelly she cried. She was also angry — angry that she hadn't had a choice. It was really important to her. Shelly's staff encouraged her to talk to her psychologist about how she felt. I didn't know if she'd be able to. But she did.

I don't hesitate to say the psychologist seemed rather furious. The report that she sent to the county expressed her opinion that we were all unethical and incompetent. We were "interfering in Shelly's behavior program." The program was that Shelly was not allowed to talk about her grief to anyone except her psychologist. The psychologist told Shelly she could choose, it was her choice. She could keep seeing her, or she could go to the group. Shelly chose the group. The psychologist sent a report saying that this would be the last time the psychologist would see Shelly since she would be getting "treatment in a new therapeutic facility." Gene says that on Shelly's first night with the group she carried herself with such poise and class that he was knocked over. The group promptly kicked Gene out of their meeting since he had not lost anyone. When the doors opened again, he found Shelly surrounded. People were talking with her, laughing with her, being with her. Others came over to Gene and reassured him all had been well. What a delight Shelly was! How insightful Shelly was! Things couldn't have gone better. Shelly beamed and said, "I helped!"

The Project and Its Effects

Even though there is no book available on how to create caring in communities, when I started out I often wished for one. There was no way of knowing how and when I should offer support to the citizens who made commitments to get involved. I started out with the idea that I, as a human service worker, should be as invisible as possible. I've come to believe that sometimes this is true and sometimes it's not. Again, there was no one answer. The challenge became to discover what our role might be, finding the ways to not impose or change the natural flow of communities but to still somehow guide them in finding and being open to the contributions their members with disabilities could make.

At times some of it seemed easy. Finding Sophie, Frank, Gene and the others, and bringing people who wanted to contribute to their attention, was tapping into a world they were trying to create anyway. Their understanding of the life experiences of isolated people with disabilities was a wonderful thing to watch unfold. Meeting regularly at the deli and hearing their many stories seemed to be an important supporting role for me to take. Also, taking the time to learn about their perceptions of their community generally was a part of the support which evolved. Several times I helped unload a pickup truck of food for the food pantry. I needed to have an understanding of their "work." Listening to their concerns and their solutions, not being this "expert" was all a part of it.

On the other hand, some experiences were pretty tough. One woman from a community group that had agreed to help began, instead of working in her neighborhoods, to visit people at our agency building. Next, she wanted to and did attend several professional "staffings" held about the people she was trying to connect. I was at a loss for what to do. It appeared to me that she was starting to get sucked into the human service world. I had told her that I was placing trust in her. Yet what should I do when I felt the focus of our efforts drifting? Was I trying to be the "expert" or was it a legitimate concern? In this particular situation, I made the decision to talk with her about my concerns. This discussion led to defensiveness, probably on both of our parts. She began to feel a lack of support from me.

As we worked through this, many things became clearer. First, she was feeling isolated even within her own community organization. Her efforts at getting involvement from others in her group had fallen on deaf ears. Also, she was becoming disillusioned with many people from her community who she thought would be open to accepting people with disabilities.

Rejection was slapping her in the face. The human service world became an attractive alternative since it was a place that was used to the presence of disabled people.

My chosen role of being in the background had been the wrong role in this instance. A stronger presence was called for and I hadn't seen it. The turning point came when she finally found an ally, someone to share in her efforts just as Sophie had Frank and Frank had Gene. Then she stopped trying to be with human service workers and started being with people from community organizations.

Fertile Ground

There is something to be said here about fertile ground. Just as new seeds cannot sprout and grow and bloom without nourishing soil, a project such as Citizen Participation cannot flourish without a supportive backdrop.

In my agency a climate of experimentation was encouraged. The soil had been nourished and tilled so that new ideas could grow. There were space and encouragement from leadership to be creative, bold, and even audacious. There is no doubt in my mind that without these ingredients, the seed of citizen participation might never have sprouted and, if by chance it did, it would have died from lack of nourishment.

Even with the fertile soil, the project itself appeared to be just this very tiny effort in the complex workings of a very large agency. But it is also possible that this insignificantly small project also represented a seed of change.

My own feeling about change was that it was natural, important and necessary. I guess what I realize now that I didn't realize then, was that there seems to be a direct relationship between change and conflict.

Something started to happen at my agency that I find very hard to describe. First, it's hard to say positively that this citizen participation project was the only variable operating that was responsible for change. But it was important, somehow. Second, there are all kinds of emotions that get wrapped up in change — feelings of joy and excitement as well as anger and pain. Finally, I'm sure others who were there would have their own valid perspectives on what was changing, what it meant, and whether it was good or bad. I respect those perspectives. But all I can do here is share how it looked, seemed and felt through my own eyes.

I can say with all certainty that the citizen participation project, which is really about Sophie, Frank, Albert, Pete, Eddie, Rob and the others, changed my life. The change was not reflected only when I was at work or only in my personal life. Somehow the change blurred these two aspects.

The stories that unfolded as people with disabilities and other citizens from their communities came together challenged the very foundation of my human service world. Those who were once clients were now evolving into citizens. Those who were untrained, inexperienced and, up to now, seen as unwilling, were now leading the way for those (including myself) who had viewed themselves as highly professional, experienced, specialized experts. Everyday simple solutions and wisdom replaced professionally driven answers. Those who always felt they knew the most knew the least. Specialized training was replaced by human caring.

In the citizen participation project, jargon was replaced by everyday language. Lists of needs and deficits got pushed aside for talents, hidden gifts and desires. Assessments in the service world got replaced by getting to know a person in the citizen world. I could go on and on but I think the message is there. Somehow our experiences started eroding the fundamental beliefs that are probably a part of every single human service agency alive. It was like knocking out the pillars of the structure one by one.

Given that citizen participation was something none of us had expertise in, and given that I was a person responsible for learning how it might work, I can tell you it was very lonely work. As my own fundamental ideas were eroding and being replaced, I found myself feeling like an alien in my own agency. I felt that no one understood what I was talking about anymore, yet I wanted so much to share it. There seemed so much resistance to these new ideas. I struggled to find words. I felt walls building between myself and many of my colleagues. I didn't want the walls there at all, yet I knew that in reality I was laying some of the mortar. The more we talked about "a new way of thinking" the higher the walls seemed. On both sides of the wall there was uncertainty, anger and self-doubt.

I struggled with many questions. How much of the conflict was me — my personality, my style? How much of it was the sheer confusion of a new undertaking? Part of the confusion may have been my colleagues'. How could I be saying this, that and the other thing just last year and now, all of a sudden, be saying something so entirely different? I also wondered how much of it was just what we were discovering and sharing. Would it have mattered who was saying and thinking all these new things? Was it just the fact that they were being said?

I remember calling our sponsors at the Developmental Disabilities Planning Council to ask them if I was losing my mind. Behind closed doors I would ask my boss if there were something wrong with me. The feelings I had were that of being an outcast. I shut the door to my office and cried a lot.

Here we all were with our foundations cracking and walls built, trying to somehow relate to each other and trying to figure out what all of this had to do with our mission. Along the way, we asked for help from the Commonwealth Institute, funded by the Council to help people like us explore our values. They came and did some workshops. The conflict continued and even escalated, bringing us to the very edge of dysfunctionality. Anger increased; factions formed. The leadership struggled to help everyone work it through. Maybe this had to happen. Maybe we had to get to a place of real conflict before we could begin to build something new.

Other things, good things, were happening too. For me, when blocks in the wall broke, it allowed me to find other people in my agency who were also starting to question their foundations. They were also struggling. Then the Council and the Commonwealth Institute connected me with others in the state and in the country who were also asking themselves if they weren't a little out of their minds to be thinking the things they were. We started to meet. This network became a lifeline for me. I was fortunate too, because my boss always listened and told me that I had something important to offer, no matter how much trouble I was helping to stir up for him. I was fortunate to have the support of my husband, children and friends. I felt myself becoming a better citizen in my own community. I saw people with disabilities and their friends working together and caring for each other in a way that I had never thought possible. It made all of it worth it.

In the tiny town with a funny name life goes on. Frank's and Sophie's formal "project" with us is done but they are still there, open and willing to lead me to others — to do what they can — to do what seems natural to them. They keep doing what they always have done, but now with people with disabilities too. They told me that their community is enriched by the contributions of Albert, Pete and the others. One day Sophie told me that she finally understood why the people with disabilities she invited to that tea long ago didn't come. She says that knowing Bonnie has helped her see that people who have been very isolated are afraid they won't be welcomed. Frank and Sophie say that we need to find more ways for people to feel welcome. They think that every community needs to think about this.

Through Frank and the others we are learning something significant about the art of asking. Frank tells this story about being appointed as chairperson of his church's historical committee. He had noticed that the group was composed of the same people who are on every other committee. It seemed that these same people were the only ones involved in anything. Frank decided to — as he describes it — "go a-calling." He called on people who never got involved in anything. He called, in particular, on the church's oldest members. It made sense to him that they had a unique perspective to offer. Their gift wasn't their ability to research the history. Their gift was that they had lived the history. He told them how the church needed their knowledge. Twelve new committee members were found, all of them over age seventy. They were delighted that someone had asked them to be a part of it. Frank says that often people don't realize they have something to offer.

So what is the "theory" of this art of asking anyway? To get people involved, Frank says, you first have to let them know that they have something valuable to offer. Then you ask them. Period.

These days when I go to the deli, I often meet with Gene. He is formally working with me to help neighboring communities find ways to welcome people with disabilities. There are some new possibilities emerging. A very exciting development is the formation of a group of people from neighboring communities who have gotten interested in starting a citizen advocacy office to be a focus for their "connecting" work. The group includes many of the people I have talked about here, other community leaders, and a local priest. They are visiting citizen advocacy offices in other Pennsylvania communities and are considering applying to the Council for a grant to get it started.

The majority of people we have helped to connect with groups in the community are still involved in them. I still hear great stories of people making contributions, about personal relationships, and about growth.

At my agency we're still struggling. A recent retreat helped us all think about the guiding principles and values that we hold as most important. We need to be careful. We need to be thoughtful. And we need to be open. We need to be careful we don't come to the conclusion that the only thing that the people that we serve need is a few community friends and connections, and everything will be fixed. We need to be open in order to learn from each other and to listen to the dreams and desires of those we serve. Ultimately, I don't know what will happen. But I don't think we will ever be the same.

As for me, I am constantly learning and constantly struggling. Maybe it will just always be this way. I want to say something like "I can never go back." It's like when you've been looking at the little symbol on your credit card and then you squint and you look at it from another angle. You find that there is this different symbol. It is a hologram. You hadn't seen it in all the times you've looked at that card, and now all of a sudden it will never look like the same thing again.

For all the times I wished I had a manual on how to do my job, I hope now that one is never published. I feel as if I need to protect something — an endangered species, if you will. To professionalize, objectify, assess and impose human service structures on communities is wrong. It's already happened too much. That's why people find it so unusual to hear about the Sophies, Franks and Glorias that I have been so fortunate to meet and learn from. I find hope in their ways, their wisdom and their stories. It is not just a hope for the lives of people with disabilities. People caring for people; people being welcomed and revered for their uniqueness and contributions; people building better communities — that is the promise for all of us. And all you have to do, to get it started, is to ask.

CHAPTER 3

Asking for Citizen Advocates in Beaver County

A.J. Hildebrand

We started meeting over kitchen tables, and over coffee in local restaurants. Our first board meetings were at the Hot Dog Shoppe. I had been used to meetings in conference rooms and formal offices. As a human services administrator for twelve years, I had worked in an agency that ran group homes, but after a number of years I had become concerned with what was happening to the people who were served by the agency. I spoke about my concerns, and my colleagues at the agency became concerned about me. After a lot of difficulty, we parted company.

I live in Beaver County, Pennsylvania, where I have lived all of my life. I know a lot of people in Beaver County, including quite a few people with disabilities. Many people with disabilities that I know are living lives of segregation and isolation. I have come to understand this loneliness as a form of social oppression of people who do not fit society's norms. I felt called to respond to this problem, but I did not feel any real call to run formal service agencies anymore. What was I going to do? My family and I spent a long time struggling with that. I had heard about a kind of program called citizen advocacy before, and knew some people who were involved with citizen advocacy in other places.

Citizen advocacy is a community effort, through which ordinary, competent citizens represent the interests and promote the well-being of other citizens who are vulnerable and at risk of social isolation. Citizen advocates strive to understand and act on another person's interests as if those interests were their own, through a freely-given, personal relationship. Citizen advocacy is a specific way of asking ordinary citizens to become involved in each other's lives. Tom Kohler, a citizen advocacy coordinator in Savannah, Georgia, once said, "the only real tool we have in citizen advocacy is asking."

I started by asking other people in Beaver County to get involved. A small group of us began meeting at the Hot Dog Shoppe to talk about citizen advocacy; reading up about it, studying its principles and strategies, and trying to understand what we as a group were

---

Mr. Hildebrand is Coordinator of One to One: Citizen Advocacy in Beaver, Pennsylvania.

going to do. We formed what in citizen advocacy is called a "core group" — a core of people who are committed to making citizen advocacy work in a community. We then formed a board of directors and incorporated, so that we would be ready to apply for a grant from the Developmental Disabilities Planning Council the next time one became available. When we successfully gained a grant, we moved our meeting place to a little office in the center of the main street in Beaver. We had a telephone installed, and some local businesses gave us some office furniture. Now we were ready to start the business of asking. The first person we asked for was Michael.

Dennis and Michael

Michael spent most of his life being served by agencies. When he was seventeen, he was institutionalized after his mother died. For the next seventeen years, he lived the life of a resident of a large state institution. Michael was then "deinstitutionalized" in 1974, and moved into a group home, one in which I lived and worked in my early group-home days. Michael "graduated" to semi-independent living and married Heather, who also lived in a supervised living arrangement. Michael and Heather eventually became fed up with semi-independence, and moved out completely on their own.

Michael later inherited a small amount of money, and he turned to another agency for help in figuring out what he should do with his inheritance. He agreed to let a local agency that serves people with mental retardation manage his money, since Michael and Heather were not very good money managers themselves. A few years after Michael received his inheritance, the money was almost gone. It turned out that the agency was not a very good money manager either. Rather than protecting their inheritance, the agency was just having Michael and Heather live off of the principal. Instead of protecting their entitlement to federal Supplemental Security Income, they were disqualified because of the way that the inheritance was handled. They would qualify again only after all the money was spent and they were totally poor again. That day was now fast approaching. Because of poor management, their one shot in life of having some financial security had been lost.

I went to see Michael and asked him if he wanted us to find an advocate who could look into their financial affairs. He said yes. Michael's landlord, James Barton, who is the leading realtor in the town where Michael lives, and who knows a lot of people, was the person I started with. I told Mr. Barton that I was looking for someone who knew something about managing money, and who could take on

Michael's cause. Since Michael liked to philosophize and was good at testing people's sincerity, I was also looking for someone who was a good listener and who was sincere. The landlord told me, "Dennis Hargrove is the person you want to talk to. Tell him that I sent you." Dennis Hargrove is well known in the county. He is a managing partner with the largest accounting firm in the area. Dennis's office is a few blocks from Michael's apartment.

Now I was faced with the real thing. I had to ask. I went home and lay on my bed for a while. Could I really do it? Could I ask? Would Dennis respond? What would I say? I sat on the edge of my bed and stared at the telephone for a while. My palms sweating, I picked up the telephone and got Dennis on the line.

I told Dennis that James had suggested that I call him. I explained that I was with a group in Beaver County called One to One: Citizen Advocacy, and I told him a little about Michael's situation. I forget how I described citizen advocacy, but since Dennis knew Michael's landlord, he was willing to listen. He sounded interested in learning more. We made an appointment to meet in Dennis's office.

Now, Dennis has his finger on the pulse of economic development in our community and is a very busy man. For this appointment, I wore a coat and tie. Sitting in the reception area of Dennis's office, I remember thinking about a principle of social role valorization, which I had studied for many years. Social role valorization says that you should enable people who are socially marginalized to enter the valued core of society. I was sitting in the valued core. Dennis's office is not luxurious, but it is comfortable. It is a place where important matters are decided and a nerve center in our local business community. I remember thinking, "How did I end up here? What business do I have approaching this man who does not know me from Adam?" And then I thought, "Just tell him about why you got involved in citizen advocacy. Tell him about Michael's situation. Ask him to help."

I spoke to Dennis from my heart, and he spoke from his. He asked me a lot of questions about who I was, about citizen advocacy, about our board, and about Michael and Heather. At one point Dennis asked me, "How many citizen advocacy relationships do you have?" I swallowed hard, and said, "Well, Dennis, you would be the first!" He smiled and said, "Oh, so I'd be sort of a guinea pig?"

I told Dennis that we had spent a lot of time learning about citizen advocacy. I told him that I had had other forms of involvement with people who are handicapped, and that I felt confident about what our group had learned, although of course we had a lot more to learn. Dennis was quiet for a minute, for what seemed like an interminable period. He sized up the situation, and said,

> "Well, it's not every day that someone comes into my office and tells me this kind of story out of the blue. There is something significant about your coming to me, and I want to meet Michael. The fact that I'd be the first advocate interests me. It tells me that I'd get a lot of your attention. I'm also interested in how organizations develop, and the fact that what I do will have an impact on what others will do later is very interesting to me. I think you've come to the right person."

I enthusiastically agreed. We shook hands, and made arrangements for Dennis to meet Michael. I walked out of Dennis's office, elated that someone had said "yes!" In fact, I found myself singing "hallelujah" in my car, and thanking God for what had happened. I kept saying to myself — out loud — this really works!

What followed in Dennis's and Michael's relationship was a long series of ups and downs. Dennis looked at Michael's and Heather's whole financial situation. He helped Michael get control of his money. Some insurance matters were straightened out. His Supplemental Security Income was reinstated. Hospital bills were taken care of. Dennis believed the agency that was handling Michael's money should have tried to protect his inheritance, and he questioned the decisions that were made. It was a very difficult process, and one in which the agency got very angry at me. At a pivotal point, Dennis had a meeting with the agency's director.

> "You know," Dennis said to me later, "I have been at a lot of difficult meetings, tense meetings, where real mismanagement has been discovered by audits; meetings in which embezzlement by bank officers was discussed; but this meeting was as tense as any meeting I've ever been in. I have seen immorality in business, but this sort of immorality boggles the mind."

The outcomes of Dennis's advocacy on behalf of Michael and Heather are mixed. Michael and Heather did not recover the money they had lived on from the inheritance. In fact, once Michael got control of his finances, he didn't want Dennis's help anymore. After Michael got control of his money, he and Heather moved to an apartment that was less expensive and not as comfortable as where they had lived before. But, *Michael* decided. For many years he had decisions made for him, including how his inheritance would be handled. Dennis helped Michael to find his own voice.

One memorable moment that Dennis shared with me was when Dennis accompanied Michael to a program plan meeting at the sheltered workshop which Michael attended. During the meeting, the workshop staff were explaining to Michael that one of his goals should be to get a haircut more often. Michael's response left a deep impression on Dennis. Michael told the workshop staff, "Y'know, whenever I have five dollars in my pocket, and I start walking to the barber shop, I pass a grocery store. Then I have to decide between bread and milk or a haircut. I usually decide that bread and milk are more important." I do not know that Michael would have made this statement without an advocate at his side.

As I began to learn more through initiating and supporting citizen advocacy relationships, I learned fairly quickly that it cannot be just a one-person crusade. We hired a part-time person, Denise Shaw, to help with the office work. My one criterion for hiring somebody was to find a person with qualities that I lacked, who would complement my strengths and offset my weaknesses. I have a background in human services; Denise does not. I make appointments to talk with people; Denise "runs into people." People would not describe me as outgoing. If you look up the word "outgoing" in the dictionary, you would find a picture of Denise. Being a citizen advocacy coordinator can be a very lonely, frustrating job. There are times when I cannot face another person who is crushed and lonely. These are the times when Denise or one of our board members will keep things going, through encouragement and support. Denise has become a competent citizen advocacy coordinator in her own right, and she shares the work of recruiting and supporting citizen advocates in our community.

Colleen and Harmony

Harmony's life has been changed through the involvement of a citizen advocate. Harmony is five years old, and she has cerebral palsy. She also has an unusual syndrome called Guillain-Barre, which causes a temporary paralysis. Harmony uses a wheelchair, and she has faced many hospitalizations in her young life. We learned of Harmony through her mother, Bridget, who had tried to start a support group for parents of children with disabilities. I had noticed a brief news article about a meeting of this support group, a very informal group of parents who were advocating for their children. When I called Bridget, we had an interesting talk about advocacy, but Bridget declined to meet with me at first. I called Bridget a couple more times over the next six months, sent her some information on citizen advocacy, and finally we got together. Upon meeting Bridget and Harmony, I realized that Bridget had not been putting me off, but that in fact all her energy was devoted to holding things together for Harmony, and that it was hard for Bridget to think of another "thing" in her schedule, such as spending time learning about citizen advocacy. But, the more we talked, the more interested Bridget became.

Bridget invited Denise and me to come to her home to meet with her and a friend of hers, Jessica, who also has a disabled child (Kristen, for whom we later found another advocate). We sat with Bridget, Harmony, Jessica and Kristen in the kitchen and talked. While I focused on explaining citizen advocacy, Denise focused on learning about Harmony.

Harmony is a very bright little girl. She talks in a quiet but determined voice. Harmony was telling us about some of her hospital stays, and she obviously liked telling her own story. Harmony and her parents live in a rural area, and she did not have much opportunity to be around other children. Harmony was receiving "homebound" instruction and therapy several times a week, in which teachers and therapists would come into the home and work with Harmony. Harmony enjoys being around people, and she is very close to her mother and father. Bridget told us that she had a hard time finding people to babysit Harmony. Bridget also told us that she has had to fight for the services that Harmony needs, and that she did not feel that enough service options were available in the area. We met Harmony in January of 1989, and she would be starting school in the fall of the same year, although it had not yet been decided where.

After spending some time with Harmony, we decided that an advocate could be helpful in the following ways:

- to help Harmony be around other children.
- to support Bridget in advocating for Harmony's needs, particularly her educational needs.
- to be available as a "sitter."
- to think of things to share and do with Harmony.
- to help her feel wanted by people other than her parents.

With these roles in mind, we began to look for an advocate. A couple of months earlier we had met Colleen Harris, a mother and home-maker who lived only a few miles from Harmony. Colleen had read a story about citizen advocacy in the local newspaper, and called us to learn more. The article Colleen had read was about a citizen advocacy relationship which involved an elderly person, so she talked to us about meeting someone in a nursing home. However, as we spent time getting to know Colleen over several visits and conversations, it became clear to us that she would be better matched with a child. Colleen has two young children of her own, and her warmth and love for children were abundantly obvious. Colleen talked about how she felt upon seeing pictures of hungry children on television, and that she often asked herself "What can I do to help?"

Colleen had worked as a legal secretary for a number of years, but decided to stay at home with her children when her second child was born. As we talked with Colleen about some of the people with disabilities for whom we have found advocates, we could see how strongly she identified with people who were vulnerable, particularly children. While we felt sure that Colleen was the right person for Harmony, we wanted to give Colleen some time to think things over, so we met with her several times, and spent more time with Harmony and Bridget before introducing them.

Denise made the introduction at Colleen's house, and stayed for a while with Colleen, her son Daniel, Bridget, and Harmony until everyone felt comfortable with each other. They discussed the role that Colleen could have in Harmony's life, and simply got to know each other. Denise excused herself so that Colleen could get to know Harmony without her "looking over her shoulder," and Harmony and Colleen spent the afternoon together. In talking with Colleen later, she told us how interesting and sweet Harmony is. It was clear that Colleen was deeply touched by Harmony. Over a period of months, Colleen and Harmony spent time doing things together and enjoying each other. It did not take long for Colleen to win both Harmony's and Bridget's confidence. With great care and sensitivity, Colleen persistently talked with Bridget about how much Harmony has to offer, and how much she enjoys being part of Harmony's life.

Colleen spent a lot of time with Harmony, and gained some insight into what Harmony's world is like. On one occasion, Colleen told us how she was watching Harmony watch her young son Daniel riding a hobby horse. Colleen noticed that when Daniel would hit the high point of his ride, Harmony's eyes would widen. In a sense, Harmony was "riding" the horse with Daniel. Seeing the world through Harmony's eyes was a powerful learning experience for Colleen. We had many support conversations with Colleen, about integration, education, friends, parenting, disability issues, and other issues that impacted Harmony's life. Colleen had to work things out for herself about what steps she should take on Harmony's behalf, and we acted as a sounding board, as a source of information, and as moral support.

Over a period of time, Colleen became absolutely convinced that Harmony should be in a regular school with typical children. Colleen's belief was based on her personal knowledge of Harmony as a person, and upon her belief in Harmony's ability to learn and grow. We shared whatever resource information we could find on special education and integration. Colleen shared her feelings with Bridget, and offered to help advocate for an integrated setting. The school psychologist who tested Harmony had made a recommendation that Harmony attend a segregated class at a rehabilitation facility some forty-five minutes away from where Harmony lived. That meant an hour and a half each day on a van or a bus to attend three or four hours of school. The psychologist stated that regular school would be too frustrating and stressful, and that it would be too much for Harmony to handle. Colleen believed this assessment underestimated Harmony. Colleen knew that Harmony could handle this frustration and stress. She handles it every day. Colleen saw how her own children enjoy and love Harmony, and felt that other kids should not be denied the opportunity to be with Harmony.

Colleen and Bridget talked things out, and decided to advocate together for a regular classroom. They would tell the psychologist she was wrong and the school officials that a segregated setting was not an option for Harmony. They would insist that the school system provide the supports that Harmony needs to participate in regular kindergarten. Colleen and Bridget talked with Harmony's home teacher, who supported their position.

Colleen, Bridget, and the teacher met with the school officials, and within fifteen minutes, the school administrators had reversed their position. Harmony would go to the kindergarten in her home community.

This was a life-changing decision for Harmony. What Harmony thinks of herself, what other kids think about her, the expectations and opportunities to learn and grow, the friendships she will develop — all have been changed in a positive, hopeful direction. Harmony is now a little less "one of them," and a lot more "one of us." Harmony is getting mostly A's on her report card, and the other children are learning from Harmony, things that they would not have learned had Harmony been sent to a special school.

Kelly and William

When we learned about William, he was almost a year old, and he was facing some serious difficulties. William was a loving, beautiful little boy who had been fighting for his life, for all of his life. William was born two months prematurely and had a number of physical problems. He had cerebral palsy, and at the time we met him, he had problems with his breathing. His nasal passages and airways were filling with fluid, and he needed to be suctioned out frequently, sometimes every half hour. He had apnea, which means that his breathing sometimes stopped. He also needed a special heart and lung monitor to ring an alarm when his breathing stopped. William had difficulty eating, and was being fed with a nasogastric tube during the night. It was possible that he also had mental retardation.

Besides William's physical problems, his family was facing a number of serious obstacles. The family's insurance carrier was threatening to cut off their insurance. William's older sister, Erica, who was four years old at the time, had her own needs as a young child. But her parents spent most of their time caring for William or attending to basic household chores. There was not much time to spare for Erica. William's mother, Eileen, had passed the point of exhaustion. She was, as she put it, "living on coffee and catnaps." The services that William and the family were receiving were fragmented and disorganized. Bills were piling up, and agencies dragged their feet.

Finally, when Eileen was really exhausted, a social worker suggested to her that maybe she should consider putting William in an institution. When we talked with Eileen, she told us, "They'll take my baby, but they won't give me what I need to keep my baby at home." When we learned about William and his situation, their private insurance was reaching its limits. If something was not done, William would not have the equipment necessary to keep him home and to keep him alive.

Denise and I dropped everything else we were doing, and focused on finding an advocate for William. We decided that we were going to ask an advocate the following questions:

- Will you advocate for William's financial needs; insurance, utility bills, etc?
- Will you bring together several people who can help out in various ways?
- Will you find people who can help take care of William at home?
- Will you help provide transportation to doctor appointments and other appointments?

We began talking to people in the community about William. Denise talked to her sister-in-law who had a friend named Karen who lives in the same community as William. Karen's husband is a township supervisor, and after talking with Karen, Denise attended a township municipal meeting to talk about William. Karen called a friend of hers, Kelly, who also lives in White Township. We called Kelly and asked if we could come talk with her, and we met with Kelly and two of her friends the next day.

When we met with Kelly, we presented William's situation, described citizen advocacy, and raised our questions. We presented the essence of what we were asking as a matter of defending William's life. We shared our view that all life is sacred, and that every human being's life has value and is important. William's vulnerability and his situation called for immediate action.

Kelly is a pastor's wife in a small close-knit church, and she is used to coordinating the efforts of lots of people. She is a leader in her church community and she has a calm, reassuring presence. We introduced Kelly to William and Eileen, and Kelly asked a lot of questions about William's needs. Within hours, William's respiratory problems had worsened. Kelly and several other friends responded immediately. One of the neighbors, Rose Ann, took Eileen to the hospital, and took care of Erica for a couple of days during the crisis. Kelly got the medical insurance straightened out and worked out arrangements with utility companies. When William came back home, Kelly arranged for someone to be available several hours each day to help around the house, to help care for William, and to assist Eileen in other ways. Kelly also helped arrange for in-home nursing care to be provided through the medical insurance.

During one of William's hospitalizations at Children's Hospital, an hour away in Pittsburgh, we called a friend of ours, Sarah, who lives and works in Pittsburgh. We asked her to be a crisis advocate during William's hospitalization. There were several decisions pending regarding William's health care, including a possible tracheotomy. Someone needed to be with William during the times when Eileen could not be there. Sarah spent time with William while he was in the hospital, holding him, reassuring him, feeding him, loving him. No scientific data will prove that the extra attention that William got from Sarah, and the confidence and hope that Eileen felt because of the support that she received from Kelly, made any difference in William's life. However, we know in our hearts that Sarah's love was strengthening and encouraging to William.

The story of William is one that calls us to examine our most fundamental values and beliefs. We maintain that each person's life has absolute, inherent value and worth. We believe, as did William's mother, that William deserved the chance to be part of a family, to live at home with the support that he needs. It was not a question of "can William live at home?" The question was, "will our society provide the support that William needs to live at home?" The advocate tried, against difficult odds, to help bring together the support that William needed. There were a number of people who cared very strongly about what happened to William and to his family. Kelly and others were a source of emotional and spiritual support for Eileen. On one occasion, when we were talking with Eileen, she told us, "I thought nobody cared enough to help. Now I feel hope."

William went through many struggles. He went through surgeries, hospital stays, emergencies, and trying times. He became stronger and his breathing improved. There was at last someone to call in an emergency. Finally, William's mother could get some sleep at night. There was someone who would get on the telephone and straighten things out. There were people who would help defend William's life. William and his mother were not alone.

Although William's physical condition improved, other circumstances resulted in his being placed in a nursing home until his mother could get the support she needed for him to return home. William's mother, facing other difficulties in her life, needed time to pull things together. She was planning to bring William home after he had some minor ear surgery. It was a deep and unexpected shock when Kelly called to tell me that William had died early Christmas morning. He had difficulty breathing on Christmas Eve and, at about 3:30 a.m. Christmas morning, William's mother got a phone call to tell her that William's condition was very serious. She requested that he be life-flighted to a major hospital, but William died while this was being arranged. He was nineteen months old.

In his short life, William touched many people. His struggle was powerful testimony to the capacity of the human spirit to endure. A citizen advocate and others who became involved in William's life through the actions of the advocate, tried in many ways to do what was necessary to keep William home, to protect his life. But it wasn't enough; William still died. Citizen advocates, like everyone else, have human limitations, and cannot solve every problem, or heal every wound.

As a citizen advocacy coordinator, I searched my soul about William. Did I do all that I could? Did I support the advocate in the ways that I should have? Should I have tried to involve more people? Did I ask the right questions of the advocate? Those who were closest to William asked themselves similar questions. It may be that everything that was humanly possible was done, that everyone involved in William's care actively defended his life. Or, it may be that our human frailties and an unresponsive human service system failed to give William what he needed. There is some truth in both statements. William's mother tried to do all that she could. The advocates tried to do all that they could. Yet, we have a system where babies die in the sterile surroundings of a hospital, and our human limitations are very real.

During William's funeral, I was struck by the fact that about a dozen or so people who attended the funeral got involved through citizen advocacy. The advocate's husband, a minister, officiated at the service. The capacity of human beings to rally together around one small child seemed indeed great. The capacity of one small child to change the lives of those who came to love him is greater still.

What are the Fruits of Citizen Advocacy?

In any new human endeavor, a group of people can start with nothing and come up with something. Citizen advocacy in Beaver, Pennsylvania has provided opportunities for learning for several hundred people in Beaver County — and perhaps many more. Advocates usually involve their families, friends, and neighbors in one way or another. Many have heard the story of citizen advocacy; we have talked to a lot of people. However, much talk and no action will not change and improve the life situations of people with disabilities. A vision of a better life must be translated into real and substantial improvements in the lives of vulnerable people if we are to claim the worth of our efforts.

So what are the "fruits" of citizen advocacy? The story of William bore fruit. William had people in his life who tried to help him to live at home as a member of a family. His mother had hope because other people were helping who also had hope. In this situation alone, at least twenty other people became directly or indirectly involved with William. Sadly, despite their efforts, William died. Yet William may have lived longer, and his life was fuller because of the advocate's involvement. Of one thing we *can* be sure. William had a tremendous impact on many people.

Personal involvements change people. Such actions change one's understanding of how people who are vulnerable are typically treated. Indeed, such experiences change how one sees the world in which we live.

As of January 1990, we have initiated over thirty-five citizen advocacy relationships in just over two years.

- One advocate has been helpful in enabling a young woman with Huntington's Chorea to live at home with her grandmother, by sharing in the daily care that the young woman needs.

- Another advocate is trying to get a communication device for a woman who cannot talk. An advocate has made a personal commitment to a man who lived in an abusive boarding home, and has found him a better place to live.

- A local high school basketball coach has become a father figure to a sixteen-year-old boy. The boy has mental retardation, lives with his mother, and was spending most of his time alone in his bedroom. The advocate is enjoying opening up the world to his young friend.

- The local Clerk of Courts has become an advocate for an elderly gentleman who is blind and lives in a nursing home.

- Another advocate helps a teenage boy who has muscular dystrophy spend time with other teenagers without his parents around. The young man asked the advocate to be his Confirmation (a sacrament of the Catholic church) sponsor.

- An advocate is arranging for a medical re-evaluation for a man who is on a respirator and cannot talk.

- The town librarian has become an advocate for a man who has spent most of his life in an institution.

- An advocate is helping a young man who was institutionalized as a child get a job with decent wages and benefits, instead of washing dishes for minimum wage.

- An advocate spent time visiting a young man who had a severe neck injury. The young man's fight for life before his death in a nursing home left a profound impact on the advocate.

Citizen advocacy is one way in which people can act on the choice to be good. I visited a citizen advocacy office in Georgia and met an advocate who summed up the essence of citizen advocacy in a few words that were plain and simple. She said,

> "I help people. That's what I do. I help people, that's who I am. I look at someone, and I look at them like they was me. I put myself in their shoes, and I help them. If there is someone in need, I help them. I believe he [the person she was helping] can learn. He may take longer, but he can learn. He's just like us, but you have to teach him things. He will always need help, but he can learn."

There are people in the world who are willing to "look at other people like they was me." An advocate is a person who represents the interests of another person, as if those interests were his or her own. "Like they was me."

Citizen advocacy is more than just fostering friendships. We ask people to defend the lives of fellow citizens who are vulnerable. We ask ordinary people to learn from people with handicaps who have contributions to make in the world. We ask citizens to stand against segregation and isolation. We ask advocates to help unemployed people with disabilities to find and keep a job. We ask families to consider adopting a child with a disability. We ask some people to make a lifetime commitment to stand by, for, and with people who are often living in oppressive situations.

In our work, we realize that we cannot change the world, but we can ask people to try to change the world for some people and we can support them while they try. We are giving ordinary citizens an opportunity to be good.

Exploring Conceptual Change through a State Developmental Disabilities Planning Council

> "...it is not (usually) the ideas of philosophers that change reality; nor, conversely, is it the practice of ordinary people. What changes history, what kindles revolutions, is the meeting of the two."
>
> — Oliver Sacks

Sharon Gretz and A.J. Hildebrand set out in their respective towns to try out a new vision of the way in which the situation of people with disabilities might be addressed. The stories of what they tried to do and are doing serve as concrete tests of the different way of thinking I have termed a new conceptual and social revolution. Both are unusual and creative people who set out to do something that was quite counter to the world view gained in their training and in their professional experience. Both, at the time I first met them, were struggling with a certain sense of restiveness in traditional professional roles in human service agencies. Each might have eventually found ways to overcome the resistance and financial obstacles inherent in trying something dramatically new. But they may have not; or it may have taken each of them a very long time. The world is full of people bound in regular jobs dreaming of some new and better way. Why did they get to try their ideas out?

Each secured a grant from the state Developmental Disabilities Planning Council with which I am associated, as part of a conscious approach to nurturing the new conception of which I have spoken. The projects and the Council serve as partners in change: the projects demonstrating new approaches, the Council serving to make successful demonstrations available.

Since the conceptual change I talk about in this book is based upon the experiences of the Pennsylvania Developmental Disabilities Planning Council, it is necessary to tell you enough about such organizations for the work that I am talking about to make sense. Let me begin at the beginning, at the point where I knew almost nothing about them myself.

My Introduction to the Council

In one of the last days of December of 1983 I found myself looking over an ornate balcony in the Pennsylvania Capitol as a child with cerebral palsy, held in the arms of the Lieutenant Governor, flipped a switch to illuminate the state Christmas tree. Harrisburg was certainly a place I had never expected to be, but there I was, singing carols with my new governmental colleagues. I had moved to the state, unpacked and found my office, a little series of rooms high above the state library. Now I needed to start work. What was my work to be?

I had just been appointed by the Governor to serve as Executive Director of the state Developmental Disabilities Planning Council, a small organization charged with improving the lives of people with developmental disabilities. It had been troubled and largely ineffective, and so as a "reform" appointee I had an opportunity to help the group try to recreate itself in a new way (if I could survive longer than my predecessors!). Despite the serious difficulties, there is an advantage in coming as a new leader into a setting which all agree is in real trouble: resistance to change is extraordinarily low. People are not strongly inclined to defend present practices if nobody likes the present very much. As the vice-chairperson of the group said when I asked his approval of some initial changes I wanted to make, "Anything you want to try is o.k. with me — you can't mess it up any worse than it is already." Under the test of initial changes not everybody came to agree with that statement, but it was in general an accurate indicator of shared sentiment at the time.[1]

Like Sharon Gretz and A.J. Hildebrand, I had been working to develop and improve services for people with disabilities, in my case in another state. It had been exciting to do such things as start group homes when they were new experiments and nobody knew what they were. But eventually conditions in that state became so technologized, so bureaucratized, so dominated by the state department of mental retardation, that it became clear to me that the developmental disabilities field had now reached a point at which the invention of little that was new would be permitted. The community service field, in a word, had become institutionalized.

Reluctantly, I broadened my gaze beyond the state's borders, with little real hope that anyplace else would be substantially different. When I got to Pennsylvania, I discovered that my generalization had been wrong. While my perception of the narrowing of community work was basically correct, there were differences in the environment of Pennsylvania which made significantly greater creativity possible.

Why states so close in proximity should differ so markedly is a question that has preoccupied me from the beginning. Certainly the Commonwealth of Pennsylvania's county-based governmental system is significant in counterbalancing the power of state departments which are unconstrained in the other state. Considerable local control and variability are thus preserved, at the cost of statewide efficiency. Constructing the community services system in the 1970s on an intensive "philosophical base" of normalization of educational workshops is surely another significant factor, as compared with a state in which community services were established with no conscious and explicitly stated system of values at all. But I reached the conclusion after searching for answers in Pennsylvania history that these were perhaps recent signs of differences that could be traced back to cultural differences inherent in the Commonwealth's origins, as compared with the first state. The contribution of the religious and cultural values of Quakerism, with its tradition of religious tolerance, may be a key factor in this, its tracings still felt centuries later in the organization of developmental disabilities services.

Thus I found myself in a new situation, with a group of Council members and other colleagues of unusual imagination, in an organization which was troubled but which was at a flexible stage and had a mandate permitting an extremely broad range of activities. It had a membership of people who were deeply committed to the welfare of people with disabilities and increasingly troubled by emerging problems in community services. Within this group, a number of leaders entertained dreams of doing something very different, were open to risk, and were intrigued by the possibility that a new approach might be possible. If a group of people found themselves involved with a small forum for social policy development such as a Developmental Disabilities Planning Council, equipped with status as a governmental agency and with grant money to give away, what could they try to do to nurture the progress of the conceptual revolution which might be underway? That is what we set out to discover.

That the impulse to nurture a new conceptual revolution is set here within the experience of a particular kind of organization called a state developmental disabilities planning council is not, I believe, its most relevant characteristic. It is merely, if its work is truly valid, one type of governmental and/or funding organization which can perform such work. All of the conceptual and social explorations described here could have been attempted from other settings, such as foundations, many of which would have been much less complicated to pursue such work through. Nonetheless, it is pertinent to examine some of the aspects of this kind of organization, both to understand it individually and to comprehend why this kind of setting which lends itself to conceptual and social change was created and exists.

Background and History[2]

Developmental Disabilities Councils, which operate exclusively at the state level, were invented in Washington. Vigorous advocacy of disabilities groups had resulted, in 1970, in the Developmental Disabilities Services and Facilities Construction Act, PL 91-517. The Act was intended to

> "assist the States in developing a plan for the provision of comprehensive services to persons affected by mental retardation and other developmental disabilities originating in childhood, to assist the States in the provision of such services in accordance with such plan,"

and for the construction of facilities. One of the key provisions of the new Act was to require each state to establish a Council on Developmental Disabilities to develop a state plan for services to people covered under the legislation, and to oversee the allocation of federal money received by states under the Act.

The 1970 Act also served to formally introduce the concept of "developmental disabilities" as a group of conditions larger than mental retardation but which required similar response. While the concept had no etiological basis, it was introduced as a broad term to avoid fragmenting approaches, diagnosis manipulation, and other problems experienced in categorical programs (Boggs, 1972).

Significant among the Act's provisions was the requirement that state Councils include representatives of all of the various interests concerned with the welfare of people with developmental disabilities: principal state agencies, local agencies, non-governmental organizations and groups, and persons with disabilities and family members themselves. Broad cooperation of all parties was intended to ensure that the efforts of different state agencies would be effectively coordinated. The involvement of persons with disabilities in policymaking was a relatively new direction in public policy, tracing its origins to the effects of the civil rights movement (Wieck, 1990) and taking its model from other recent federal legislation such as the Vocational Rehabilitation Act (Boggs, 1990). This involvement brought democratic participation into policymaking and service development.

While Councils were granted decision-making authority over how federal funds were to be spent, this responsibility was in fact handled jointly with one or more state agencies termed "administrative agencies." Writers of the act, who originally envisioned a financially substantial formula grant program to states, didn't want to set Councils up as new agencies in state government. Councils were intended "to remain relatively free from entanglement with ongoing problems and struggles inherent to any bureaucratic structure" (Sheerenberger, 1987). This turned out not to work, although the planning direction seemed reasonable in terms of the original goal which was to bring large amounts of funds into states to extend service to people under the new "developmental disabilities" definition who would not be served by states otherwise. Domestic funding shortages caused by the Vietnam War, however, caused this original formula grant function of Councils to be abandoned, and their function contracted to that of planning and advocacy. The vestigial provision for separate administrative agencies, however, remained (Boggs, 1990).

Although subsequent revisions of the Act have reduced the ability of state administrative agencies (often mental retardation departments) to control funds, limitations on Council activity by the state departments and consequent conflict have remained problems in many states.

When I arrived in Pennsylvania, one of the first things I found was that the fiscal person who actually wrote the contracts for Council grants was in an agency across town and did not report to me. In fact, I could obtain almost no financial information. When I tried to order a modest tracking wall-chart to monitor grant processing, he turned me down, claiming that there was not enough money in our multimillion dollar budget! Obviously, this had to be remedied before one could attempt to do anything else, and we were successful in eventually bringing fiscal control internally and into the service of the Council's program and policy decisions. Even under these best possible circumstances, however, all fiscal and personnel actions must be transacted through the immense and resistant bureaucracy of a large state administrative agency.

Pennsylvania's Council, like those in all other states, develops a state plan every three years in which it sets forth the objectives it intends to pursue over the next period. From these objectives, Requests for Proposals are issued and proposals are received. Proposals are subsequently chosen for funding by proposal selection committees which are conflict-of-interest free and at an arm's length from Council decision making. Grants, which usually run for a three-year period, are then awarded.

The Setting in Which Developmental Disabilities Planning Councils Function

Human service settings are fickle creatures, subject to the whims and fluctuations of many internal and external influences. Among such settings, Developmental Disabilities Councils, despite their great advantages, tend to be particularly subject to the ills, fallibilities, and instabilities likely to beset creatures of such complex and negotiated design. Not quite governmental bureau, not quite voluntary association, not quite foundation, they have proven as an organizational type to be quite problematic to raise to great effectiveness, despite the high quality of people often associated with them. Balanced between the the three cross-winds of an advocacy constituency, a governmental bureaucracy, and grant-seekers, Councils are settings which often require a significant ongoing expenditure of energy to maintain autonomy and stability amidst strongly conflicting forces.

The Dance of the Advocates

Any social movement is a highly charged, unstable aggregation of people and groups, each of whom have their (often conflicting) passionate view of what will better the lot of mankind. Social activists are a scrappy bunch. This is exactly the nature of the developmental disabilities advocacy movement, where argument, insurrection, and passionate disagreement reign. Developmental Disabilities Councils, as a creation of this advocacy movement and its representative in state government, often serve as a focus for the varied views of what to do about the needs of their diverse constituencies. Since Councils influence state policy and they give out money, one can expect great passion over how the money should be spent. Should one reform the "system" or should one protect individuals? Should one attend to the needs of people with mental retardation or those with spinal injuries? Should one think mostly about the needs of cities, or reach to rural areas? All such spirited discussions are never-ending, as of course they must be.

A pertinent example of the political dynamics of the advocacy community is the attrition in the unique flexibility of Developmental Disabilities Planning Councils' through "demands by special interest groups for mandated targeting" (Boggs, 1977). Because the original Act was "deliberately non-specific in its interpretation" (Stedman, 1975), there is ongoing action by such groups to insert restrictive language into successive federal reauthorizations. Each mandated activity, of course, gains what a particular interest group believes will produce results for its constituency by sacrificing Council flexibility and autonomy on the state level. Thus the groups that, acting together, created Councils will, acting alone, progressively reduce their ability to function over the long term. De Tocqueville's observations on the social dynamic apparent here are contained in Chapter 10.

The Morass of the Bureaucracy

Keeping an organization stable that has its life completely within the advocacy community is difficult enough, as the leadership of any voluntary association can attest. Developmental Disabilities Councils, however, carry the discussions of the advocacy world into their home which is within the bureaucracy of state government. The bureaucratic setting of government, of course, plays by rules that are just as specific, if different, and just as perilous, if more deeply embedded.

Government, like every large bureaucracy, is tied up by a myriad of laws, rules, and procedures designed to ensure long-term stability and avoid scandal. The ever-expanding morass of these procedures makes it extremely difficult and frustrating, as any activist governmental administrator can attest, to get anything done. Bureaucracies don't like to change, and resent those who try to change them. As Jerry Miller (who never had a long tenure in any state government) once said: "If you want to change a system overnight, you'd better be ready to leave in the morning."

Government is, after all, the most extreme example of the professional/bureaucratic world view at work. The resistance of such large bureaucracies to unusual ideas is well-known.[3] On a practical level, government is set up to deal with large, professional organizations while "new world view" settings are usually small and unsophisticated. It is often technically difficult to be able to successfully make grants to small settings. As Byron Kennard explains:

> "Here is the awful irony we are facing: *The only efforts that the system will permit are those firmly rooted in the old assumptions.* An example: When the government, after years of prodding by citizen groups, finally began to support solar energy development, it set things up so that most of the grants, contracts, and subsidies went to big institutions and corporations. Now, it so happens, big institutions and corporations do not really believe in solar energy, nor do they understand how to develop it. By its very nature, solar energy is best applied in decentralized ways. By their very nature, centralized institutions cannot comprehend decentralization. Handing over the control of solar energy's development to big companies is like asking elitists to promote the values of populists, never the twain shall meet. But big institutions and corporations mouth the assumptions recognized and trusted by the system. They are as comfortable as an old shoe so they get the financial support.
>
> "New efforts rooted in fresh assumptions will be opposed and even repressed by the prevailing system simply because this system is programmed less to learn than to endure. Accordingly, it learns poorly but endures well." (1983, pp.xiii-xiv)

The gulf of differences between a governmental system which is necessarily rooted in old assumptions and settings experimenting with new ones is so great it could not be successfully bridged without the sympathetic and skilled help of numerous individual people charged with operating various aspects of the system. These individuals, after all, are not all unfeeling bureaucrats, but people working within a setting in which the prevailing world view emphasizes values such as stability, order, clear power relationships and career development. As individual people they have their individual values, relatives with disabilities, and an orientation to stretch an interpretation for those in whom reason to trust has been proven.

Contrary to popular impression, comptrollers, government lawyers, procurement specialists, and others can want to see life improved for people with disabilities if you go about it in a way that is possible for them within their roles. In some states, as noted, bureaucratic and political control is so strong that organizations such as Councils are virtually prohibited from doing anything significant. In Pennsylvania, thankfully, we have been indulged with an unusual measure of understanding and tolerance, considering what we ask.

An established agency, serving as interpreter, can sometimes translate the words of one language to the other and so make the meeting of the "oil and water" of small associational settings and government bureaucracy more successful. Under such an arrangement the new setting can fulfill the necessary requirements for funding and government can feel comfortable. These requirements may be reinterpreted to meet the distinctive features of the small settings for funding, reducing the pressure for the informal group to professionalize itself in order to be able to talk the language of funding, contracts, and reporting. Sharon Gretz's project is an example of this arrangement.

Yet even with the understanding help of individuals, attempting to pursue this work can be frustrating. Only extreme clarity of purpose, high esprit de corps, and a wry sense of humor on the part of a small, wily staff group make it possible at all. When you need more help, you find that staff have to be hired through the civil service system — only they're not giving the exam. It takes six years of filing forms to get some office computers — and then the software order is canceled to fund prison repair. Interoffice mail delivery stops because the government police start ticketing the mail van for parking in front of the building. Grants are held up by scores of signatures and procedures while projects face closing for lack of federal funds which are due to expire if not spent immediately. When it gets particularly bad I have a fantasy of wrapping myself with dynamite and going, plunger in hand, to the departmental office where a contract has gotten hopelessly stuck. "Issue that grant now or I'll blow us all to kingdom come!" I'll yell, as terrified clerks and bureaucratic supervisors crawl about the floor frantically searching for my blue-back contract in the stacks of backed-up paperwork.

Developmental Disabilities Councils, by bringing the divisive activism of a social movement into the resistant bulk of government, set up an inherent conflict. Activists want things to change, and right away. Bureaucrats want things to go on pretty much the way that they are. This is the context in which those who aspire to promote major conceptual changes in world view must operate. A thorough understanding of the dynamics involved is essential.

Such inherent tension, incidentally, is one reason why people in governmental positions who actually try to *do* something tend not to last very long.[4] State commissioners of mental retardation, by way of example, have an average tenure nationally of only 22 months. The curious thing is they tend to be "killed off" by the advocates rather than the bureaucracy. The former mental retardation commissioner of one state, by way of illustration, transferred some years ago to be commissioner of corrections. In an interview shortly after the change, he confessed that he found running the state's problematic prison system to be a less stressful job than his former one. And this was a week after a major prison riot! The difference? No advocates. It seems a high price to pay for peace, somehow.

Grant Seekers

Grants administrators, as Byron Kennard (1972) once wrote,

> "are constantly on the receiving end of desperate, impassioned pleas and brazen maniacal sales pitches intended to break them down and to wring a grant out of them by any means, fair or foul. To maintain simple human dignity they develop psychological defenses, just as surgeons learn to turn a deaf ear to the groans of the sick and dying." (p.72)

Giving out money in the developmental disabilities field is hard business. For one thing, there is so little "free" money around, especially to do innovative or controversial things, while human need and misery are, of course, limitless. It is as if one arrived with a few small bags of seed in the midst of a refugee camp in starving Ethiopia. As people surge for the bags, it is clear that the seed will be quickly devoured by a small fraction of the dying. The only hope to do some lasting good is to carefully plan how to help a few people plant gardens. It is the old "teach a man to fish" question. Holding out on the seed for planned and careful use will label you, of course, as unfeeling and heartless in the eyes of some.

A Developmental Disabilities Council director, as a grants administrator, must become inured to being more or less constantly besieged by people who are extremely unhappy when they don't get a grant. Councils develop procedures and funding cycles in order to create enough predictability and peace to be able to have a space to think. Those that do not defend themselves behind a reasonably strong series of funding procedures quickly become food for the vultures, struggling to function while being picked over like carrion by a variety of providers of all types, advocates, consultants, and anybody with the strength or wit or cunning to dart in between the bigger jaws to tear off a tasty piece of an ear. In this regard, the high level of procedural structures within government can be useful. On the other hand, the necessity of living in relatively peaceful coexistence within a bureaucracy means that a great many good ideas cannot be funded at all, or at least not in the way one would like.

These dynamics can conspire to make the council director who is interested in self-preservation hesitate about answering his or her phone at the beginning of a grant cycle. One cannot be blamed for starting to feel like one is walking down a threatening alley on a dark night, with the glint of reflected eyes and unsheathed steel flashing from behind every boarded-up window and dumpster. After a particularly hard day you can feel like pulling your wallet out, throwing it into the middle of the sidewalk and carefully fleeing backwards down the street, yelling out "take the money, for God sakes — just maybe drop the wallet into a mailbox when you are through!"

Results in Practice

Developmental Disabilities Planning Councils were a new form created to attempt social change. As an idea, it seemed very promising. But how well has the idea actually worked?

As organizations charged with coordination of the efforts of others through cooperation, Councils have succeeded about as well as any other attempt at this kind of endeavor, which is to say not particularly. The mandated presence of people with disabilities and family members themselves in a government policy-making body was, on the other hand, a unique and even visionary invention. The regular rubbing of elbows of state officials and people with disabilities at board meetings has been a productive experience over the years. Finally, the availability of money to sponsor new efforts has held the potential to be uniquely productive and to allow the ideas of such a group to enter the actual practice of social policy. There is the flexibility under such Councils' broad mandate to pursue ideas which are too new for anyone else to feel comfortable funding yet. Historically, Councils funded the creation of group homes when they were new, and may as well live to fund their replacement. It is rare to have a governmentally funded organization in which a cross-section of the citizenry concerned and those who direct the systems that serve them sit together to consider the question, "What can we do and spend money on that will make life better for people in our state?" Developmental Disabilities Planning Councils, when they operate effectively, are able to consider this question.

One obvious impediment to the effectiveness of Councils is the provision for "administrative agencies," which can become enormously problematic in attempting to do anything innovative, and have even largely prevented effective action in certain states. Yet this alone is not sufficient to explain often limited results. Why does one see so many need assessments, report compilations, and computer analyses, and so few "attempts to consider the impossible?" Why, with so many possibilities, were we not accomplishing more?

Upon reflecting on a multi-state Developmental Disabilities meeting I had attended, I once wrote about the group as a truly integrated society of people with and without disabilities, where only the form of the work and not the form of the body seemed to matter:

> "Yet the problems themselves seemed pallid objects for such human passion: bylaw modifications, budget analyses, annual leave policies ... It seemed hard to find how these meetings and memoranda to government offices and to ourselves would improve the lives of people with disabilities. Our work seemed to be about modifying systems.
>
> "I reflect in my corner of the meeting-room that I am seeing two parts of our work. The first is the enthusiastic and characteristically American way we join together to accomplish some common end, as de Tocqueville so long ago observed. Yet that impulse to accomplish something gets pulled into the terms and forms of that same system that the people originally set about to change. Our own discussions, I note, are often so complex and technical that few newcomers could understand what we are talking about." (1988, p.6)

This was not only observable elsewhere; it was observable at times within my own Council, among my own friends, and in myself. Our primary limitation seemed not to be administrative and other difficulties, formidable as they were, but our own failure of imagination. Looking at the situation of people with disabilities, and of our society generally, we often could conceive of no action other than that which was most familiar to us. That imaginative action should be a rare commodity in general is no surprise. Most of us work in settings in which creativity is far from fostered. But one would not expect it to be rare in social instruments with the broadest possible charter for imaginative action. This points more to a limitation in what we believe possible than to any inherent constraints in the social form.

The process in which Developmental Disabilities Councils were supposed to engage was quite straightforward. You did an analysis of all of the programs for people in the state, located the gaps, and conducted need surveys to pinpoint the exact type and scope of the need. Then you "filled gaps" in the service system by starting new programs or by adjusting bureaucratic systems. Eventually, perhaps all of the gaps might be filled.

The more that some of us thought about this approach, the less sense it made. Surely society was more subtle and complex than that. From that point, we started trying to figure out what *did* make sense. This brought us to a path we didn't expect. Eventually, some of us began to believe that the promotion of new social experiments was one way of working towards a new change in social conditions. We were trying to get to something larger than conventional "systems change". Developmental Disabilities Councils were in fact extremely useful, and perhaps even designed, for such imaginative ends.

Government and Creativity

Many of the dynamics described above can be found in one way or another in all organizations that provide funding for new projects in the developmental disabilities field. But our own experience with a Developmental Disabilities Planning Council may be particularly relevant for government. For it is possible, in our experience, for government, necessarily bound as it is in an old world view, to support the emergence of the new. This is particularly true on the state level. "Many states stifle creativity," Steve Taylor reported finding from his national research on community integration. "They create an atmosphere in which bureaucratic compliance is rewarded and innovation and risk-taking are punished. Just as states can inhibit innovation and creativity, they can also foster them" (Taylor, 1988). There is no question that this is true. But creativity, as two family policy writers recently pointed out, is part of the American design:

> "Two hundred years ago, when they designed our basic Constitutional framework, the founding fathers reserved substantial powers and responsibilities to state governments so that they might serve, as Jefferson put it, as 'civic laboratories' for exploring alternative solutions to the problems that would inevitably arise in the course of human progress." (Edwards and Snyder,1987, p. 2)

Developmental Disabilities Planning Councils represent, at their best, an opportunity to capitalize on the possible role of states as civic laboratories by using their broad charter to experiment in new and creative ways. It is by using this rare capacity to experiment that new conceptual and social revolutions may emerge.

I spoke in the opening chapter of such revolutions in the metaphor of a sea voyage. In considering that voyage we took an initial glance in Chapters 2 and 3 at what a far shore might look like, through the experiences of Sharon Gretz and A.J. Hildebrand. In this chapter we have examined one ship available for the journey, a state Developmental Disabilities Council. In the next chapter we will look at the near shore: the current situation in community services. What is it now like in the land in which we live? What conditions would possibly induce us to consider a voyage away from all that we know, to new shores across an unknown sea?

End Notes

1. Readers who assume from this short summary of this initial period that I was full of confidence in the outcome have never taken over responsibility for a setting in crisis. Suffice it to say that I rented an apartment on a month-to-month basis.

2. To explore the complex and interesting history of Developmental Disabilities Councils and of their establishing Act is not possible in a brief space. This extremely simplified overview is intended only to orient the reader not familiar with them to their basic characteristics.

3. A splendid and amusing exposition of the rules bureaucracies operate under is Kharasch's *The Institutional Imperative: How to Understand the United States Government and Other Bulky Objects (1973)*.

4. From a psychological perspective, public officials are also available to receive the projections of those activists who have unresolved power conflicts which they need to play out in opposition to an external figure. These "shadow" dynamics, which run beyond the valid tension of opposition based upon issues, work upon the same inherent emotionality of crowds that leads nations to war. One of the liabilities inherent in such roles for practitioners of any form of statecraft is, of course, vulnerability to personalized attacks.

CHAPTER 5

Context for a New Conceptual Revolution: The Current Situation

"If the misery of the poor be not caused by the laws of nature, but by our institutions, great is our sin."

— Charles Darwin

Some mornings in the wintertime I stop to drive out the cold with a warm breakfast at the counter of the Alva Restaurant, a little family-owned place across from the train station in Harrisburg. Like most diners it is a community center of sorts. Each morning finds the same people trading the same banter back and forth. Over to the side of the counter a special table is reserved for the railroad workers' coffee break. You get the impression that trainmen have been drinking coffee there since the Alva was founded in 1916, and it is probably true.

Every Tuesday morning at ten a long table is set up in the restaurant's dining room. A group of fifteen or twenty men, all obviously retired, filter in and spend an hour or so talking over coffee and a Danish. One day I finally got curious and asked the cashier who they were. They turned out to be retired trainmen. Having come to the Alva together for coffee breaks for so many working years, they continue to unite their old work crews once a week at the old place. They see their old friends, and they get out of the house. Their warmth and ease with each other are readily apparent.

A sociologist might refer to these trainmen's Tuesday mornings as an example of an "informal associational group." All this means is that it is an example of the countless semistructured groups that serve as associational glues to hold society together, bonding us around various purposes with each other.[1]

If you did a study of the effect of the Alva group upon the members' lives, you would undoubtedly discover greatly significant results. In our culture retired people are subject to great loss of meaning in their lives, and consequently to increased risk of depression and physical decline. Yet the Alva group requires no funds, no professional supervision, no requests for proposals to be mailed out and reviewed. The professionally supervised adult activity centers across town seem empty and juvenile by comparison.

Finishing my coffee, I muse on the fact that my task at the office today is to develop formal program funding in the state for similar needs. The biggest problem of persons with developmental disabilities seems to me to be their exclusion from the common life of society. People in the developmental disabilities field have tried, with some success, to remedy this problem in a variety of ways. Yet all of us, including my organization, try to accomplish this by the conventional means of human service programs. Is there a limitation inherent in what we do? Or is there another way we can approach our work? How can we help to develop something with our millions of government dollars that is as useful to people with developmental disabilities as the Alva trainmen's group is to them?

As I walk into my office, the telephone is ringing. Message slips litter the desk. I glance through the morning's mail: invitations to governmental and advocacy meetings to address various serious problems in mental retardation services. Other meetings to plan the creation of a system for people with physical disabilities who as yet have no services. A news clipping about a young man who died in one of our state institutions after being restrained. An announcement of a workshop teaching a kind of restraint; a modified martial art for staff to learn to control and protect themselves from people with disabilities. A pleading message from an elderly mother whose adult son, for years on an "emergency waiting list" for admission to a group home, is beating her up in their home. Advocacy "alerts" on funding shortfalls for residential services, and an announcement of a rally at the legislature to demonstrate for increases in the budget. New regulations from Washington to force people with disabilities out of nursing homes if they need "active treatment." What in the world, I muse, is "active treatment?"

One doesn't have to stay very long in an office like mine to notice that a lot seems to be going wrong in community services for people with disabilities. Of course in such work there is no quiet time, has been no quiet time, in this or any other field of human welfare. Yet the feeling of what is going wrong seems somehow different than it was even a few years ago. Our task once seemed to be fairly straightforward: close the institutions, and replace them with a humane system of community services. Yet now community services themselves seem increasingly immersed in serious difficulties. There are community agencies at risk of bankruptcy, and county programs in fiscal distress so severe that people with mental retardation are actually being returned to institutions. Lack of resources, money and staff are alleged to be at the root of such crises. Advocacy groups and task forces form and work to pull in the resources that the service system so desperately needs. Yet fiscal resource issues, while very real, often serve as a focus of what can be a much more complex situation with deeper meaning than a simple lack of money.

Various issues arising in community services, if examined to-gether, emerge as symptoms of a larger process of change at work within the field. These issues, in my experience, tend to cluster in five basic areas:

1. Abuse, neglect, and psychotropic drug use
2. A staff "retention and recruitment" crisis
3. Isolation of people served
4. Increasing clinicalization of the field
5. Retarding effects of the system itself upon those dependent upon it.

The Current Situation in Community Services

Abuse, Neglect, and Psychotropic Drug Use

"We can state unequivocally that adults with mental retardation are being abused and neglected in their residences and elsewhere."

— Eileen Furey and Melanie Haber, Connecticut Protection and Advocacy Office; Connecticut University Affiliated Program (1989)

To the generation of young workers who started group homes, the work had much of the character of a rescue operation. Those of us who found people in abusive institutions and brought them out to commu-nity services can never forget what the experience was like. The stories of getting "key raps" on the head from an attendant's weighty key ring, the scars on the shoulders from being pushed up against the steam radiators until the flesh sizzled, the massive overdrugging, the criminally inadequate medical care — one does not push such images easily from one's mind. As we steadily got people out we breathed a sigh of relief. They were now safe. It is thus deeply unsettling, almost unimaginable, to start to see reports of neglect and abuse beginning to emerge from community services themselves.

Evidence thus far is largely anecdotal, although statistical records now exist in certain state protection and advocacy offices. Yet the problem is great enough that it occasionally emerges in the newspa-pers. Evaluators in community settings using such instruments as PASS or PASSING[2] say that problems are quietly pervasive. One hears rare — but deeply disturbing — stories of people in community residences who are neglected, or run over in the road, or who choked to death. Certainly the reality is that abuse and neglect in institutions were vastly, incomparably, more prevalent, and that ill treatment is often just more visible in community settings, if harder to traditionally monitor. Yet such incidents are exactly what "pro-institutional" parents opposing community placement feared. This is not to say they were "right:" institutions were clearly enormously worse. But the fact is that such incidents were not supposed to happen in our community programs at all. It was just not supposed to happen here.

We now see the use of aversive treatments in community programs. Even more significantly, it is now a rare but regular occurrence for states to go so far as to close the occasional community program for health and safety reasons. Given the known and understandable reluctance of states to take such an extreme step, this tells us a great deal about just how far conditions in community services can deteriorate.

While extremes do not show the mean, they can sometimes show the leading edge of trends. To find out what life conditions are really like in services, the best thing to do is to to ask the people whose lives are dependent upon them. It is difficult, of course, to elicit frank responses from people whose lives are controlled by systems, because of the threat of retribution for complaining. One of the rare settings in which people with the label of mental retardation feel safe enough to tell such stories is in adult self-advocacy organizations. Listening here one can discover a great deal.

At a recent self-advocacy retreat, the talk turned spontaneously to stories of abuse that members were subject to in their group homes. Women tentatively volunteered stories of unwanted sexual approaches by staff they were powerless to repel. One of the organization's advisors, who knew them very well and for many years, dating back to when many of them had lived in institutions, was completely shocked. She knew there were problems, but could it really be *this* bad? Recovering slightly, she posed one quiet question. "How many of you," she asked, "are afraid of your staff?" All over the room hands went up.

If good, caring people are attracted to this work, how could such a situation have come about?

One of the few areas in which data on injurious conditions in community services exist is the use of psychotropic drugs. Again, the work of starting community residences involved getting people off the psychotropic drugs they had been given in institutions for years. Staff convictions about this were often fierce; doctors were challenged. It was somewhat of a rarity in those days to have people in your program on psychotropics. It always felt a little bit like defeat.

Recent research, in contrast, has documented routinely high rates of psychotropic drug use in community programs. One recent Pennsylvania study found that over half (51%) of people served in community settings received psychotropic medications (Nowell, et. al., 1989); another found a rate of 42% for former residents of Pennhurst State School (Conroy and Feinstein, 1988). A recent study in Ontario established a rate of 40% (Gowdey, 1987); one in Illinois, 29% (Buck and Sprague, 1989). Increasing attention in the literature indicates this is a phenomenon drawing enough concern to warrant investigation. Only the day before I was writing this, *Mental Retardation* published the first reported account of a person with mental retardation who had developed neuroleptic malignant syndrome, a rare but deadly iatrogenic disease caused by psychotropic drugs (McNally and Calamari, 1988). The list of drugs which had been administered to this young man looked exactly like the kind of polypharmacy I used to see in state mental institutions fifteen years ago.

There are those, of course, who point out that people with significantly higher levels of behavioral difficulties are living in community services today than could gain admission to them in the past. They attribute the rise in drug use to this change. Yet this alone is not satisfactory in explaining increased drug use. We now have institutions which seem to have lower rates than those emerging from some community studies, although institutions retain people with much more severe behavioral difficulties than are found in community services. When more extensive comparative studies are done, we may find that many community services now have higher psychotropic prescription rates than the institutions to which they relate, and with a population of people with less severe disabilities. The drug use rate, like the frequency of other types of abuse and neglect, serves as an indicator of changes within the community service system.

The "Retention and Recruitment" Crisis

Probably the most pressing and intractable problem affecting the community system has been termed the "retention and recruitment" crisis. What this term means is that residential provider agencies cannot find enough staff to hire, and those they do hire don't tend to stay long. Agencies in certain areas of my state routinely operate with many unfilled positions, with other staff and supervisors stretched to the limit to take up the extra workload. Annual turnover rates for mental retardation and mental health residential workers in Pennsylvania, according to a recent survey, average 66%, with rates of over 100% far from uncommon (Pennsylvania Association of Resources for the Retarded, 1988). One executive director I recently met told me that she had turnover rates of 250% in some houses, that is, two and a half new people in each position each year. Another commented to me that the recruitment problem was so severe that she just wished she didn't have to hire people with criminal records.

Hospitals are an example of another human service with a critical shortage of workers. Hospitals are experiencing such severe problems getting a sufficient supply of nurses they have in desperation recently begun to recruit nurses from foreign countries. One could predict that one might see this in community services next and, in fact, some agencies are now starting to pursue foreign recruitment. The practice of hiring people from other countries for jobs that are so unattractive that locally qualified members of a field will not take them has long defined the hiring of physicians in institutions, we may recall.

Human services programs are not the only industry with a severe shortage of workers. Fast-food franchises are a well-known example of another. Almost every fast food restaurant that one goes into these days has signs up trying to recruit housewives, retired people — anybody — to work there. When in Connecticut last year I discovered the shortage was so severe that employers were sending commuter buses to New York City to bring in people poor enough to be interested in working at such jobs.

From a management perspective, most industries could not long survive under conditions of such massive turnover. Fast food operations are one example of how adaptations can apparently be successfully made, at least for a time. These combine simple, routinized jobs which pay low salaries with quick, effective training. The cost of constant employee replacement can thus be reduced to a minimum. For a McDonald's, it probably doesn't matter a great deal if everybody behind the counter is new every six months, as long as there are enough people behind the counter.

When we hear the words "retention and recruitment crisis" in *our* field of work, we know that the terms and concepts which govern the world of business and industries like fast-food franchises have been borrowed to help to understand our difficulties. From a management point of view, if we can just manage to fix the system sufficiently to have enough people behind the counter of our community settings, with recruitment balancing attrition and training costs manageable, we will have stabilized the caring system. The recruitment and retention crisis will be solved.

This phenomenon, however, can be looked at in ways other than through management concepts. One might say instead that a caring enterprise such as ours has its true being in the reality of relationships between people, particularly between people with disabilities and their staff. In these community settings, in which relationships are the essence of the enterprise, each relationship that a person dependent upon the service forms is likely to be broken frequently and predictably. If such a person resides for ten years in a group home with three staff and a 100% turnover rate, he or she must form thirty new relationships in that time. And this is in the residential program alone, without looking at work programs, case managers, social workers, behavioral specialists, and the many other people who dance in and out of the dependent person's life in a regular fashion.

If I were faced with a constant disruption in my emotional and personal life, if I could never depend on anyone really "being there" for me, I would probably become deeply bewildered. I would probably retreat into myself and avoid making new relationships as freely, knowing as I did that they were only destined to end. I might, when I had a problem in such a discouraging environment, even descend into abusing myself and have to be treated behaviorally for "Self Injurious Behavior."[3] Or I might become disturbed and have to receive psychotropic drugs to treat my psychiatric problem. The rise in psychotropic prescription rates is, I suspect, directly related to this constant discontinuity of relationships in people's lives.

In fact what we now believe to be a "retention and recruitment" crisis is not that crisis at all. It is in reality something far more serious. *It is a managerial description of settings in which those with the economic freedom to leave consistently do so.* Only those without the freedom to leave remain. This is one sure way to tell "clients" from "staff" — by how long they have been there.

What is curious about this is that perceptive and dedicated administrators have recognized the problem of constantly broken relationships as it has steadily escalated. Yet it was only when the problem of recruitment of replacements became so severe that it threatened the very managerial ability to keep enough bodies behind the counter that a crisis was declared. The crisis, in fact, was there all along. For one must question whether "care" settings in which the very medium of caring, the relationship, has grown moribund, can be considered valid, no matter what their objective goals or other beneficial characteristics.

In truth, the retention and recruitment crisis, although naming the crisis in the wrong way entirely, does serve to make us aware that a crisis exists. But it is as if an epidemic of pneumonia were suddenly declared to be sweeping off the population, when all of the people who succumbed were suffering from underlying malnutrition. It is easy to confuse symptom for cause.

Isolation from the Real Community

Related to the lack of enduring relationships with staff is the lack of relationships with ordinary citizens outside the service system. It is now increasingly recognized that by moving people from large remote service settings to small service settings in neighborhoods we often only managed to bring about physical integration, a necessary but not sufficient condition for actual social integration to occur. The involvement of residents of group homes in the life in their neighborhoods and communities once they could be physically present has been well documented. [See Robert Perske's *New Life in the Neighborhood* (1980).] But there is another and neglected side — the degree to which the kind of isolation seen in institutions still, in subtle form, pervades community services.

David Spect and Michael Nagy, in particularly interesting research, conducted an inventory of the kinds of relationships that residents had in community residential settings in one area of Massachusetts. Confirming casual impressions, Spect found that few people had freely given, unpaid relationships with members of the communities in which they lived. Almost all relationships were with staff (who, as noted above, change frequently). An unexpected and surprising finding was that the staff *themselves* had few ties to the communities in which they worked. Although the community residences were tolerated, many were not in any sense really part of their communities.

One can imagine hovering over such a group home's neighborhood in a helicopter. You look down, and to the naked eye the home looks like just another home on another street; just part of the community. It looks splendidly integrated. But then suppose that you have some advanced military "spy scope" that shows only the path of ordinary relationships in and out of the house. Paid services, social workers, day programs, and staff would not show up on the screen. While most homes on the block would be spiderwebs of lines to neighbors, schools, clubs, and friends, the people congregated in many group homes would stand alone.

This is not to say, again, that relationships do not occur in community services, and that they do not occur dramatically more frequently than they did in physically isolated settings. We know from our experience that this is true. But we also, when we stop to think about it, know many people who know only staff. We know many people who have no one but staff to give them a Christmas present, or to notice their birthday, just like in an institution. If we took our special "relationship-scope" and viewed all of the community residential settings in the country from the air, how much real isolation would we paradoxically find still there?

Increasing Clinicalization

When we look at community services of a few years ago compared with those of today, one of the most striking differences is seen in the clinical and technical language and procedures used. Most group homes were put together by young people with no particular human services background. There were no training programs, no behavioral specialists, no independent living plans, few, if any, regulations, no real "field" at all. Like most new enterprises, it was made up as we went along. There were many joys in this, but many disadvantages as well. Without sophisticated clinical support, people with really serious needs didn't get to live in community services. And there was constant confusion and disorder. To try to organize things better and to support people in their needs, we strove for more clinical sophistication. We developed clinical management systems. As the size of services spread, these practices increased so as to manage what was becoming a large enterprise. People had to be certified to give out pills. Houses had to have consultant behavioral psychologists. Records had to be kept.

The change in the underlying world view of residential workers corresponding to this development has been rather clearly observable through a community residence management simulation that some colleagues and I developed and have offered for some years through Cornell University. These Simulations are games in which participants play a decision-making role, in this case a residential administrator, balancing aspects of "real life" work (Schwartz, et al., 1983). Simulations are a particularly useful educational method because they illustrate in condensed form the interrelationship of factors and decisions which actually take place over a long time period. In this simulation three days corresponds to a year of "real time." The most interesting aspect of this simulation, however, turned out to be unexpected: it allowed participants playing the role of administrator to "live out" their usually unconscious world views in projection. It was like giving people an "ink blot" test combined with psychodrama. What do you see in this situation? Based upon what you see, what will you do?

The responses of players to typical problems concerning people served have been fascinating. In one "incident" (all drawn from actual events), a person living in a group home starts to act very disturbed. In reality, the incident is a simple one. The man has been sexually approached by a male staff member at the sheltered workshop. His "acting out" (in psychological terminology) is his distress and substitute for language in a frightening and conflict-ridden situation. If simulation participants investigate, they soon unearth the underlying reason for the behavior. They discover what the man concerned is, in his behavioral language, "saying." When the game was first developed, participant teams used to frequently pursue this and figure it out. But that seldom happens when the game is played these days. Instead, an immediate referral is frequently made to the consulting psychologist to construct a behavioral program to bring the behavior under control.

This change, noted in one incident, from seeing a person to detecting a problem, tends to pervade all responses throughout the game. What we are seeing is an expression of a change in the way that participants view the world. Responses vary, of course. Workers in Oregon still tend to see incidents more as human problems, rather than as clinical manifestations of pathology. Responses in Pennsylvania usually lie somewhere in the middle. New York is now highly pervaded with a clinical/technical perspective, with programs in the New York City area marked in this regard. I once had a simulation group that used so many technical terms to describe people and what they did that I made a list of them all on an overhead transparency and showed them at the end. "Food intake area," I recall, was one of them. It meant dining room.

Clinical and technical concepts, in short, have become so pervasive in community services that it sometimes has become difficult within them to think of any other way to approach a person with a handicap. Many residential workers, who no longer live with the people concerned, but work shifts in connection with other employees, seem increasingly unable to see the people that they work with as other than a collection of symptoms calling for the proper interventions. The power of socialization in these distancing technical values can be seen in the speed with which they are picked up by new workers who have been in these settings only months or even weeks. Experience with the simulation, in observation of programs over time, and in following the field's applied literature, indicates that the rate of clinicalization of the work is taking place very quickly.[4]

When I read that changes in this field often take place quite quickly, I am struck by the realization that I have been in it myself now just long enough to see certain developments come almost full circle. For the kind of clinical/technical orientation beginning to appear now in community services is precisely the kind of thing that I saw in advanced form in institutions when I first began. When I first walked the wards of a state hospital and encountered an old frail man tied in a wheelchair crying out plaintively "help me, help me," I had to be "educated" to see that this really was "attention-seeking behavior" to which I must not respond to avoid reinforcing it. Yet the man was crying out for help — he really was! One might have to listen very carefully to puzzle out exactly what kind of help he wanted — and maybe the help he needed was impossible to get for him. But one had to see him as a person in order to begin to hear.

There is compelling evidence, I think, to suggest that this process of not listening, of not seeing community service clients as people, is proceeding in community settings just as it did in institutional ones. Of course, with institutions we saw the final stage of a process that here may be only beginning. I wonder, as I look at many community services operating in the current environment, whether the clinical sophistication that we pursued has made these programs better. I do see people with tremendously challenging behavior living in community settings, and I marvel at the skill necessary to accomplish such a wonderful thing. But for the greater number of people, I wonder whether life conditions in this technically sophisticated system really feel as good or as rich as they felt in its messy origins, when nobody really knew what they were doing except to try to live together somehow. It is supposed to be better. We know so much more what we are doing now.

Retarding Effects of the System Itself Upon Those Dependent Upon It

The community services system was intended to foster the kind of expectations and personal growth which were so deplorably absent in institutions. Impressive and even astonishing growth is certainly still seen in people in community settings. Yet evidence of low expectations and limitations here seems to be emerging. It was recently recognized, for example, that the long-held assumption that sheltered workshops prepare people for competitive employment is virtually a complete fiction. People prepare for years in many of these workshops and never get ready for a real job. People work on learning their numbers and colors in day programs for ten years and never learn them. Also, sheltered workshops have economic and labor pressures to retain their most capable clientele, similar to those evident in the state institutions of a decade or two ago. The development of supported employment was intended to increase expectations, support people on real jobs, and get them out of what some critics are now calling "institutions in the community."[5]

The experience of what it feels like to live in the modern community services system was documented in a quite remarkable study produced a few years ago by a self-advocacy group in California. Under a grant from the California Developmental Disabilities Council, this group of people with mental retardation went about the state and interviewed their peers about their lives in relation to the services they were receiving. They hired a writer with no human services background to help write it up. They called their report *Surviving in the System: Mental Retardation and the Retarding Environment* (California Developmental Disabilities Planning Council, 1984).

In their report they complained about low expectations and limited opportunities. An interviewee complained of a sheltered workshop where "they make you more retarded." They talked about being limited and controlled by staff. They spoke of feeling held back for their economic worth to the system. "The difficult thing," one person said, "was that wherever I tried to go, people wanted me for my money instead of myself." As a friend of mine who used to live in Pennhurst State School once said, "I don't want to go back there — no way. But the people try to run your lives out here just the same."

In fact, one doesn't have to go very far to encounter numerous stories of community services founded recently on high expectations which now actually hold back the growth of people. In a recent instance, a residential worker who befriended a man in a supervised apartment learned of the man's burning desire to get a real job near where he lived, rather than to keep going to the sheltered workshop some miles away where he was bored, felt isolated, and made almost no money. The worker, innocently, talked to a friend of his who had a small family restaurant and got the man a job. It worked out very well; both the employer and employee were very satisfied, and the man began to become part of the town where he lived.

Soon, however, the sheltered workshop found out that its ex-client had found a job, was working, had *not* gone through the workshop placement office and, even worse, had been assisted by a staff member of a *residential* provider agency rather than by a vocational agency specialist. In the ensuing confrontation the restaurant worker was removed from his job,[6] returned to the workshop's supervision, and placed at a work enclave job site some miles from his home. Although he worked at a "real job," he remained in actuality an employee of the sheltered workshop which performed the community job under contract with the local business. The sheltered workshop, of course, retained a portion of contract earnings for administrative costs, a practice defended by the administrator as a way to help others by ensuring the continued economic health of the facility.

The Deterioration of Settings

Abuse, neglect, drugging, discontinuity of relationships, pervasive isolation, the reduction of people to aggregations of clinical syndromes, feelings by those served that they are being "retarded" by services: these are serious indictments indeed of a service system founded to free people from abuse and to promote growth and freedom. They are profoundly unsettling to see. Yet the evidence is there, and it seems to be accumulating.

There will be those who say that I am far too negative in my appraisal; that I am not taking into account all of the impressive evidence of growth and improvement in life that community services offer to people. It might even be said that by listing serious problems within community services I could put ammunition into the hands of those people (and they still very much exist) who wish to see people with disabilities reinstitutionalized. This frankly caused me considerable hesitancy in setting this down.

I could write a book about the incredible benefits of community services to people with disabilities. Many such books have been written. But that is not the purpose of this book. My intent here is to examine serious problems within community services for a purpose. That purpose has been to discern the nature of the difficulties, to understand just how serious they may be, and to discover what to do next.

It might be challenged, as well, that my analysis, for personal reasons, harks back too much to the "good old days" of the early community movement. That my concerns are little more than nostalgia for the past. For the moment let me just reply that those aspects of that time worth appreciating in memory have less to do with periods of past life romanticized by memory, or with anything particular about the community services themselves, than with the feeling of having participated in the establishment of new and uncharted settings. The founding of community services was but one of such creative times. This subject will be explored in greater detail later.

That most of the problems that I have listed are indeed seen as serious by those concerned about people with disabilities is evident from the multitude of efforts increasingly initiated to try to manage, control, or solve them. Task forces meet on employee recruitment and retention. Legislation is introduced, and state offices set up, to detect and monitor abuse. In one state a special program to train community residential staff in police investigation techniques was started so that staff could properly investigate each other when abuse occurred. Centralized systems to monitor drug prescriptions in community settings are proposed. Regulations are increased. The number of meetings held each month within a four-block walk from my office on various pressing problems in the community services system is significant.

Despite the sincerity of the concern, most of these efforts seem less than promising in truly resolving the issues. The issue of low staff salaries in my own state is a pertinent example. There is absolutely no question that the salaries paid to residential workers in Pennsylvania and most other states are indefensibly low. They are so low, in fact, that there is some risk of developing an entire underclass of poor residential workers. Raising salaries is the only moral thing to do. To continue to expand the system while paying people so poorly simply seems indefensible.

When one attempts to raise salaries, however, one is immediately caught in a quandary. First, the amount of money required to raise them even minimally is simply not likely to be obtainable. Second, current population demographics suggest that even if salaries were more attractive there still might not be enough workers to fill all of the necessary positions. Third, it is far from guaranteed that higher salaries would directly translate into increased retention or job tenure.

What keeps people in certain kinds of work, in fact, is often a complex series of factors, not all of which are economic. As I write this, for example, I am in a rural area in upstate New York with lots of family farms. Small-scale farming is a perfect case of an occupation that doesn't pay. But I know a number of people who want to farm so much that they work at regular jobs just so they can get out at three in the afternoon and grow things. The economic policies which make it necessary for the growers of food to do this are, to my mind, as indefensible as those which pay very low salaries to those who care for and about people with disabilities. Still, people do both. An agency with high morale that I am familiar with surveyed their staff and found that they had comparatively high qualifications and long tenure but continued to work for salaries considerably lower than they could command elsewhere in the current job market. What makes people come and stay in this work may, like farming, be more complex than money alone.

Thus with staff issues, and abuse, and all of the other difficulties arising from the current system, traditional solutions may simply be insufficient. For all of the remedies proposed are, in one way or another, technologies. If what we are dealing with are simply failed technologies of caring, then an application of new and better technologies should fix the problems. If, on the other hand, the problems are symptomatic of the error of technological approaches themselves, then an additional application of technology will only speed the underlying process of increasing dysfunctionality. In this case our solutions would be like the face-powder used in Elizabethan times, which gained its nice white color from the high content of lead. The lead caused lead poisoning sores on people's faces. To cover the sores, they used more lead.

At root, such symptoms as I have described indicate an underlying process best described as the deterioration of settings. Community settings, which started in an air of excitement, now seem bogged down in difficulties. This is not the first collection of settings, or the first social movement, to experience such a problem. In fact, the deterioration shows quite typical signs. There has been a loss of shared mission. Work which was once inspired by a higher sense of group and community vision has now succumbed to routine. Leadership has been succeeded by supervision. Organizational charts and job descriptions, once rare, have become dominant. Social visionaries are not attracted to the movement very much anymore because it is no longer a movement; instead, organizations seek employees. It is all not as much fun, frankly, as it used to be. This is important because the staff of such programs no longer are finding them fruitful scenes for their own personal growth.[7]

Where have we seen all of these symptoms before? In fact, we don't have to think back very far. We saw them in institutions. As Michael Smull (1989) points out, these symptoms are precisely in kind, if not yet in degree, the types of conditions in institutions which led to the reaction of the community services movement. Institutions, I well recall from my first day as an employee (when I was welcomed to the professional staff by being fingerprinted), were scenes of abuse, neglect, drugging, and isolation. Staff turnover and recruitment were troubling issues.[8] They were places where everything had a clinical character and people tended to be seen as clinical entities and less than fully human. Staff were, in the system where I worked, termed "items" in personnel language. There was a clear organizational chart. There was an abundance of supervision and little leadership. And people who were the inhabitants of institutional settings, whether staff or residents, did not flourish. They were places where nobody grew.

History, Technology, and Professionalism

How did we reach this point in the evolution of community services? To understand this, it is worth examining the picture that has emerged thus far from three additional perspectives. These include taking a brief look at some factors related to the historical development of residential services, examining the significance of the impulse toward technological solutions, and considering the concept of professionalism as an influence on the way that caring services are conceived, with some of its economic consequences.

Historical Trends in the Configuration of Services

"The founding of the early institutions was accompanied by a pride, hope, and euphoria we can scarcely comprehend."
— Wolf Wolfensberger

It is useful to remember that the institutions in which we found the deplorable conditions alluded to previously did not start that way. Indeed, the first American residential institutions were founded in the mid-1800's with as much optimism and hope as any of the first community settings a hundred years later. The founders, charismatic leaders like Edouard Seguin and Hervey Wilbur, believed that people with mental retardation could learn and flourish beyond the limits of any then-existing expectations.

This first generation of institutional leadership, as Wolfensberger has pointed out, eventually succeeded to a second generation of facility superintendents who were far more interested in managerial efficiency than in the individual potential of their charges.[9] Dramatic expansion of institutions took place, along with the routinization of operation and care. By the early part of this century, when the segregating ideology of eugenics became dominant, the early vision of the founders had been entirely displaced. Settings that had been born as places for the unfolding of individual potential had become concentration camps for a people regarded as an alien and dangerously infectious seed within society, to be confined lest they breed criminality and dependence.

The conceptual shift in the 1960s and '70s to pursuing community rather than institutional service seemed to be a radical departure from institutional forms, an entirely new way of doing things. Yet the new service model had deep roots in its predecessor. Such inventions as the early parent-run activity programs in church basements were, it is true, a huge leap back into the community. But these were a short-lived exception, as the record of programmatic and physical architecture shows. For the early prevailing forms of community services were almost completely institutionally based in character, if not actually in location. State institutions, for example, were still built; they were just newer, closer to population centers, and contemporary in architecture.

The shift toward community services took place in the closely allied worlds of mental retardation and mental health (mental retardation still fell under the jurisdiction of mental health departments in most states) at approximately the same time, although with some differences. Mental health architecture provides a particularly illustrative example of this transitional period in the form of a state psychiatric hospital that I saw opened in Elmira, New York in the early 1970s. Emblematic of the new ideology of "community psychiatry," the center was one of the first to be located in a downtown residential neighborhood. Driving past, the award-winning design presents a variegated facade of interconnected small brick complexes that fade as cunningly as a print by Escher into the matching brick of a surrounding low-income housing complex. Entering the front walk, on the other hand, brings you into an institutional courtyard bounded by hospital wards. The flat walls of these wings face a row of simulated "community" shops — although the real shops of downtown Elmira are only blocks away.

Externally, this new center and its architectural predecessor by almost exactly a century, located forty miles away, look completely different. Yet if you compare the internal arrangements of wards and hallways of the Elmira center with the 1869 asylum, it is evident that the internal structures of the remote nineteenth-century facility and the "community" twentieth-century one are essentially the same. Blueprints of both, laid side by side, show the same lines of rooms along hallways, just as in any hospital or dormitory. It is as if an institution is trying to disguise itself within a community, without actually changing its identity. It is the concrete expression of a human services world view with one foot still planted firmly in the old way of doing things, the other tentatively trying the new ground outside of its walls.[10]

The same movement which tried to make an institution at least architecturally part of a community gave birth to a key piece of legislation announcing a change from institutional psychiatric orientation to community orientation. The federal Community Mental Health Centers Act of 1963, which was supposed to make local psychiatric services available to all people, spawned a network of such local centers throughout the country. Compared to the existing tradition of "the asylum on the hill" it seemed a major conceptual leap forward. Yet these centers quickly fell short of the community ideal. As Sarason observed, after noting that such centers had increased the readmission rate to state hospitals in Connecticut by over four hundred percent:

"The community mental health center virtually guarantees the continued existence of the state hospital even though its initial rationale was
opposed to that of the state hospital! It could hardly have been otherwise
because these centers were conceived within the same traditions of
professional practice and theory — the same nomenclature, administrative hierarchical structure, professional preciousness, and professional
responsibility — that are the basis for state hospitals."(1974, p. 191)

Community mental health centers did deflect admissions to state
hospitals in many cases. But they also became a source of referrals for
state hospitals in others. This is because they were really part of the
same system, born, as Sarason points out, of the same beliefs. They
illustrate how community service forms that at first may seem dramatically different from their predecessors can carry unrecognized
within them the seeds of their true origin. Given time, these seeds give
evidence of the familial connection.

Returning to the field of mental retardation, one can see considerable evidence of such "seeds" in new growth. Some of these have
already been mentioned. Other examples arise readily. A first of these
is the reinstitutionalization of people from community settings under
the pressure of budget limitations in community programs. This, just
as Sarason observed in mental health, bears witness to the invisible
link that exists between the two.

A second and more striking piece of evidence relates to the ease
with which reversion to frankly institutional forms of an earlier era
can take place. The transition from institutional to community forms
was of course evolutionary. The first buildings used for group homes
were frequently small institutions cast off by other organizations in a
period of decline: convents. Some were homes located directly on
institutional grounds. After this early experience, some states, like
Pennsylvania, leapt ahead by establishing homes for no more than
three or four people each. The ongoing trend has thus been to smaller
and more physically integrated settings. Large group homes like old
convents have become conceptual and practical anomalies, "white
elephants" of the early days of the movement.[11]

It is thus surprising and instructive to see this trend reversing in
some places. New York State, for instance, has in recent years abandoned policies which kept the size of group homes under the already
quite large size of twelve. Most striking of all, this state has also been
pursuing a massive building program placing group homes *directly
back on the grounds of institutions!* Such homes were even serviced in
some cases by the central institutional kitchens, with trucked delivery
of food just like that to other outlying buildings. Plans for one group
home "housing development" alone proposed 152 "beds" of this type

on the institutional campus.

New York's institutional group homes are, of course, simply a recreation of the old nineteenth century "cottage plan" under another name. If you compare them with the architectural plan of the Craig Colony for Epileptics, founded in 1894, it is clear again that the underlying arrangement is identical. In fact, one can find architectural analogs from different centuries even on the same campus, something that nobody involved seems to notice.

How can it be that those involved in planning and erecting community services with such clear physical, organizational, and administrative resemblances to institutional practices and forms (and such dissimilarity to actual communities) fail to recognize them? Sarason, again, offers an observation in describing those responsible for carrying out the deinstitutionalization movement:

> "...they had absolutely — and I think 'absolutely' is not an exaggeration — no understanding of communities: how they are organized and work, how they would respond to those who would return to their communities, and the crucial importance of developing formal and informal constituencies and support services. In their hands, deinstitutionalization became a technical-fiscal problem..." (1988, p.384)

The emergence of problems in community services evocative of institutions (erosion in practice and size, readmissions, belief that problems can be solved through fiscal and other technologies) is therefore not as surprising as it may seem. For it may prove that revolution in thought and practice away from institutional forms was not as thorough a revolution as it seemed at the time. Some seeds, it seems, may have come along.

Craig Colony for Epileptics was located in the little town of Sonyea, a hamlet in the western part of the state. I drove through that town occasionally for years, and always assumed that Sonyea was an Indian name, no doubt from when the Senecas used to live in that region. There are many Indian names in that part of New York. One day I found out that my assumption was completely wrong. Sonyea stands for this: State of New York Epileptic Asylum. The post office had been established when the institution was founded. There had been no town there before, despite the name on my map. They had built an institution, and called it a community. Perhaps we, in our own modern way, have done something similar.

The Impulse Toward Technological Solutions

"I do not accept the argument, and haven't for years, that technology is value-free. It's laden with values. And by values I refer in this case to technology's tendency to reinforce controlling, systematizing, ordering behavior. These values have permeated our culture in this century."

— Thomas P. Hughes

The other night I called a friend who is in the hospital. She has multiple sclerosis, and is there for treatments with a powerful drug that may reduce the constant pain in her legs and perhaps help her to regain her ability to walk for a while. It is understandably a frightening and rather overwhelming time for her. A beautiful young woman, once a dancer and an international model, it has not been easy for her to get used to being so completely dependent and bedridden much of the time. She went to this hospital because it has a reputation for being a very good one.

She is getting the drug, and is hopeful that it will work. Yet in the whole week since her admission, she told me, very upset, she has not been able to get any nursing assistance to help her bathe or to wash her hair. She is not able to even get her toothbrush to brush her teeth until about noon each day. Finally, her sister came in and gave her a sponge bath to make her feel a little bit better.

This inattention to my friend's personal hygiene, this neglect of what anybody's sister would consider basic nursing care, is not the fault of uncaring nurses. It was just, she told me, that they were all so very busy, and there were simply not enough of them to attend to other than major nursing tasks and the volumes of paperwork they were responsible for. There were many excellent specialists in this hospital, and the best and most sophisticated life-saving equipment, along with highly trained technicians to operate it all. There was just no one to give somebody a bath or a toothbrush. This example of the allocation of resources within hospitals tells us something important about the world view governing the operation of these services. It tells us that in the world view of hospital management, feeling clean and as attractive as possible is no longer seen as having as significant a role in healing as, let us say, a CAT scanning machine. Since allocation of resources always follows values, we know immediately from this seemingly isolated observation what is more valued within this caring enterprise.[12]

The emphasis on the value of technological approaches in hospitals is, of course, merely another example of the current importance of technology in human services of all kinds. This may be a frank technology of equipment, as we see in hospitals, or a technology of clinicalism, classification, and management, as we see in institutions and increasingly in community services as well. From this perspective, many efforts to improve and reform current community services can be viewed as variations on a theme of technological improvement. Activists may envision the path to the improvement of conditions for people with disabilities through legal techniques, through increased management efficiency, by the restructuring of funding streams through Medicaid reform, through surgery to correct the facial stigmata of Down Syndrome, or in myriad other ways. That many of these things may be valid and even important things to do is as little at issue as whether hospitals should have CAT scans: they certainly should. The question is, rather, how the human problem is conceived and where the emphasis of value is placed. Each emphasis has hidden costs.

Management technologies, as John O'Brien (1987) pointed out, may be "very costly in their potential for misdirecting attention" from important issues in their attempt to make the world a more manageable and orderly place. Thus federal funding may exchange increased money for local ownership and flexibility. Handing an association's social issues over to lawyers or other technical specialists may secure objective successes at the cost of organizational vitality and investment in the ongoing struggle.[13]

The glorification of technology in the field of human services is a reflection, in turn, of technological values in the larger culture. This pervasive emphasis in the culture, as Wolfensberger explains, is based upon our unconscious faith that "science and technology can lift the human race above its nature and, indeed, above nature itself." "The world," he continues, "is full of policymakers, planners, administrators, law makers, and government leaders who are inflicting the same classes of mistakes on human services as they are transacting in the realm of industry and manufacturing, business, raw materials, conservation, energy, and so on."[14] The administrators at Three Mile Island still really believe that the technology of nuclear power is failsafe. Yet operators can still apparently fall asleep at control panels. If they do so at the wrong moment, I will lose my life.

The application of technological approaches in caring services brings to mind the experience of foundling homes and orphan asylums when they were the prevalent way of dealing with infants without families. Even in well-organized nurseries in such places, babies used to die at inexplicable rates. One could provide the best scientifically calculated and nutritionally balanced infant formulae on precise feeding schedules, have the most germ-free environments, the optimal amounts of light and air. Yet many babies continued to give up the ghost. This phenomenon came to be called "hospitalism" (Spitz, 1946). They were failing to thrive in these hospitals and other institutions, just as surely as if an essential vitamin were missing from their sterilized formula bottles. Nobody, for a while, could figure out what was wrong. It was a mystery.

We know now, of course, that the babies were dying from lack of love, an essential and evanescent nutrient of the human soul that was somehow overlooked. They needed to be held, and loved, and sung to, and stroked. It turned out that these were things that you just couldn't provide in an institution, no matter how hard you tried or how well you managed it. There was only one place that you could get this nutrient: a mother. That we don't have orphan asylums anymore in this society is not, as Thomas Szasz once pointed out, because we found a cure for being an orphan.

This same phenomenon is currently being rediscovered in the dense technological environment of neonatal intensive care units where premature, high-risk infants who would have died only a few years ago are saved. Research by practitioners of the new specialty of environmental neonatology is now finding that feeding babies on demand rather than on schedule, introducing natural rhythms of lighting, and other "anti-technical" practices, seem to add to thriving significantly and even to reduce the incidence of disability appearing in later developmental stages. A campaign to temper the dominance of technological efficiency on such units with nurturing practices has apparently been greeted with reasonable acceptance by neonatal nurses, but is reportedly frequently resisted strongly by many physician neonatologists in charge.

Professionalism and its Consequences

"The siren of one ambulance can destroy Samaritan attitudes in a whole Chilean town."

— Ivan Illich

Technology, as Illich points out, is closely related to the issue of professionalization. In order to understand the significance of increasing technology in community services and in the culture at large, one must therefore pay some attention to what we think about the importance of professionals in solving problems that the society faces. One hears constantly, of course, about the shortage of professionals necessary to solve various human problems. One reads in the newspaper from time to time of supposed shortages of physicians, especially in certain regions. During the brief era of community psychiatry in the 1960s and '70s, one used to read newspaper reports showing the desperate scarcity of psychiatrists in the country, compared to the incidence of mental illness. The shortage of such trained clinicians was seen as a grave and almost insurmountable national health

problem. Efforts were made to increase the production of psychiatrists and other clinical personnel to improve the mental health of the
nation.

There is no evidence, years later, to show that the mental health
problems of the country are on their way to being solved, whatever
benefits an increased number of trained clinicians may have offered
to individuals. In fact, the severity and frequency of mental disorder
is probably either worse or no different. The insurmountable national
problem of mental disorder seems impervious to all of the techniques
and manpower the mental health field has been able to muster. Either
professionals cannot solve the problem, or there are not enough of
them, or both. But even if professionals *can* solve the problem, it is now
clear that there will *never* be enough.

This comes as little surprise. For the "disease of professionalism,"
as Sarason noted in 1979, always involves "the tendency to define
human problems in ways that require highly educated professionals
for their solution, thus rendering the problem unsolvable." In addition, as we have seen with the related question of technology, it always
comes with a significant cost. "I have no doubt," Sarason wrote
elsewhere, "that when the final history of the human race is written,
high on the list of diseases contributing to its downfall will be
professionalization which, whatever its origins in social virtue, dia-
lectically gave rise to its own destruction." (1977, p.254)

Professionalism not only defines problems in ways that devour all
human and financial resources and thus guarantees failure, but it
displaces indigenous community ways of living and healing. There is
no longer any old woman healer living down the street, no longer a
neighbor lady who knows how to deliver babies, because their roles
have been displaced by the physician on the corner and, increasingly,
by the medical center. This is not entirely a bad thing: I would much
rather go to my doctor (and have a CAT scan, if necessary) for gall
bladder disease. Still, it is undeniable that something has been lost.
The herbal healer, and the lay midwife, knew things about healing
that modern medical technology, despite its benefits, has forgotten. It
is unlikely, for instance, that either "folk" healer would allow a
woman in her charge to go unbathed for a week. Such "ordinary"
contributions to the process of healing as feeling clean and present-
able have been largely displaced by new concerns. As one consequence of this, the neighborhood roles of healer or midwife have
disappeared (and in fact become illegal).

Why is the rush to professionalization so pervasive in society?
Such a question is complex, and begs easy answers. Certainly professionalization offers benefits in a variety of important ways in many

fields. But a number of social observers have increasingly suggested that factors tying professionalization to changes in the economy of society are significant. It is common knowledge, this line of reasoning goes, that the economies of developed countries are moving far away from an original basis of agriculture and primary production. As this change progresses, jobs are lost in farming, manufacturing and related occupations. These must be made up somewhere if widespread unemployment and social and economic collapse are not to result. The change of the economic base to one relying upon service activities is well understood and documented.[15]

Human services are a highly significant part of the growth of the service sector of society, as economic statistics and the interest of business corporations in human services of various types will attest. As I write, rural towns and counties in upstate New York are in the midst of a vigorous campaign to convince the state corrections commissioner to locate in their areas new prisons demanded by the increasing size of the incarcerated population. The number of Americans in prison is growing perhaps as fast as 8 percent a year, according to The Sentencing Project (*Atlantic*, 1989).

Prisons are being wooed by such localities as businesses once were, although prisons, as pointed out by local officials, don't pollute and are likely to be around longer. Although the prisoners are predominately from downstate areas near New York City, the need for jobs is greatest upstate. Economic and political pressures thus demand that these people be incarcerated far from their homes. Wolfensberger notes this enforced separation from one's family and community seems to be correlated with increased recidivism.

In the Adirondack region of New York, the *New York Times* reports, "prisons now rival the timber industry as one of the area's largest employers" (1979). Modern imprisonment requires a considerable number, and an ongoing supply, of corrections professionals. Corrections officers are required, along with administrators, psychologists, nurses, and industrial trainers. An associate degree program in corrections science is needed at the local community college. Such professional employment offers one of the few ways to make a living and find a career in areas in which farming, timber, and manufacturing are no longer viable.

The vast increase in inpatient psychiatric beds for troubled teenagers represents a more entrepreneurial example of professionalization. In 1985 congressional hearings, the economic recruitment of teenagers as inpatients of psychiatric facilities run by corporations was revealed to have become a widespread practice, even while research and practice shows that less severe interventions work much better. Inpatient services, however, are covered by medical insurance. Television ads for such facilities, aimed at worried parents, can now be seen in many cities in the United States.

A clear picture of the role of professional service employment in modern economies has been captured in an illuminating economic analysis performed in Chicago. Kallenback and Lyons (1989) added up all of the public funds of all types that were spent on poor people in the county. Then they divided the total by the number of poor people it was spent on. What they found was this: that if you divided up the total amount and gave it to everyone in cash, it would bring every poor person in the county above the poverty line. Since more than half of all anti-poverty spending is for services, this money goes to professionals who provide the services specified. Poor people have no control over these services. Most service money, for example, is spent on medical services. One could use medically designated money, for instance, to get treatment for medical symptoms of malnutrition, but not for the cause: that would fall under food stamps, if you qualify. The poor live in a complex world of such programs.

Despite constant attempts at "welfare reform," this basic situation always remains unchanged, no matter the level of money allocated for "poverty." What happens as a result of this, as John McKnight has pointed out, is that the reliance upon professional services as a way of approaching the problems of poverty causes a fundamental change in the conditions under which poor people live. As the number of service programs increase, they create a new environment which is greater than each program's individual contribution. According to the Chicago report, "as the total number of programs increases, they begin to replace the normal social and economic environments with a world of their own." In this dense environment of interlocking programs, people live in a strange and highly controlled world different from the rest of society. "They are surrounded by programs," in the words of the Chicago study, "that effectively institutionalize them in their own communities." Such a statement is highly evocative of Spect's findings, mentioned earlier, of the isolation of people with disabilities in group homes.

From this perspective many of the problems in community services discussed earlier in this chapter can be seen as but one instance of a larger dynamic affecting all people who are economically dependent upon public support. Professionalism, despite its benefits, displaces ordinary community processes in both cases, substituting an environment of service which can institutionalize people, even in their own homes. As McKnight has said, we once built institutions with high walls. Then we learned to build institutions with low walls.

Now we can build institutions that have no walls at all.

Looking from our imaginary helicopter at the isolated people in group homes, surveying the clinicalization and other symptoms just like those seen in physical institutions, hearing the endless need for more resources to fuel the professional approach that we have conceived to help people with disabilities thrive, it becomes increasingly clear that we have created a monster. If people who are poor live in institutionalized environments created by a network of services, what must the lives of people with developmental disabilities, frequently dependent upon a professional service system that by definition is responsible for every moment and every aspect of their lives, be like? At the end of a logical progression in the erection of formal services, we have created a system that still serves as a significant obstacle to their freedom, in part so that economic forces of professional employment may be fueled. We have created the community services system out of love, and operate it out of love. Yet, in the deep collective unconscious of society, love may not be all that is at work. Writes McKnight:

> "Removing the mask of love shows us the face of servicers who need income, and an economic system that needs growth. Within this framework, the client is less a person in need than a person who is needed. In business terms, the client is less the consumer than the raw material for the servicing system... His essential function is to meet the needs of servicers, the servicing system, and the national economy. The central political issue becomes the servicers' capacity to manufacture needs in order to expand the economy of the servicing system." (1977, p.2)

Is this, after all, what our work and efforts have brought about, a system of diffuse community services that helps to serve in the end the same need for professional employment which influenced the location of the old rural employment-producing institutions, and today's prisons? Is it possible that, despite our individual caring, compassion, and desire to serve, our serving system expresses darker unconscious intentions within society as well? Might it be true that some of the problems that we see today are due to the living out of old pressures for human services to isolate devalued people and provide economic utility? Just as Samuel Gridley Howe warned against institutions in the midst of the last century's unbounded enthusiasm for them, are such people as McKnight, Wolfensberger, Thomas Szasz, Sarason, and the late Burton Blatt cautioning us today?

This, as I mentioned earlier, has not been an easy chapter to write. No one likes to dwell upon the serious afflictions of an approach to human service upon which so many people completely depend, and to which one has oneself devoted so many years of professional life. Besides, it tends to make people angry. Those who, early on, believed that the institutions were failing and worked to change them certainly earned a full measure of that. Yet until people were generally persuaded that institutions were outmoded as a way of serving people, there was no reason to pursue a better way. Enumerating the emerging problems in community services serves the same purpose.

In attempting the unpopular task of examining what I am persuaded is indeed failing, I document not the failure of service systems or people, but of an idea. For the way that we conceive of a task, our theory about how that aspect of the world works and therefore what might have an effect, determines what we do. As Coleman Lyles once summarized the philosopher Rudolf Steiner:

> "Most of what passes for social theory breaks down in the face of actual life. It is as if a theory of bridge building when applied to the task of building a bridge utterly failed to produce a serviceable bridge. The only difference is that the inadequacies of the bridge-building theory quickly become obvious whereas in social life the connection between suffering and bungling is not so readily recognized."[16]

When a theory fails, when the bridge that was erected begins to sway and fall into the water below, it is a tormenting and difficult time for the people involved. There is always a strong tendency to cling to the old conception, even in the most evident stages of decay. But decay is only one part of life; more importantly, there is growth. And so new ideas always arise to take the place of the old. The process through which this succession of ideas takes place is known as a conceptual revolution.

If the theory called professional service by which human needs are addressed is indeed in decline, then there must be a new idea emerging as part of the process of conceptual revolution. Since a new idea may seem as small as the first group home did when compared to the dominance of the then-vast institutional system, one may have to look carefully to find the seeds of what the future may hold. The next chapter, therefore, discusses how such conceptual revolutions take place, by looking at a field seemingly far distant from our own; that of winemaking.

End Notes

1.   Roy Oldenburg's *The Great Good Place* (1989) develops an elegant and delightful theory about the role of such settings as the Alva in society.

2.   *Program Analysis of Services Systems,* Wolfensberger & Glenn (1975), *Program Analysis of Service System's Implementation of Normalization Goals,* Wolfensberger & Thomas (1983).

3.   See Wolfensberger, Wolf, "Self Injurious Behavior, Behavioristic Responses, and Social Role Valorization: A Reply to Mulick and Kedesy" (1989) for a fuller exploration of this issue.

4.   For a view of the perception of clinical sophistication from the perspective of the person reliant on services, one is reminded of Ira Goldenberg's work in creating a community setting for troubled urban youth. In a survey of residents, Goldenberg's study revealed that staff with the *most* academic qualifications in such work were rated lowest in competence by those whom they served (Goldenberg, 1971).

5.   Sheltered workshops, the service now under attack as "institutional," were the first real community service, predating group homes by some years. That their "institutional" limitations and character are being recognized now probably has more to do with the fact that they are older than residential service forms, rather than any inherent difference.

6.   This was apparently accomplished by harassing the restaurant owner with the threat of reports to social security offices and other means, until the employer let the worker go.

7.   For a detailed description of the dynamics surrounding the creation and deterioration of settings, see Seymour Sarason's *The Creation of Settings and the Future Societies,* (1972), discussed later. The same phenomenon is also briefly described as it occurred in the nuclear power industry in Freeman Dyson's *Disturbing the Universe,* (1979). According to Dyson, "The fundamental problem of the [nuclear power] industry is that nobody any longer has any fun building reactors."

8.   Turnover was a significant problem in urban areas, where job-seekers had a choice of employment, although not so in rural areas, where they didn't. Recruitment of qualified professional staff was a problem everywhere, and especially in remote facilities. Union salaries, of course, moderate the picture significantly in comparison to community settings. These dynamics remain the same today.

9.   An excellent history of this subject is Wolf Wolfensberger's *The Origin and Nature of our Institutional Models,* (1975c). A particularly interesting, detailed portrait of one of these leaders is Bernard Graney's *Hervey Backus Wilbur and the Evolution of Policies Toward Mentally Retarded People,* (1979).

10. If you visit someone at the "community" facility today, incidentally, you will find that there are many more locked doors than in its sister rural institution. The field of community psychiatry, as Sarason (1988) points out, was a short-lived venture.

11. The concept of the "continuum of care," in which people must progress from most restrictive to least restrictive settings, (e.g., institution to quarter-way house, to half-way house, and onward to independent living; or segregated

school, to segregated classroom, to "resource room," to full classroom integration, etc.) expresses the thinking behind this historical progression in a programmatic ideal. It serves by definition to validate the most restrictive setting as the inevitable "anchor" to this progress toward liberty and thus assures its continued existence as the basis and origin of the rest. It demands in a curious way that "ontogeny recapitulates phylogeny," in requiring individuals to relive evolutionary stages of service forms in the same way that embryos were once believed to relive anatomical stages in the evolution of life. Steven Taylor (1988), among others, critiques the continuum concept as outmoded.

12.   Readers are encouraged to read Sarason's *Caring and Compassion in Clinical Services* (1985) for a fuller understanding of the dynamics behind the fading of ordinary caring in human services.

13.   One recalls Saul Alinsky's caution to neighborhood organizers never to let a group hire a lawyer to solve a problem for them.

14.   Wolfensberger's short piece "A Brief Reflection on Where We Stand and Where We are Going in Human Services" (1983c) is a disturbingly powerful summary of this issue.

15.   Wars, of course, have served to absorb surplus manpower. Military-related occupations make up a significant amount of the employment of the United States, even now in a time of peace. This economic role of the military, some argue, is now being supplemented by the development of an army of human service professionals recruited and trained to "attack" various social problems. One thinks of the "War on Poverty," to which so many social researchers owe their training, or the current "War on Drugs." In the once richly agricultural county where I sometimes live there are now only two major employers: the state regional mental hospital, and the Army munitions depot where the neutron bomb is stored. A drug-treatment prison is shortly to begin construction. It's on the site of an abandoned army hospital.

16.   This comparison has been made by Elizabeth Boggs in discussions, as well.

CHAPTER 6

How Conceptual Revolutions Take Place

"...novelty emerges only with difficulty, manifested by resistance, against a background provided by expectation."

— Thomas Kuhn

When I first moved to the Finger Lakes region of New York State, the hillsides behind my house were covered with vineyards. The grapes which grew in these vineyards were of the species labrusca, called sometimes "native American," or hybrids of these. They were varieties like concord, from which grape jelly is made, and they supplied the big wineries over on the next lake from us.

Labrusca grapes didn't make particularly notable wine. The kind of grapes from which you made really good wine, like the wines of France and more recently California, were of a species called vinifera. These had names like chardonnay or reisling. You couldn't grow these kinds of grapes in the eastern United States, unfortunately. It was too cold. People had tried and failed for 350 years. Everybody knew that. The state university knew that, and taught how to grow the kinds of grapes that would grow in that climate.

Things would have stayed exactly this way, if it hadn't been for an incident that seemed completely insignificant when it had taken place almost twenty years before the time that I am describing. In 1951 a Russian immigrant named Dr. Konstantin Frank had stepped off a boat in New York City with his wife, three children, and almost no English. He was fifty-one years old and had no prospects. As it turned out, he had been a professor, a specialist in growing grapes at a university research station in the Ukraine, a very cold region. He got a map and looked up the closest area to New York City where grapes were grown. It was the Finger Lakes. He bought a bus ticket.

Dr. Frank found his way to the the New York State Agricultural Research Station in Geneva. He looked at the labrusca and hybrid grapes they were growing. Then he said to them, in his broken English, something along the lines of "Why are you growing this junk? You should grow vinifera. You could make good wines instead of this garbage! It is no colder here than it was in Russia!" The researchers were not amused. They told him they were busy.

But Dr. Frank was a persistent guy as well as a not particularly subtle one, and he was hard to get rid of. So they eventually gave him a job. The job was hoeing blueberries. He was now fifty-two years old and working as a field hand, tending blueberries and the labrusca hybrid grapes for which he felt such contempt. Grape-growing and wine-making went on as before. And there things would have stood if it were not for another small event which seemed inconsequential at the time.

One day there was a wine-growing conference at the research station. Attending the conference was a famous winemaker from the Gold Seal Winery named Charles Fournier. Dr. Frank buttonholed Fournier with his theories, as he had been doing with everyone else. But Fournier, an elegant and cosmopolitan gentleman originally from the Champagne district of France, did what no one had ever done before. He listened to him. He was intrigued. And he hired him to try his ideas out at his winery.

Frank and Fournier labored for several years trying to perfect a way to keep delicate vinifera vines from freezing in the wintertime. When the vines were old enough to produce grapes, they made wine. When it was ready, they released it. The world of winemaking was astonished. This was not like the fruity wines of New York State at all. This was like the wine of France! It was impossible. But it had been done.

Dr. Frank was an irascible old iconoclast who expected rejection and, some people said, was not averse to encouraging it. He held some frankly strange opinions. (He believed, for instance, that wine made from French-American hybrids was poisonous and would kill pigeons.) But he was the one man in the western world who had the vision and the knowledge to make European-style wines in cold climates. New, young grape-growers flocked to his house from everywhere. They would sit on his porch, sip wines such as they had tasted only from Europe or California, and listen to the master. If they were favored they would go home with a trunk full of grapevine cuttings and a head full of new techniques. From these material and conceptual cuttings grew many of the small wineries operating in the eastern United States today, the legislation in most states permitting them to be established, and a virtually complete change in the face of wine-making in a large part of the United States and Canada.

Today, the hills behind my home in New York are still covered with vines. But if you look at them closely, you will discover that a great many of them are a different kind. They are no longer labrusca. They are vinifera, the species that was supposedly impossible to grow there only three decades ago. Grape-growers plant vinifera as a matter of routine. Eventually, the most interesting change of all happened. The state university said that it could be done. They made technical assistance to do it available, in fact. Of course there was a considerable amount of money involved in growing vinifera by then.

Understanding How Conceptual Change Takes Place

What does a story from the field of winemaking have to do with the field of developmental disabilities? Only this: it is a particularly clear example of how a dominant conception or world view in a field of human enterprise can be radically displaced by a new conception which appeared, at first sight, to fly in the face of all reason and experience. It illustrates as well how progress in theory and practice in fields are made: not through the slow and progressive accumulation of knowledge, but through conceptual revolutions.

A theory of how such conceptual changes take place in the field of science is set forth in Thomas Kuhn's *The Structure of Scientific Revolutions* (1962), a landmark work of intellectual history well known to scientists but generally little known in our field.[1] While Kuhn confines himself to the specific and unique enterprise of science, much can be learned from his examination which seems generally applicable to human knowledge. He examines with great precision the mechanisms through which revolutions in thought, such as the one described above, take place. Some of the characteristics of the process that he delineated may well be pertinent later for understanding our current situation in developmental disabilities. The first of these is the role of anomalies in precipitating conceptual change.[2]

Anomalies

Anomalies, in Kuhn's definition, are "violations of expectation." Dr. Konstantin Frank was an anomaly in the field of winemaking, for his work completely violated the dominant expectation that vinifera grapes wouldn't grow in cold climates. It remained an anomaly as long as it was a small violation of the dominant expectation. As more and more anomalies (in the form of vinifera vineyards) became established, the strange new idea of Dr. Frank's became more and more accepted. Eventually there was a change in conceptions, and the view that these grapes could indeed be grown became the dominant one, displacing its predecessor. The child of any grape-farmer in the northeast today knows and assumes that vinifera can be grown. If you were to tell him or her that this was once — a very short time ago — thought to be impossible, you would get the same kind of response as if you had said that people once thought tomatoes were poisonous. But they did, of course.

Anomalies are thus the key events which usher in a change in world view. Anomalies are demonstrations of a new theory of the world. Such demonstrations, not their formative theories, force changes in conceptions. It is not the idea of growing vinifera in cold climates that has power, but the thriving vine beneath the snow, the glass of wine in one's hand. It is not the idea that a tomato is nontoxic, but eating one and not dying that makes people rethink their position.

Crisis and Resistance

Each of us, Sarason points out in *Caring and Compassion in Clinical Practice*, operates from a world view as solid and as unexamined as that of the farmer's child I used as an example above. Each of us is:

> "...possessed by a world view resting on axioms that are unarticulated precisely because they seem so natural, right, and proper. The process by which we are socialized into society is one by which we assimilate axioms requiring no articulation. They are self-evidently 'right.' They are silent but bedrock to our view of what the world is and should be. These axioms do not become blind spots (that is, they are not recognized as such) until events in the larger society force us to challenge what was heretofore unchallengable." (1985, p.58)

The presence of anomalies themselves, in other words, is only one of the conditions necessary for conceptual change to take place. Anomalies are, of course, essential: in science, in Kuhn's words, it is only when "the profession can no longer evade anomalies that subvert the existing tradition of scientific practice" that "the extraordinary investigations that lead the profession at last to a new set of commitments, a new basis for the practice of science," begin. Yet the "seed" of anomalous theory and practice is always related to the "ground" in which it rests. If existing practice is proceeding relatively smoothly, based upon an existing world view, there is little reason to pay attention to anxiety-provoking new ideas that suggest a completely new order of things.

Dr. Frank, for instance, would have been just a fellow up on a blowy hillside planting some vines that nobody had ever heard of, if other events in the larger society had not put the existing approach to winemaking under considerable stress. This had to do, in simple terms, with an increased interest in fine wines which began to sweep the country in the 1960's. It became clear that continued popularity of the old labrusca wines was far from guaranteed, although some large wineries reacted to the changed consumer demand for vinifera as blindly as General Motors reacted to the increased popularity of small foreign cars at about the same time. It took a considerable amount of unsettledness — of a sense that reliance upon the old world view was no longer safe, and that something of a crisis was at hand — for Dr. Frank's conception to be heard. The ground, one might say, needed to be disturbed before the seed could sprout.

Novel, conception-shifting anomalies, Kuhn points out, always emerge against resistance. The new world view always challenges the established order of a field, in which people are deeply psychologically invested. In science, he noted, "the emergence of new theories is generally preceded by a period of pronounced professional insecurity." In most cases, new scientific conceptions have been accepted only after "the awareness of the anomaly had lasted so long and penetrated so deep that one can appropriately describe the fields affected by it as in a state of growing crisis."

The Minds of a Few

A final point to be culled from Kuhn's observations on science is this: "Any new interpretation of nature, whether a discovery or a theory, emerges first in the mind of one or a few individuals." There is always, in other words, a Dr. Frank at the root of such changes. Interestingly enough, Kuhn points out that most new ideas come from either young people who are not yet fully socialized into the particular field, or from those who come from outside of a field entirely.

Kuhn additionally says of the one or few individuals who begin to see the world differently that "invariably their attention has been intensely concentrated upon the crisis-provoking problems" they are considering. Most scientific investigators, he explains, are like chess players who, with the board before them, try out

> "various alternative moves in search of a solution. These trial attempts, whether by the chess player or by the scientist, are trials only of themselves, not of the rules of the game. They are possible only so long as the paradigm itself, [the "chessboard"] is taken for granted. Therefore, paradigm testing only occurs after persistent failure to solve a noteworthy puzzle has given rise to crisis. And even then it occurs only after the sense of crisis has evoked an alternative candidate for paradigm."

He points out, later, that conceptual revolutions in science, "involving a certain sort of reconstruction of group commitments," can take place on a very small scale, even within scientific communities of fewer than twenty-five people, and can be unrecognized by those outside of that community.

Current Potential Revolutions

As I write this, a most interesting example of a potential conceptual revolution in science is much in the newspapers. Two researchers recently announced that they had successfully demonstrated something that according to current scientific knowledge should be completely impossible: that nuclear fusion can be made to take place under normal temperatures, and in fact in a table-top laboratory apparatus. The implications of this, if true, are tremendous. It means that the energy of the stars can be harnessed with a simple mechanism, producing a safe, unlimited, and inexpensive source of power. Such a discovery would literally transform human civilization. The New York Times reported the opinion that this new source of energy "would rival the discovery of fire" (Broad, 1989). That they characterized the new assertion of the truth of this discovery with the term "earth-shaking" clearly indicated what such an anomalous finding would do to the scientific community. It would force such a change in the way that scientists view the world that it would be as if the very world were felt to shake beneath their feet.

Predictably, the announcement of this "discovery" has kindled a furor in scientific circles — so much so that a major conference has now been held to argue over whether the supposed anomaly is actually true or not. This, of course, is Kuhn's phenomenon of resistance in action. The new "truth" will be put to a strenuous test. At the moment I write this, the general opinion from the conference is strongly negative, with a small group of participants still siding with the paradigm-challenging researchers.

Will this small group turn out to be the "few minds" described by Kuhn who actually see the emerging future? Or will history show them to have been merely chasing a hopeful illusion? I know nothing about nuclear physics. But by understanding the process described by Kuhn I can follow the unfolding of this drama with a comprehension of the main themes. I know, for instance, that the chance of such an expectation-shattering finding being true is quite small. Since this example is taking place in the realm of science, I know that it will ultimately be put to rigorous tests of its validity. I know that the greatest probability is that, by the time that my words are published, the allegation that "cold fusion" works will be completely disproven and forgotten. Yet I also know that if, by some small chance it *is* someday found to be true, today's events would have looked exactly the same. The claim of anomaly or the mustering of resistance are no indicators of validity, or of the lack of it.

The picture of scientists from all over the world scurrying to the conference in Santa Fe puts me in mind of an anthill stirred up by a stick — it is a crisis; it is "earth-shaking." The forces of resistance must be mustered to put the world back in order. They will either be successful, or the world will change. If it changes, it will be a new world of a kind now thought impossible. Understanding the interplay of anomalies, crisis and resistance, and the power of the minds of a few, we can follow the drama as we can follow an Italian opera, even if we do not know the actual language. We know that when Priestley discovered oxygen in the 1770s, he was "seeing" something in the air — an invisible gas — that nobody else could then see. People who see things that nobody else sees are frequently thought to be hallucinating, deluded, willfully wrong, or possessed, depending upon the situation, the commentator, and the historical time. We shall see, given time, whether the "cold fusion" researchers are paradigm-changing Priestleys or just plain wrong. It is too early to tell.

The current historical period brims with similar examples. Is pollution of the atmosphere creating a "greenhouse effect?" Some scientists say yes; that we must make massive and rapid reduction in pollutants to avoid climatic warming and an environmental crisis. They submit a report to the federal government. But such changes would have negative economic consequences, so the administration rewrites the report to say that it's really not all that bad. A cabinet official says that sunglasses ought to take care of it. Meanwhile, in a small technical publication you can observe that a viticultural researcher in New Zealand has published an article instructing growers how to adjust vineyard practices for a world that may be significantly warmer. Eventually, thermometers will tell us who is right.

Conceptual Change in Medicine

Examining viticulture and science may reveal much, but they are not directly about people. Medicine, on the other hand, brings the question of conceptual change into an arena in which changes in world view can be easily seen to have an impact upon the ways that human beings are treated when in need. Medical history, in fact, is a fascinating if daunting compilation of procedures once practiced with great fervor, based upon conceptions of the world now commonly acknowledged to be completely inaccurate. One thinks about the practice of bloodletting and the view of physiology upon which it was based. Yet it was vigorously championed as wholly scientific in its time.

The interplay of anomaly and resistance, too, can be clearly observed in the stressful process through which new conceptions and procedures in medicine have been and continue to be adopted. One recalls the introduction of anesthesia, and the enormous resistance of some contemporary surgeons to using it, believing as they did that the intense pain of surgery was necessary for healing. One chuckles over not-so-remote cigarette ads in old magazines of the thirties and forties containing doctors' testimonials for the positive effect of Lucky Strikes or Camels on the digestion. Then one remembers how bitterly the research establishing the connection between cigarettes and lung cancer was fought, and how tobacco-company researchers still fight a last-ditch battle of resistance against it even to this day.

Certainly many doctors knew of the link between cigarettes and cancer long before the famous Surgeon General's report on smoking and cancer was made public. But medical inventions, even when positive, have, as with anesthesia, been slow to translate into commonly accepted practice. "Birthing rooms" in hospitals were strongly resisted for a long time, although they have gained a foothold after many years. Radical mastectomy for cancer, although rarely practiced in England anymore, still takes place with some frequency in American hospitals. Quadruple bypass heart surgery and hysterectomy remain two operations performed with very high frequency, despite the presence of a number of "anomalous" practitioners and emerging research to show that these operations may be unnecessary much of the time. Each change in practice, and consequent change in world view which has taken place, has typically run a gauntlet precisely like that seen in the scientific world described by Kuhn.

Closer to the field of developmental disabilities, the medical specialty of psychiatry has been an area of human service in which conceptual changes can be observed, often in a dramatic way. One brief example pertains to the practice of physical restraint of people confined in asylums. Restraints such as straitjackets, handcuffs, immobilizing chairs and cribs, and other similarly diabolical devices, were considered essential for successful treatment of people with mental disorders at the dawn of the nineteenth century. The proper management of an asylum was inconceivable without them. Yet, under the leadership of asylum superintendents in England and spurred by the death of a patient in a straitjacket in 1829, English practice began to witness an elimination of restraints from entire asylums. Resisted bitterly by American asylum superintendents, the demonstrations of their English counterparts nonetheless put considerable public pressure on them. First proclaiming that it would not work, the American doctors finally resorted to the classic "but it won't work here" defense by objecting that "the patients in European institutions, accustomed as they were to unquestioned acceptance of authority, might willingly submit to 'moral' restraint, but not your liberty-loving American who, sane or insane, would never agree placidly to the imposition of authority by an individual, and hence could be restrained only by mechanical means" (Isaac Ray, 1844, in Deutsch, 1949).

What happened as a result of this battle over medical practice was curious, and demonstrated one additional characteristic of conceptual change that may be most observable in the regions furthest from the rigorous testing that defines the practice of science. It is that new conceptions, once established, have no more guarantee of immortality than their predecessors. In the question of restraint, for example, the anomaly of nonrestraint demonstration worked. By the late 1800s the annual report to the legislature of one New York State asylum, for instance, reported that restraint had been virtually eliminated, a claim which they obviously felt they should advertise to their funding source. Yet a couple of decades later at that same institution and at virtually all others in the country, physical restraint was once again the norm, and staff in such places once again found it inconceivable that one could do without it. This remained commonly accepted practice until the introduction of the powerful tranquilizer thorazine in the 1950s. There are those who claim that in fact this revolution in practice, at least as it applies to restraint, represented no change at all but merely an exchange of physical for chemical bonds.

In areas of social practice like psychiatry, one sees an ever-oscillating change in conception and practice. In the early 1800s, mental disorder was "discovered" to be curable through "moral treatment" aimed at educating lost reason. By the end of the century it was "discovered" to have biological malfunction of the brain at its root, caused, if you dissected the brain, by a detectable lesion or (if you could not find it) by a "hidden lesion."

By the time that I got into the field, in 1970, this biological determinism was being slightly displaced by a view of mental disorder as a social problem, and by the development of an emphasis on "community psychiatry" and social programs. I noted the architectural tracings of this change in the last chapter.

Today the emphasis in psychiatry has swung once again to the biological; an understanding of mental disorder as a brain disorder, and a belief that sufficient research will find the true physical cause. It is, of course, the "hidden lesion" all over again, if only at a vastly more sophisticated level. The cycle has taken just about a century.[3]

I have attempted to make the case, in this chapter, that changes in the way that the world is conceived, and in any field's practices deriving from such conceptions, follow a comprehensible process as described by Thomas Kuhn. We have started in the vineyard, and looked in turn at science, at medicine, and at its subspecialty of psychiatry. Finding the elements of this common process applicable to these disparate human endeavors, let us return to the field of developmental disabilities.

Endnotes

1. Two exceptions are William McCord's 1982 article "From Theory to Reality: Obstacles to the Implementation of the Normalization Principle in Human Services," and Robert Perske's "Attitudes, Acceptance, and Awareness: The Changing View Toward Persons with Down Syndrome" (1987).

2. Kuhn uses the term "paradigm," a word that in common usage means "model" or "pattern," to denote "universally recognized scientific achievements that for a time provide model problems and solutions to a community of practitioners." Thus, a paradigm in science may be the scientific conception that the sun revolved around the earth or, later, that the earth revolves around the sun. I use "paradigm" in Kuhn's sense as a synonym for "conception" or "world view" in this text.

3. This is not to say that the current reversion to a biological orientation may not yield helpful discoveries. There are often advantages and disadvantages on both sides. The inappropriate treatment of psychological symptoms of the vitamin-deficiency disease of pellagra by psychotherapy before the cause was discovered is frequently cited by biological psychiatrists in defense of a biological orientation and against "talking" therapies. But one wonders about the current enthusiasm for chemically-specific treatments for such conditions as obsessive-compulsive disorder, or agoraphobia, or stage fright. And one remembers, of course, the historically observable deterioration in the condition of people with mental disorders the last time a biological deterministic world view held the stage.

CHAPTER 7

Conceptual Revolutions in Developmental Disabilities

"My real-life organizing experience, I freely confess, leaves me convinced that nothing can be done to solve social problems by conventional means. Virtually every conventional response will actually make things worse."

— Byron Kennard

The field of developmental disabilities, it could be claimed, was founded on an anomaly. That anomaly was the belief by Dr. Jean-Marc-Garpard Itard (1771-1838) that a man with apparent mental retardation who was found living naked in a forest could learn. The man, as everyone studying our field is taught, was Victor, "The Wild Boy of Aveyron." Itard's experience in attempting to "civilize" Victor appeared in a book of the same name. It was the world's first published account of an attempt to educate a person with mental retardation. Itard set out to bring the "wild boy" to civilization.

Itard did not achieve his original expectations. He had expected Victor to learn more rapidly and more successfully than he actually did. Despite his five-year effort, Victor remained a person with severe impairments. Yet Itard succeeded in producing a demonstration of great power. Not only did he have the highly anomalous expectation that a person with severe intellectual deficits could learn, but he showed that such a person could indeed develop intellectually through educational means, if not admittedly to the high level that Itard had originally hoped.

This evident learning made it a true anomaly, in that it could not be predicted or expected under the reigning world view of the time. But just as we can see in the case of other successful emerging anomalies, it arose against a background of expectation that provided a fertile ground for the new finding to appear. As Burton Blatt notes in his discussion of Itard, the latter's beliefs must be viewed as part of the dynamic culture of post-revolutionary France, in which an enlightened philosophy proclaiming human improvability permeated the society.[1] Itard, Sheerenburger notes, ended up later transferring his experience with Victor to educating people who were deaf, significantly contributing to the field of oral communication. He believed that people could learn, whatever their outward appearance of disability might be. This was a dramatically new idea.

The course of the early history of the field of mental retardation is like all fields in being marked by a series of leaders who challenged the world view of the day. Like Itard, each believed that people labeled as mentally retarded had far greater potential than contemporary expectations allowed. Our current reverence for such names as Edouard Seguin, Maria Montessori, Samuel Gridley Howe and Dorothea Dix is due to the fact that each in his time challenged existing expectations and pursued demonstrations in which his beliefs gained more general acceptance. Each encountered his share of resistance as he attempted to advance these beliefs. When Seguin successfully taught a person with mental retardation to talk, write, and count, the greatest authority of the day, according to Blatt, judged that such progress showed that his pupil must not have been mentally retarded after all, although he may have seemed to be so. People with real mental retardation, as everyone knew, couldn't learn.

Tracings of the iconoclastic expectations of the early leaders are visible today in the vast changes which have taken place in expectations and social conditions for people with disabilities. That the educability of children with disabilities should be publicly accepted, and that there should even be a federal law requiring schools to address their needs, is a great leap forward from attempting to demonstrate that one particular person, Victor, could learn. That people with disabilities are no longer predominately incarcerated in large institutions but are physically living in ordinary communities is an astonishing advance from the time when the first tentative group homes were opened. That all of this has taken place within two or three decades indicates a change in world view which has taken place with lightning speed. Even the time dividing the publication of a book such as *The Mongol in Our Midst* in 1924 (what picture does this chilling title conjure up of the attitude towards people with mental retardation in society?) and the appearance of highly valued roles for characters with mental retardation on popular television shows today has been scarcely sixty years.

Recent Conceptual Change

The developmental disabilities field shows clearly that the process of conceptual change is a constant one. One reason for this is that ideas, even visionary ones, are inevitably subject to deterioration in actual social practice. Surely the eventual conditions within mental retardation institutions were far removed from those planned and even maintained for a while by their original founders. A second is that the new paradigm of one age became the old paradigm of a succeeding one. Sheltered workshops are one of the most visible current examples of this.

Sheltered workshops, as noted in Chapter 5, were one of the earliest of community services. When I worked in an institution we could bus people daily out to the "community" to work, long before we could find anyplace there for them to live. Sheltered work was what you got if you had a disability and you wanted to work. Because sheltered workers had limited skills, work needed to be uncomplicated. I ran a sheltered workshop in an institution and spent a great deal of time puzzling over how paying jobs could be made so simple with jigs and fixtures that they would only admit a screw or a saw-cut in one way, so that people could work successfully. Then I went to Toronto to see a fellow named Marc Gold hold a workshop called "Try Another Way."

"Try Another Way" was an expectation-shattering challenge to the beliefs of vocational potential upon which the enterprise of sheltered work was built. Gold provoked great excitement as well as great resistance by traveling around the country showing how people with severe retardation, dismissed as having "no vocational potential" and left to rock on some ward, could be quickly taught to perform such complex tasks as assembling an intricate bicycle brake. He did it in front of my eyes, in front of an audience of several hundred, with a person whom he had never met before, using a simple sorting-board. It was astonishing: it was magic. I returned home to the workshop and built a sorting-board just like his. I got hold of a bunch of old heavy institutional door locks, took them all apart, broke down each step of the assembly into the smallest gestures, and practiced assembling them so they would work until I knew the job intimately. Then I got Mitch, the person in the workshop whom we all believed to be the least capable of learning there, and who spent all day sanding (often across the grain), and asked him if he would work on putting together locks with me. After a very short time it was completely clear that Mitch could learn to put locks together, tiny reversible parts and all, and that I could teach him to do it. I cannot believe that students of Itard or Seguin could have felt any differently about what they were going to have to stop believing and what they would have to start believing than I did then.

The power of Gold's demonstrations was revealed in the fact that it tended to rock not only conceptions of vocational training; it had the potential to shake the very foundation of the mental retardation field. If what the field held to be true about intelligence, IQ, and the predictive value of diagnostic tests *was* true, then what Gold was doing should have been absolutely impossible. Yet the evidence was there. Gold's violation of the expectations of the old mental retardation paradigm shot a large and permanent hole through it, a hole later widened by the work of Bellamy and Wehman in supported employment. In a fragment of historical time, industry-integrated, supported employment programs have become the new norm for vocational work. The relevance of sheltered workshops is so in doubt that my own organization now issues grants to convert sheltered workshop programs to ones that place people in supported jobs in community businesses.

Similarly, at a time in which group homes are the norm, John McKnight and others have encountered the concept with curiosity. McKnight is a particularly good example of someone who comes from outside the field entirely, just as Kuhn noted, with a different sense of what is reasonable and what is possible. "Why would you put six labeled people together?" he questioned innocently when he started to meet with developmental disabilities groups. "Why would you make such a thing as a group home? Where did you get such an idea?" It was a question that virtually nobody in the field had thought to ask because, as Sarason pointed out earlier, nobody in a field usually *can* ask such questions. The approach to assisting people through a service form called group homes was part of a world view that was "self-evidently 'right'."

Kuhn, we may remember, says that such challenges are often developed in "the minds of a few." A notable example of what Kuhn describes, in our own field, relates to the contributions of Wolf Wolfensberger. Many people currently in the field know only that Wolfensberger is regarded as one of the "fathers" of normalization, and that he is now a highly vocal critic of human services. It is hard to describe Wolfensberger's present role in the field by such terms as teacher, researcher, and program designer, although these once applied. In many ways he has embraced the role of a "prophet" who proclaims truths that he feels nobody wants to hear. Yet it must be remembered that Wolfensberger once was probably the most skilled systems architect in the field, served as the designer of the first comprehensive service system in the world (ENCOR, in Nebraska)[2] and has been a prime influence on policy and practice in both the United States and Canada, as well as in other countries.

If one goes back and reads Wolfensberger's "Twenty Predictions about the Future of Residential Services in Mental Retardation," published in 1969 when he was only thirty-five, one sees a completely different world view than the one evident in Wolfensberger's published work today. He discusses anticipated progress in the field in an essentially optimistic way. He predicted the eventual disappearance of institutions and their replacement by community services.[3] But after a considerable period of (in Kuhn's words) "intensely concentrating upon crisis-provoking problems" involved in attempting to implement his vision of community services, he made an acute shift in world view. In a very few years he shifted from offering workshops on how to create and operate good residential and vocational services to ones on "How to Function with Personal Moral Coherency in a Dysfunctional (Human Service) World," on contemporary human services as technologies and the consequent rising abuse of psychotropic and behavioral interventions, and on what he terms "death-making" and the sanctity of life. He speaks and writes now mostly on what he terms "higher order issues" in which two interrelated themes are prominent: how human services pose a threat to the life of vulnerable people by carrying out essentially genocidal unconscious social impulses against them, and why personal relationships will be the only protection for such persons in the collapse of the social order he feels is imminent. It is as if a world-famous architect of skyscrapers suddenly came to the conclusion that all buildings were unsafe, warned users against them, and henceforth refused to go in them anymore, living only in tents set lightly on the land. What wrenching change of belief could cause such an architect to renounce his tools?

Those who wish to trace the development of community service programs will inevitably come to Wolfensberger, and an extended network surrounding him, as one collection of a relatively few minds with a different world view. It was he and his students who staged many of the original demonstrations. The powerful conception of the institutional world view eventually fell to demonstrations by a few people like these as surely as the shape of vineyards was changed by the influence of Dr. Frank. Slowly, and against enormous resistance, some of his current and very different work seems to be gaining some influence. Who is to say if Wolfensberger's current work will take hold? Or, if it does take hold, where it will do so? It is interesting to note that while his workshops in the United States have been sparsely attended for some time, he has begun lately to speak to capacity crowds in Australia. Is Australia, for Wolfensberger, today's low-resistance Nebraska? We will have to wait and see.

Most of us who are workers in the field of developmental disabilities, like the scientists Kuhn writes about, are players on an assumed chessboard. We calculate moves within the cognitive constructs of the game itself. What is the ideal size of a group home? How do you start a state-wide day-program system? How do you monitor quality? It is always a very few (in our case, probably the Burton Blatts, the Seymour Sarasons,[4] the Wolf Wolfensbergers, and later the John McKnights and John O'Briens) who speculate after concentrated study on the nature of the game itself and propose entirely new and upsetting rules.

The late Burton Blatt, after a stint as Massachusetts Mental Retardation Commissioner, wrote in 1970 of his realization that the traditional methods of systemic reform — the "rules of the game" — were not working. One, for instance, was always trying to improve conditions in the institution by adding new and "better" staff. Complained Blatt,

> "Adding new 'good' people to a sick System does not make the System appreciably healthier, but it does infect the 'good' people and they, eventually, behave in much the same way as those they've replaced. Our goal, then, should be to change a System which promotes inadequate and inhuman care and treatment. Whereas, till now, our goal has been to change the people, and, thus, rescue a System which is, in fact, without hope." (p.314)

What Blatt was talking about in 1970, of course, was the painful realization that he could not reform the institutional system, as he had set out with great vigor to do. He saw adopting a community model as the change that would set people with developmental disabilities free. He lived long enough to begin to see the kinds of community problems so reminiscent of institutions begin to emerge. Were he alive today what would he be saying about current moves on the chessboard, and the nature of the game itself?

Potential Conceptual Change in Developmental Disabilities and the Current World View

The world view from which human services currently operates, which has sometimes been termed the "professional/bureaucratic" paradigm, is well known. It assumes, as John McKnight points out, that human needs can be met through structures and methods that are no different than those used to build automobiles or to run a ship. One creates a bureaucratic hierarchy with one person at the top and various tasks and job descriptions carefully delineated. If management is good and resources are in sufficient supply, then "caring" should be delivered by service systems as predictably as automobiles roll off of the assembly line. Given sufficient technology and professional manpower, it is assumed that most personal and social problems are fixable.

In part of my own professional training I was exposed to a particularly poignant example of the extremes to which this set of beliefs has been taken in our culture. It was something termed "systematic counseling," a then newly developed school of thought about how personal counseling of people in distress should be conducted. Upon enrolling in this graduate school, we were given a copy of an extremely complex flow chart full of boxes, arrows, numbers and captions showing the stages of the counseling process. As students, we were advised that when we began counseling practice we should put this diagram under the glass tops of our desks, so that we could refer to it as we counseled the troubled human being on the other side who had come to seek our assistance.

I still remember clearly the opening lecture of the graduate program in which this approach was introduced. The diagram was shown on an overhead projector and the work of the year ahead in learning the individual tasks of counseling (such as "identify concerns [box 5.1], or establish intermediate objective" [box 7.2]) was explained. Setting his pointer down, the presenting author asked for questions. Tentatively, from the back of the room, I raised my hand. I must be misunderstanding this, somehow, I thought. So I asked if he meant — he surely didn't, did he? — that anyone, no matter what their personal characteristics, could be trained by this system to be a competent counselor. The instructor paused for a moment to consider it, and then replied, "No, anyone, as long as they have an IQ of at least 100."

The systematic counseling approach and the beliefs attendant to it delineate the current world view of the human services enterprise with precision. In fact, the flowchart that was used can be seen as a virtual "snapshot" of the professional/bureaucratic conception of caring. If you set this flowchart and a flowchart for the assembly-line production of automobiles at a General Motors plant near the university side by side, you cannot tell one from the other unless you read the labels. If even the most subtle and intimate of interpersonal caring relationships, that of counseling and psychotherapy, can be successfully pursued this way, then what caring activity cannot be? Is this the same attempt to deeply understand a person that an analytic psychotherapist once described to me as being rather like "explicating a poem?"

Since one's world view is, as noted, generally unexamined and unconscious, there would be no reason to question such ideas as systematic counseling or group homes or comprehensive service systems if they only worked. For this, historically, is the meaning of the crisis of failure of existing world views. If the community services system would only work, or if it could only be made to work with all of our energies and our money, it would be a great relief. We would then not have to consider such queasy questions as whole new "chessboards." We would not have to say, like Dr. Frank, "what else might grow here other than what we are used to planting?"

Can a significant conceptual change occur in the field of developmental disabilities at this historical moment? Is it just possible that the time is ripe for such a shift? The answer to this question cannot yet be known. Even if one believes that the current world view is exhausted, there is ample evidence of the kind of growing resistance and rigidity that always arises at times of such crises: the professional insecurity, the increased and anxious clinging to traditional approaches. The systematic counseling approach has its parallels everywhere in the healing professions: the new biological reductionism of psychiatry, the institutional group homes in New York, the bewildering technological research studies that now fill the developmental disabilities literature.

I asked John McKnight this question, late one evening at some hotel where we were both speaking, in a slightly different way. "Why were you attracted to our field?" I asked him. "What did you see in developmental disabilities that seemed worth your time in promoting social change?" McKnight's reply was thought-provoking. As an "outsider," he had noticed a number of particular characteristics of our field. First, it had recently been through a massive revolution in thought and practice (the parents movement) organized by ordinary citizens. Second, it had as yet few ties to universities, although he felt that the increasing development of these was troubling. These characteristics showed him, he said, that this was a field which still had significant plasticity and thus potential for change. Knowledge and practice were not fully settled. Things were still in some upheaval.

De Tocqueville, writing in *Democracy in America* in 1835, described optimal periods for social change in another context in this way. He saw in the flux of history

> "...an intermediate period — a period as glorious as it is agitated —
> when the conditions of men are not sufficiently settled for the mind to
> be lulled in torpor, when they are sufficiently unequal for men to exert
> a vast power on the minds of one another, and when some few may
> modify the convictions of all. It is at such times that great reformers start
> up, and new opinions suddenly change the face of the world." (p.311)

We may thus be at a time, agitated as it is, when anomalous new ideas may bear fruit. It is possible that a conceptual revolution is indeed underway.

Yet the heavy social costs that championing social anomalies often requires should be at least mentioned in fair coverage of the process of conceptual change in society. Dr. Frank's story had a happy ending; he lived long enough to be honored by the governor and die a respected and honored (if still somewhat irascible) man. Many pioneers do not. The payment demanded by the phenomenon of resistance to new ideas can be very great.

Dr. Ignaz Semmelweis, in a classic example, was a Hungarian physician who invented aseptic hospital procedure in Vienna in the 1840s. The death rate from "child-bed fever" was then disastrous; any woman giving birth in a hospital stood a good chance of dying of infection. Semmelweis correctly concluded that the source of the infection was bacteria carried on the doctor's hands, and prescribed washing with an antiseptic solution. The results were immediate, and the death rate was reduced tremendously, not only there but later all over the world. All sterile procedures since and the saving of millions of lives can be traced back to Semmelweis' discovery. His name is one of great distinction in the history of medicine.

Semmelweis's physician colleagues at the time, however, were deeply affronted by his "discovery." Not only was he claiming that death was caused by something (bacteria) that no one could see, but the invisible cause was not carried by something negative or neutral — rats in the sewers, unclean floors, stuffy air. Semmelweis said that it was the doctors themselves that were causing the deaths of the very patients they were trying to help! This was such a completely unacceptable thought, such a horrifying assertion for physicians, that they rejected him. Semmelweis was forced to resign and was driven from Vienna by the medical profession. Although he was able to eventually continue his work in Hungary, he ultimately died at a young age, broken in health and in fortune. Galileo, similarly, was rewarded for his researches in support of the heretical belief that the earth revolved around the sun, rather than the reverse, by being sentenced to house arrest. Perhaps, as Saul Alinsky might have suggested, it was a good opportunity for him to think.

Endnotes

1.   R. C. Sheerenburger notes the influence of a particular philosopher named Etienne Bonnet de Condillac (1750-1780) upon Itard's beliefs. A much more thorough discussion of early leaders than this brief summary permits may be found in Burton Blatt's *The Conquest of Mental Retardation* (1987) or in Sheerenberger's *A History of Mental Retardation* (1983). The influence of the life of Kaspar Hauser (Pietzner, 1983) is another historical stream which I do not mention here.

2.   Relevant to the matter of resistance, it is significant to point out that Wolfensberger and his colleague Frank Menolascino were successful in bringing their ideas to

social reality first in a relatively remote state. As they wrote: "One national authority, upon visiting Nebraska, commented that in some of the large seaboard states, one would have to execute hundreds of ossified reactionaries before being able to reform retardation services. In Nebraska, he felt, one had only to execute a half dozen." (Wolfensberger and Menolascino, 1970)

3. Wolfensberger's own analysis is that his twenty predictions have "proven remarkably correct, but that considering that most of the 20 predictions have been positive ones, my perception at that time failed to anticipate concomitant negative developments" (1990).

4. Sarason's *Psychological Problems in Mental Deficiency*, published in 1949, was, for instance, the first book that set forth the idea that people with mental retardation had psychological problems, had an inner life which could be described and understood through psychology, and hence were fully human in this way too.

CHAPTER 8
The New Conceptual Revolution

"In this asylum-ridden country, is it not time to take a new departure
in this matter?"   — Hervey Backus Wilbur (1877)

"...they would have to harvest his beans in a symbolic manner, every
person who had signed the petition picking a handful of beans. They
would harvest them in the same way churches had been built in the old
days, with every family contributing some adobe bricks and pitching in
with labor so that it was a symbolic labor of all with a part of everyone's
earth in it."   — John Nichols, *The Milagro Beanfield War*

"Without the human community, one single human being cannot
survive."   — H.H. The Dalai Lama

Nora Ellen Groce was visiting Martha's Vineyard in 1978 when she
ran across what seemed a curious historical fact: for almost two
centuries, up until fairly recently, an unusually large number of
people with deafness had been born and had lived on the island. The
cause, she eventually discovered, had been a kind of genetically
transmitted deafness confined to the isolated community. But beyond
this interesting fact, she discovered something virtually incredible to
contemplate: apparently nobody had thought deafness was particularly worthy of notice there. Nobody really thought of deafness as a
handicap. But how, she wondered to a friend, were people who could
not hear or speak able to work and marry "hearing" wives and
husbands and raise families like everybody else? Oh, well, he replied,
everybody back then spoke sign language. You mean the relatives and
friends, who interpreted for them? No, he replied, everybody. So
began Groce's investigation which led to her book, *Everyone Here
Spoke Sign Language* (1978).

An elderly resident recalled:

"We would sit around and wait for the mail to come in and just talk. And
the deaf would be there, everyone would be there. And they would be
part of the crowd, and they were accepted. They were fishermen and
farmers and everything else. And they wanted to find out the news just
as much as the rest of us. And oftentimes people would tell stories and
make signs at the same time so everyone could follow [him] together. Of
course, sometimes, if there were more deaf than hearing there, everyone
would speak sign language — just to be polite, you know."

The experience of someone with the "disability" of deafness on
Martha's Vineyard years ago seems remarkable both because it feels
so natural and because it seems so unusual. It was a better situation for

people with disabilities, with a few rare exceptions, than anything which can be produced by knowledge or money in the professional field of disabilities today. Considering the primitive nature of the former society and the presumably advanced state of our own, that seems a strange thing. Yet people with deafness in that particular isolated time and location were able to take for granted that essential sense of "place" in a community that seems to be so very hard for people with disabilities to attain today. In Wolfensberger's theory of human services called "Social Role Valorization" (a successor to normalization) one could say that they had opportunity to live valued social roles to a degree rarely found elsewhere.

The way that people with deafness were perceived and treated on Martha's Vineyard could be contrasted even at that time with the way that people with deafness were perceived and treated a few miles away on the mainland. There such people were perceived to have a defect in need of remediation. Special institutions were erected for their welfare.[1]

As Groce points out, when you compare the circumstances in the nineteenth century of people with deafness on the mainland with those on the island, you find marked contrasts. On Martha's Vineyard, about 80% of nonhearing people got married, about the same rate as hearing people there. In the rest of the country only 45% married. On the Vineyard, only 35% married other nonhearing people, a much better rate of integration than the 79% then estimated nationally and the 80% of marriages in which both partners are deaf in the case of the United States today. People who were deaf on the island were just as likely to have children, and to have as large families, as their hearing neighbors, while comparative national figures were much lower. Nonhearing residents on Martha's Vineyard worked at the same variety of jobs and had the same range of economic success as anyone else. On the mainland a disproportionate number of people who were deaf tended to be limited to menial jobs and to earn substantially less than other workers. Even today, men and women who are deaf earn on the average of 30 and 40 percent less than hearing workers.

Thus at precisely the same time, with the same kinds of basic cultures separated only by a short stretch of water, even with an incidence of "disability" much greater on the island, deaf people on the mainland where professional services were available fared far worse than those on the island where there were no services at all. There was apparently no need for such services.

Today the phenomenon of Martha's Vineyard itself is gone, as hereditary deafness has faded with increased transportation and with marriage outside of the old limited gene pool. Yet apparently many old people there still casually and unconsciously gesture when they talk. It is only when you see the same gestures repeated by someone else that you realize that these gestures of the hands are not random. They are not an idiosyncratic behavior of elderly people, but a vestige of another social era. They recall a day when everybody spoke sign language, now embedded in the very fabric of the community mind, in the very dreams of those who once spoke in sign.

The Context of Caring and the Psychological Sense of Community

Caring always occurs in a cultural context, in what Oliver Sacks has referred to as the "moral space" of a community setting. This is the ancient truth that we lost in our attempt to build, in McKnight's phrase, a "system that would care." But care, as noted earlier, cannot be rendered by machinery, whether it is a CAT scan device on its sterile hospital altar, or the architectural machinery of an institution for deaf people, or the systemic machinery of a comprehensive community services system. In our modern caring systems the shadows of the ancient social rituals of community caring are like the vestigial gestures of old people on Martha's Vineyard — almost, but not quite, forgotten.

What is so significant about the situation of a deaf person living some time ago in Martha's Vineyard, or a person with Tourette's Syndrome living today in the Mennonite farming village of LaCrete, Alberta (Sacks, 1988), where genetic conditions again cause a high incidence of that particular disability, and where it is similarly accepted? What is similar about the experience of people in these settings to people who are in certain types of intentional communities or who are fortunate enough to live in other communities in which they feel deeply part of their social surroundings? What differentiates such situations from those of the many people who feel isolated and alone, despite the level of sophisticated assistance that may surround them? How may one describe the sense of being embedded in a world of others in which one plays a role? What is it that is missing when this sense is not present?

Sarason, to my mind, captured the essence of this issue in his term "the psychological sense of community," set forth in his 1977 book of the same name. The psychological sense of community, in his conception, is "the sense that one is part of a readily available, mutually supportive network of relationships upon which one could depend and as a result of which one did not experience sustained feelings of loneliness that impel one to actions or to adapting a lifestyle of living masking anxiety and setting the stage for later and more destructive anguish." To explore why this sense is of key importance it is worth quoting from that work at length:

"No one would deny that the psychological sense of community is an important need the absence or weakness of which can have debilitating consequences. But are there not other important needs which when unsatisfied also have grave consequences? Of course. Is it not danger-ous, if not foolish, to suggest an overarching criterion which emphasizes a single need? It is dangerous but not foolish, and at this particular time in our society one must risk the dangers. The phrase 'at this particular time in our society' implies both the danger in and the justification for emphasizing one particular need. One risks the danger that a distorted or narrow time perspective will contribute to a confusion between symptom and cause and lead us to see discontinuities and overlook continuities, but there is a difference between an economical and an oversimplified explanation — an economical explanation suggests that a choice has been made among alternatives. The justification inheres in the possibility that there are times in a society when a myriad of social phenomena indicate that a particular human need is so seriously frustrated, with consequences sufficiently widespread and ominous, as to force us to give it special emphasis. We are living in such times. The young and the old; residents of any geographic area; the more and less educated; the political left, right, and center; the professional and the non-professional; the rich and the poor — within each of these group-ings sizable numbers of people feel alone, unwanted, and unneeded. They may spend a large part of their time in densely populated settings, interacting with other people in a transient or sustained way, and yet be plagued by feelings of aloneness and the stabbing knowledge that physical proximity and psychological closeness can be amazingly unre-lated. They may be involved in all kinds of 'giving and taking' activities and relationships, but always aware that the boundaries and the per-meability of their private world are unaltered. They may be by personal knowledge in roles that are by definition necessary and even crucial, and yet this personal knowledge mystifyingly has little or no positive effect to bolster the fragile feeling that one is needed for what one is as a person. And these dysphoric feelings, related to family, work, and local community, are increasingly exacerbated by the perception that there are forces in the nation and the world that make one feel as autonomous and safe as an atom in a nuclear accelerator. The point is not whether these feelings are 'objectively' justified, or to what extent they are justified, but that increasingly people feel they are justified, and that they are impotent to change the situation in which they experience the anxiety of perceived personal isolation." (pp. 214-15)

Sarason's concept is a particularly clear and useful one with which to examine what is productive and what is counterproductive in current practice in the developmental disabilities field. In analogy, one might remember the orphan asylum in which infants died from what was later discovered to be lack of love. In the world view of the orphanage, love could not be seen, or was not seen as important; it could not be named. The concept of the sense of psychological community is helpful mostly because it helps us see and name that which we have sensed was the essential and missing element in all of our work. We know how to look at settings in which people with disabilities are located from a number of different perspectives: by clinical sophistication, by increase in adaptive behavior scores, in cleanliness, safety, and staffing ratios, to name a few. But Sarason helps us to phrase the essential question of a new concept of service. The question is: does a sense of psychological community exist here?

Where is a psychological sense of community found in society? When one starts asking such a question, one first finds where it tends *not* to be found. It is least likely to be found in managed, professional systems. This is not surprising, for the world view previously described as "professional/bureaucratic" arises from a completely different conception of things. This is not to say that this world view is bad; the question rather to ask is "bad for what?" The professional/bureaucratic way of looking at the world is good, as noted, for producing automobiles. It is not good for nurturing the creation of settings in which the caring of one person for another is likely to arise.[3] As McKnight has pointed out, it is as if we had two tools for pursuing our work of encouraging caring: the first the professional/bureaucratic one, the second one having to do with the encouragement and recognition of associational life. It is as if, he said, we have been consistently using the wrong tool for our work.

The correct tool for caring, we are just beginning to see, arises from an understanding of a contrasting world view which we can term *associational*. It recognizes that caring always arises in a cultural setting, and that it always is something that happens between people. It understands that the psychological sense of community is the key concept which lets us know if a cultural context exists in which caring is likely to arise. It recognizes that while the psychological sense of community cannot be produced, it is always being created naturally by the free action of societies, a tendency that can be either supported or suppressed by public policy. It understands that no matter how efficiently managed an orphanage you have, you cannot produce love. Yet love can always be found, growing naturally in the world, in the hearts of human beings.

The contrast between the *professional/bureaucratic* and *associational* world views can be seen especially clearly when they suddenly shift. Everyone is aware of how the psychological sense of community can suddenly arise among a group of neighbors who scarcely know each other, during an emergency like a flood or fire or hurricane. In New York City a few years ago there was a garbage strike that lasted so long and posed such a health hazard that high-rise apartment dwellers had to come out into their halls and band together if they were to avoid having their buildings taken over by rats. A friend of mine told me this was the first time, after many years of living in her apartment, that she had met her neighbors on the same floor.

When this sense of community suddenly forms in a setting dominated by the professional/bureaucratic world view it is even more striking. A particularly touching example can be found in the records of the San Francisco earthquake of 1906. The Agnew Asylum, an institution for people with mental disorders, was severely damaged. In an instant the clockwork regularity of institutional life was rent beyond repair. As an observer at the time wrote:

> "I was astonished to see how nicely the patients got along under the circumstances. Men and women who had been more or less constantly violent and untidy when confined to the building were getting along peacefully, seldom quarreling, and showing more desire to keep clean than they had done when restricted to the limits of the building and the airing courts. They all seemed more comfortable and contented in the tents and on the open grounds... Immediately following the catastrophe ... many worked like Trojans in the effort to rescue those caught in the wreck and in caring for the wounded... Even the epileptics have had fewer attacks." (Hoisholt, 1906, in Caplan, 1969)

What happened in this instance is that catastrophe turned the professional/bureaucratic world view on its head, and the natural associational tendency of people rushed in. One is certain that as order was restored, the former regained its acendency, and that inmates slipped from their highly valued roles as "rescuers" to their former poorly valued roles as inmates of wards being cared for because of their needs.

If we develop eyes to see associational life at work, we can begin to see the invisible structure of society beneath the formal structures of which, by common consent, it is believed to be composed. They form the "glue" which actually holds any society together. The settings making up this subtle matrix have been referred to by Peter Berger and Richard John Neuhaus by the interesting name of *mediating structures*.

Mediating Structures

> "To be attached to the subdivision, to love the little platoon we belong to in society, is the first principle...of public affections.
> — Edmund Burke

In Berger and Neuhaus's incisive *To Empower People: The Role of Mediating Structures and Public Policy*, they define mediating structures as "those institutions standing between the individual in his private life and the large institutions of public life." They are such things as the family, the church, the voluntary association. They are the informal groupings of society through which society works.

Berger and Neuhaus believe that because we have ignored mediating structures our public policy has been traditionally pursued in counterproductive and even hazardous ways. They cite Emile Durkheim's study of suicide, in which he describes "the 'tempest' of modernization sweeping away the 'little aggregations' in which people formerly found community, leaving only the state on the one hand and a mass of individuals, 'like so many liquid molecules,' on the other." As mediating structures are displaced, the "value-generating and value-maintaining agencies in society" disappear. Without them there remain only the values of the state. When all of the strength of the mediating structures is gone, one has left only totalitarianism; an all-powerful state acting directly on the individual. In their excellent work they analyze the nature and reasons for the neglect of mediating structures, and outline a thoughtful approach to public policies that would respect and enhance the value of associational life in American society.

In another book in the series to which Berger and Neuhaus's volume provides the introduction, Robert L. Woodson further explores the applicability of a policy based upon the recognition of the importance of mediating structures to specific areas. In one study he cites, people who had been in some kind of distress were asked to list whom they turned to first when they were in need. Seven kinds of people were listed most frequently, and all had neighborhood roles such as ministers, friends, and hairdressers. The eighth category, professional assistance, was turned to only after all the previous kinds had been tried.[4] As Woodson writes:

> "It has been clearly demonstrated that informal networks (mediating structures) have the strength to solve a range of social problems that have defied solution by traditional bureaucratic organizations. Yet public policy continues to ignore these indigenous institutions and instead vests most of its resources in the institutions that neighborhood residents rank as their last choice." (1981, p.128)

Northwestern University's Center for Urban Affairs and Policy Research, in a 1988 study, set out to find out how many "invisible" associational groupings actually existed under the surface of one Chicago neighborhood. In that one neighborhood of 24 square blocks alone they were able to find 575: the hidden organs and muscles of that particular social body.

Associational Life and Developmental Disabilities

There are three visions of society, McKnight tells us, which underlie various options for social action on behalf of labeled people. The first he calls the *therapeutic vision*, which "sees the well-being of individuals as growing from an environment composed of professionals and their services." The second he somewhat confusingly terms the *advocacy vision*, which "conceives an individual whose world is guarded by legal advocates, support people, self-help groups, job developers, and housing locators." The advocacy vision "conceives a defensive wall of helpers to protect an individual against an alien community." McKnight describes the third approach as the *community vision*. Unlike the others, it aims for the "recommunalization" of "exiled and labeled individuals." It "understands the community as the basic context for enabling people to contribute their gifts" (1987b).

Because McKnight uses "advocacy," which has become a misused and confusing term, it is necessary to pause to be clear what it means in this context. In its most common usage, advocacy has come to mean speaking on behalf of a person or an issue. The emergence of the Association for Retarded Citizens is the classic example in the disabilities field of how social conditions for people who have difficulty speaking for themselves can be transformed through advocacy efforts. While the great and obvious benefits of vigorous advocacy are understood, McKnight indicates the inherent limitations of an approach in which advocacy has become a movement that tends to usually be against something, a something which at root is a world which it believes will reject vulnerable people if not prevented by vigilant strategies. But because of the various ways in which this term is used, one can have terms such as citizen advocacy, which McKnight would class under his "community" vision and not as part of the "advocacy" vision at all.[5]

Placed into our earlier conception of paradigms, it is clear that a professional vision relates to the professional/bureaucratic world view. But one may see that what McKnight calls the advocacy vision has also come to relate to this view as well, for the advocacy vision emerged as a counterbalance to the power of the unrestrained therapeutic vision. Despite the incredible improvement which the advocacy vision has caused in the lives of people with mental retardation, it unconsciously embraced the same view of the world in which help must come for people with needs solely from professionals and their systems. The Association for Retarded Citizens, for instance, started organizing to improve conditions in institutions, and later to build alternative community systems. This advocacy achieved success of virtually historic note. Yet it should come as no surprise that the mature systems created by such advocacy should suffer from a lack of the psychological sense of community for those within them, for they are at root professional/bureaucratic structures, not mediating ones. Under the conditions of formation of new settings, they were, it is true, markedly associational in character. Once the initial formative period passed and formalization proceeded, however, their essential professional/bureaucratic nature increasingly became evident.

The solution to the symptoms of the decline of a community service system bereft of a "heart" of community sense is not, frustratingly, to advocate more. Systemic advocacy, no matter how systemic or how forceful the advocacy, can only advocate for systems. Writes Woodson: "Continued support of...traditional delivery systems, which view those in need of help as 'clients,' will lead to continued failure and worsening of the conditions that breed despair. The solution is not merely to improve coordination among bureaucratic agencies, nor is it to centralize and restructure bureaucracies.... There must be a renegotiation of the values and interest on which public policies are established" (1981).

As opposed to the traditional response of advocacy for systemic change, one is beginning to witness the emergence of the new approach to policy and practice based upon valuing the importance of associational life. One of the first of these was Wolfensberger's concept of citizen advocacy, which called for the building of freely given relationships between people at risk of social devaluation and valued members of society. Intentional communities composed of persons with and without disabilities are another expression of action based upon associational values, and are discussed in more detail in a later chapter. More recently, one has begun to hear of a multitude of approaches to encourage friendship between people with disabilities and others, particularly children in school settings.[6] The concept that people with disabilities must be surrounded by "a defensive wall of helpers" lest they be rejected by others has begun to be refuted by such relationships as are captured in Robert and Martha Perske's *Circles of Friends* (1988). There is a new emphasis on the role of families and friends in the lives of people with disabilities.

This new conception is arising against much resistance, a phenomenon that should engender no surprise to those familiar with Kuhn's theory of how conceptual revolutions take place. The most significant resistance often comes, curiously enough, not from those in charge of bureaucratic systems (probably because the movement to promote this concept is yet too small to pose any threat) but from the field's most energetic and committed advocates. To such persons, making friends and supporting the inclusion of people with disabilities into the associational life of their communities can seem pitifully soft and small-scale actions to take in the face of tragic and escalating needs for the basic necessities of life. What is needed for this, many think, is more and stronger advocacy, more responsive and better-coordinated bureaucratic systems, and more money. It is only through such strong action, they reason, that people with disabilities may hope to get what they so desperately require.

Rud Turnbull and Gary Brunk (1990) cast much light upon the nature of this resistance to the associational world view by proponents of the traditional advocacy approach. We note, for instance, that the language of the federal Developmental Disabilities Act speaks in such terms as "independence." Where does this term come from? Why does it say *inde*pendence rather than *inter*dependence? Turnbull and Brunk revealingly point out that the traditional thinking in the developmental disabilities field rests upon the social philosophy of "philosophic liberalism." Such a philosophy, which is strongly rooted in American cultural history, holds that "the development of an independent person is an assertion that independence is a valued goal in and of itself." The "individualistic cast" of philosophic liberalism means "that people must compete for their place in the world." Programs and legal rights were aimed at helping each individual to attain the maximum possible independence. "The belief that people with disabilities should have a place in the mainstream, which is to say in a society that is dominated by individualistic, economically oriented philosophic liberalism," they claim, "became the public philosophy rationale for the plethora of rights that federal and state laws now create."

Against the tradition of philosophic liberalism they discuss a second dominant theme of American public philosophy termed "civic republicanism." Civic republicanism, in contrast to philosophic liberalism, speaks in terms of such questions as "cooperation" and "volume." It speaks, in other words, in the language of an associational world view. Civic republicanism, according to William M. Sullivan (1982), as Turnbull and Brunk point out, believes that "the protection of human dignity depends upon the moral quality of social relationships." Turnbull and Brunk share their view that the kinds of associational world view interests of the developmental disabilities field mentioned earlier flow from the civic republicanism. In many ways the struggle over paradigm shift we have been discussing may be seen in the interplay between these two political philosophies, with philosophic liberalism currently dominant and the source of resistance against associational ideas.

Policy Directions for an Associational World View in Developmental Disabilities

We have traced in this book, up to this point, the current crisis in the developmental disabilities field, and have interpreted it in terms of the failure of the professional/bureaucratic world view underlying policy and practice. We have talked about how old world views are overthrown in the course of history and replaced by new ones. We have, in this chapter, made an argument that a new world view based upon the value of associational life is the new idea which is struggling for succession.

What, then, is the proper role of an enlightened public policy to be at this particular stage in history, in the midst of this crisis? If we believe that a new associational world view is emerging, and that its emergence is important now for people with disabilities, what can we do to aid this process? If we have taken Sarason's psychological sense of community as our compass, and have begun to see the mediating structures in and through which this sense is generated, what is to be our course?

It is not, surely, to try to recreate the ancient lost world of clan and kinship in which the psychological sense of community was as innate as the earth beneath one's feet. Then, the world was composed of mediating structures. The role and power of professional and bureaucratic structures was small. History tells us that there is no returning to a longed-for past. Much as we may hunger for the sense of place and order afforded by Garrison Keillor's radio stories from an imaginary Lake Wobegon, the world is not about to be created in that form soon again. Yet we do have many live and vital areas in which to look for associational life in American society as it is today. They are the new clans; clans and ties not of kinship, but of voluntary affiliation. How to discover them and nurture their capacity to support and include people with disabilities is work of a different world view than the one which has dominated our lives and the developmental disabilities field. The emergence of this idea is the new conceptual revolution.

In Chapters 2 and 3 , Sharon Gretz and A. J. Hildebrand told the stories of two efforts which attempted to live out this different world view. In the next chapter we will look at some other efforts and explore how one may move from theory to demonstrating the power of the theory in specific social experiments through funding and governmental support.

Endnotes

1. Sign language was actually prohibited in some of the institutional "oral" schools then dominant, to force deaf residents to rely on lip-reading. As Oliver Sacks has pointed out, the students, starved for communication, actually invented their own clandestine sign (Sacks, 1986).

2. This has also been pointed out by McKnight (1989).

3. A psychological sense of community can arise, of course, in professional/bureaucratic settings ("the boys at the office," "our" division of the company, the Marines) but such a sense always develops counter to centralized control and systemization.

4. Additional research supporting these findings is Emory L. Cowen's "Help is Where You Find It: Four Informal Helping Groups" (1982).

5. An excellent monograph which clarifies basic issues in advocacy is Wolfensberger's 1977 "A Balanced Multi-Component Advocacy/Protection Schema."

6. These are arising because it has become clear that the physical integration mandated by PL 94-142, The Education for All Handicapped Children Act, has not been sufficient to bring about social integration, as was expected by its framers. The social isolation of students in special education classrooms within schools, in fact, can parallel the isolation of residents of group homes noted earlier.

CHAPTER 9
Funding Orientation and Overview of Project Types

> "If you want to change the system, you don't worry about petty reforms, because that just strengthens the system."
>
> — Myles Horton

Moving from theory to practice is always fraught with challenge. Attempting to practice a theory based upon the importance of associational life and the "psychological sense of community" is, of course, merely one example. I started this work with at least one established belief: that all society is made up of relationships between two or more people. No matter how complex and confusing society may seem to be (and is) you can always come back to that fact; that the caring and the sense of psychological community which can surround each person with a disability must start with at least one relationship. Society is held together by tiny relationships just as a vast planet is held together by tiny molecular forces.[1] Although this may have seemed like a tiny focus of attention, in light of the vast and troubling issues obviously besetting the thousands of people it was our public charge to worry about, it set us to trying to learn as much as we could about such relationships and how to foster their emergence. An understanding of Wolfensberger's work on "Social Role Valorization"[2] was also helpful as a "map" to understanding. Relationships were, after all, key in approaching valued roles for people with disabilities in society. We in Pennsylvania were, as mentioned earlier, in a state in which tracings of the old Quaker historical values of community and of tolerance still seemed to have some effect upon the workings of society. Pennsylvania also was a state in which the community service system itself had been erected some years earlier upon the base of an intensive immersion in Wolfensberger's principle of normalization, the predecessor theory to social role valorization. This was the "ground" on which social change might find it possible to arise.

We also started by learning that there were a vast number of mediating structures in society which might afford a context of relationship and a psychological sense of community to those who could become part of them. We concentrated on learning to see these hidden structures of society more clearly, and to see what we could find out about how people with disabilities could be invited into them for their inclusion and protection, for mutual enrichment and, we believed, the ultimate improvement of our society in some way. We agreed with Berger and Neuhaus that public policy should protect and foster mediating structures, and part of our responsibility as an organization was to help to contribute to public policy.

We also, as I noted, sensed to a greater or lesser degree that the current system upon which the lives of people with disabilities depended was in a rapidly escalating crisis. We knew that by taking part of our attention to pursue these interests, we would be perceived by many colleagues as doing something at least irrelevant and at worst inattentive to the "real" problems of the day. Would we, by devoting money and energy to the tiniest of relationships for a limited number of people, be "fiddling while Rome burns?"

As it turns out, considerable encouragement in our course emerged from the unlikely direction of a 1988 book by Samuel P. and Pearl M. Oliner called *The Altruistic Personality: Rescuers of Jews in Nazi Europe.* It examines another period of crisis — this one a vastly greater crisis than our own — the Holocaust unleashed by the Nazis upon the Jewish people. In the great tragedy of that era, a small phenomenon emerged which has drawn increasing attention recently: the saving of individual Jewish people by non-Jews. More than a few "ordinary" people, it now emerges, hid those under the threat of extermination at the risk of their own lives.[3] Why did they do it? The Oliners, in studying six hundred people who helped Jewish people escape the Holocaust, found that 32 percent said they did it on their own initiative. Sixty-seven percent, however, did it because someone asked them to. Of these, only 27 percent were asked for help by the victims themselves. Fully 70 percent were asked by intermediaries.

What characterized rescuers from a psychological perspective? What kinds of people would undertake such commitments at such great personal risk? The Oliners' research concluded the following:

> "What distinguished rescuers was not their lack of concern with self, external approval, or achievement, but rather their capacity for exten-sive relationships — their stronger sense of attachment to others and their feeling of responsibility for the welfare of others, including those outside their immediate familial or communal circles." (p.249)

Rescuers were not individuals acting in isolation but people who had a strong capacity to develop and maintain networks. Thus, according to the Oliners:

> "...support from others was not simply a matter of circumstances; networks did not suddenly appear. They were the products of the efforts of individuals who deliberately cultivated every contact they could." (p. 101)

Did people have the same "altruistic" potential in Pennsylvania today as they were found to have even during the darkest days of the Holocaust? Would ordinary citizens invite people with disabilities into their families, their communities, and their associational life if one asked them in the right way? What was the right way to ask? It made sense to set out to find as many ways of successfully asking as we could. These kinds of concepts: relationships, valued social roles, the psychological sense of community, mediating structures, and learning how to "ask" were the basis upon which we attempted to evolve a public policy supportive of an associational world view which some of us believed was emerging from the smoke and confusion of current events.

In attempting to assist in the emergence of that world view, we have been occasionally misunderstood as believing that professional services were unnecessary. This, of course, was and is not the case. One might rather, as John O'Brien put it, think about the current society as a seesaw in which all the weight and the emphasis is on the professional/bureaucratic side of the fulcrum; one side all the way down on the ground, the other up in the air. It's as if a huge man were sitting on one side and a small child on the other. In a situation in which things are so very much out of balance and in which one has, comparatively speaking, an infinitesimally small amount of weight and influence, the only thing to do is to work for balance by leaping on the child's side of the seesaw with as much weight as one can muster. This, in the framework of public policy, is what those of us who saw things in this way set out to do.

Theory and Practice

A few additional comments might be made about our general orientation towards the practice of social policy. The first is that it quickly became clear that policy and practice were completely intertwined. If one holds certain values which are summarized as a "policy," these values are far from constituting an abstract or "pure" theory which one then applies to the world. Although this kind of approach to social policy is frequently attempted, holding abstract values over the concrete experience of people affected by them always makes for a Procrustean bed. To understand how good ideas can end up hurting people, one has only to examine the ways that normalization, when misunderstood and viewed as a sacrosanct and inviolate concept, has driven and legitimized all sorts of injurious practices for people with disabilities.[4]

One advantage of conceiving and funding new ideas is the continual testing of theory which takes place. The constant interaction between theory and actual practice in the unforgiving reality of the world affords continual, rich, and even painful opportunities to refine one's theoretical conceptions. Sometimes one's idea of how things work simply isn't correct. Furthermore, the experience of fostering the creation of projects in diverse areas results in the opportunity to pick up "themes" which arise across them. "If you want to understand society, try to change it," Sarason once wrote. This project afforded an opportunity to try to understand society through continuing attempts at change.

Anomalies

Second, our practice has been guided by an understanding of conceptual change as delineated by Thomas Kuhn. As John O'Brien once pointed out, all conceptual "revolutionaries" must have some idea of how change takes place to sustain them through the long days when everyone is constantly telling them they are wrong. Kuhn provides such an idea of how change takes place. It would be more accurate to say, however, that those who come up with what Kuhn terms anomalies could more accurately be termed explorers — recognizing that their role is in an active search, not in the mere passive emergence of a new phenomenon. We thus tend to see ourselves principally as allies of explorers who are seeking to help particular new anomalies emerge in the field's practice. It is from such anomalies, we are sure, that significant conceptual and social change will occur. Understanding the question of resistance to new ideas, it is clear that when new leaders emerge with a different vision of the world, these potential inventors will be unthinkingly suppressed by the existing human service system. Our most useful role as a Council has been to identify such explorers, to legitimize them with recognition, and to fund them to try out their new vision.

This recognition has helped to protect explorers pursuing ideas that people didn't yet understand. In one instance, the immediate superior of a project leader had never been to see the project until I came out from the state capital and spent the afternoon there with local officials; she visited the next week and became interested. In another, the sponsoring agency suddenly came through with extra financial support and agency investment after we extended a project's grant due to outstanding achievement. Our role has been in nurturing and "fertilizing," if you will, the seeds of emerging anomalies expressing the associational world view. We have a little cartoon logo in the office that shows a manure spreader kicking out rich clods on a field of sprouting plants, the flower of each one of which is an "idea" light bulb. "The Pennsylvania Developmental Disabilities Planning Council," the caption reads; "Fertilizing a Few Good Ideas."

Diversity

> "Diversity is the great gift which life has brought to our planet and may one day bring to the rest of the universe. The preservation and fostering of diversity is the great goal which I would like to see embodied in our ethical principles and in our political actions."
>
> — Freeman Dyson

Third, we believe it is best to plan for diversity. If one wishes to deal with anomalies, one must set aside customary practices based in the professional/bureaucratic world view typical of large organizations and governmental planning. As Berger and Neuhaus explain:

> "The management mindset of the megastructure — whether of HEW, Sears Roebuck, or the AFL-CIO — is biased toward the unitary solution. The neat and comprehensive answer is impatient of 'irrational' particularities...The challenge of public policy is to...cast aside its adversary posture toward particularism and embrace as its goal the advancement of the multitude of common interests that in fact constitute the common weal" (p. 41).

In the beginning, we conceived an approach to grantmaking that started with traditional ideas; one based upon such concepts as quantitative evaluation, model replication, and "systems advocacy." As we noticed what actually worked and didn't work in grantmaking, we gradually had to abandon these concepts. Could social programs actually be *purchased?* Some of us lost faith that they could be. In truth, we seemed to be making the most impact when we were, as mentioned, "gardening" — nurturing and fertilizing the emergent seeds of conceptions that were arising here and there around the state. We could scatter a few seeds, as well. Depending upon the soil, they might well sprout.

Each project arose around a specific leader. Leaders were different people, and each locality in Pennsylvania was different, too. We therefore needed to respect the different paths that different leaders in different places evolved in developing their own visions of the emerging world view, while holding them to basic and agreed-upon principles. We knew the greatest resource shortage is always leadership, and that the development of projects was perhaps most importantly understood as providing media for skilled leadership to develop in the state. People are diverse, and we needed to respect their diversity as well as that of their creations.

The importance of fostering diversity is now increasingly recognized in business, particularly in the creation of new businesses. As Paul Hawken, Chairman of the entrepreneurial "star" Smith and Hawken horticultural products company, recently remarked, diversity is essential for change, particularly at times in which society is changing fast. This is especially true at times of stress, when one often sees many new ideas coming to the surface. "When the rate of social change outstrips the ability of large enterprises to adapt," he explained to an audience of businessmen, "you get the entrepreneurial bloom that we have been witnessing, simply because small enterprises respond more quickly to how you and I are changing. We are inventing new lives, new patterns of living together, new values, and new ideas" (Hawken, 1989, p. 73). In our own field, new business settings are analogous to new settings for what, in its original sense, was called "social work." Such settings, principally voluntary associations, as Berger and Neuhaus point out, are "laboratories for innovation in social services," and "sustain the expression of the rich pluralism of American life." There are many more tensions inherent in pursuing such pluralism, of course, than in a simpler traditional unitary solution.

The Creation of Settings

Last, we understood our work as social experiments in what Sarason has termed "the creation of settings." In providing funding for new projects we were essentially supporting the creation of new settings. Each starts with one or more persons who has a dream, and our funds provide a way for them to attempt this dream's realization. Until Sarason wrote *The Creation of Settings and the Future Societies* it was not generally understood that the creation of settings, which are the medium of all work in human services, follows a discoverable process and set of dynamics. These dynamics have been highly visible in the settings whose creation we have supported. Resource scarcity, emerging conflict between the new setting and its "parent" when created within an existing organization, dynamics surrounding the leader's role, and numerous other issues typical to this process have been visible not only in the projects, but in us, the sponsoring organization, ourselves. In this we have continued to learn two things. First, the purpose of the creation of all of these settings is not only in the external task which they have set themselves, but it exists as importantly in the growth of the members of the core group of creators themselves. Second, Sarason once said something about the creation of settings being one of the most complicated obstacle courses devised by man or by God. This has turned out to be an accurate statement.

Translation into Action

To put this orientation into action, the Developmental Disabilities Planning Council issued requests for proposals (RFPs) in specified categories of work that they wished to encourage. While thousands of proposals are issued by government agencies, foundations, and others, these were a little different from the norm. Rather than containing a paragraph or two of information, or a mere listing of technical requirements, these documents explained in some detail the idea that was being presented, the rationale for the new social approach called for, and examples of possible activities which proposers might pursue. The primary purpose of the RFPs was to capture the attention of people around the state who had visionary ideas that would not ordinarily qualify for funding. There were secondary purposes as well. Through the process of developing them, Council committees attempted to clarify and make coherent social visions which might otherwise have remained vague. Readers and possible proposers could follow the central idea presented and understand why the creation of new types of social experiments were called for. Together, they made a statement of what the Council thought of certain social issues, what it suggested might be done about them, and what progressive public policy might be. In these ways, they served an educational function.

An Overview of Types of Projects Funded

Just as sunlight passed through a prism fractions into the colors of a rainbow, so the light of an idea can express itself through individual imagination in a rainbow of settings. Although such settings may at first glance seem as different as yellow and red, they may all derive to a greater or lesser extent from the inspiration of a single concept. In our case, the concept has been the striving for a psychological sense of community. Each setting tries to strengthen the mediating structures of community life through which this sense is created.

The progress of a conceptual revolution, Kuhn has stated, requires anomalies. These anomalies demonstrate the truth of an emerging paradigm. Chapters by Sharon Gretz and A. J. Hildebrand presented some of the experiences of two explorers of project anomalies in some detail. Just like the proof of theory in the physicist's laboratory, funded projects can provide experimental evidence of whether the theory underlying them is correct. Is it possible to respond to the situation of people with disabilities in society in other than professionalistic ways? Will ordinary people become involved in the lives of people with disabilities if asked? How do you ask? Is there more than one way? These are the kinds of questions we have been asking.

It is early to make a final judgment about how well this process of asking actually works. The development of these new settings must be viewed as experiments in progress. Nonetheless, early evidence is persuasive. People are asked, and many respond. It is from the daily experience of such enterprises that evidence is beginning to emerge, which we continually use to refine our approach in sketching out the types of activities for which we entertain proposals for funding, criteria by which we select them, and activities through which we nurture them.

Although projects comprise a conscious plurality of experimental approaches, they fall into basic categories or types. Some requests for proposals have called people to create variations on the theme of community around the topic of housing, others around inclusion in associational life, others around one-to-one relationships. Thus the categories are analogous to spectral colors in that they may describe a basic color such as red, that itself may contain many shades. The following sections briefly describe each category in which anomalies have been nurtured.

Citizen Advocacy

Citizen advocacy, which A. J. Hildebrand described in practice, is the most highly evolved, consciously conducted, asking form. Originally proposed by Wolfensberger in 1966, it was greeted with great resistance, resistance which continues in many quarters of the advocacy movement today. In citizen advocacy, as described by Wolfensberger in 1972:

> "First of all ... competent citizen volunteers represent — as if they were their own — the interests of other individuals who are in some way impaired, handicapped, or disadvantaged. Secondly, this relationship is structured on an individualized one-to-one, or at least one-to-a-few, basis. Thirdly, many of these relationships will be established on a sustained and often life-long basis. Fourthly, the functions of the advocate will be highly differentiated in order to meet a wide range of "protege" needs, while only providing the minimal amount of protection that is needed. Fifthly, the efforts of the volunteer advocates will be coordinated and supported by a citizen advocacy office." (p.218)

Citizen advocacy is practiced by a number of offices in various states. Many of the leaders of these offices form a national "culture" of citizen advocacy coordinators who constantly refine successful ways of asking, who mentor new coordinators, and who continually evaluate each other's programs. In starting a citizen advocacy office one has not only the advantage of careful design and long experience, but the availability of this culture to tap into.

The Council currently supports five offices in Pennsylvania, which range in degree of success to date. Success seems closely correlated to the degree to which the individual offices participate in the national citizen advocacy culture. The Pennsylvania citizen advocacy offices leaned heavily for assistance on the citizen advocacy offices of Georgia, which mentored coordinators during the starting years. After six years, there is now the beginning of a culture established in Pennsylvania in which new coordinators can be mentored, current coordinators sustained, and quality of practice maintained.[5]

Citizen Participation

Where citizen advocacy shows similarity of form, citizen participation projects show diversity. According to the tenets of citizen advocacy, one should be able to perform an evaluation on an office anywhere in the world following certain standards. This cannot be said for projects funded under our category of citizen participation. Originally, the Council issued a request for proposals (RFP) which called for projects to "encourage and support the meaningful involvement of people with developmental disabilities in decision-making processes that affect their lives." We funded a number of valid projects which had traditional collective advocacy as their goal: gaining improved services, increasing accessible transportation, and related tasks. Others, however, were inspired by a vision similar to citizen advocacy.

Unlike citizen advocacy, however, these other projects do not place their main focus on the one-to-one relationship. Following the ideas of John McKnight, these settings view the inclusion of people with disabilities into the associational life of their communities as their goal. In successful projects of this type, such as that described by Sharon Gretz, it is becoming clear that such introductions into mediating structures seem to follow the path of a one-to-one relationship.

The citizen participation category has been the most interesting in terms of diversity of invention. One project in Lancaster County, for example, decided that involvement in the public life of that political city was its goal. It first looked at the long-established civic leadership program called "Leadership Lancaster." In this program, common to many cities, young men and women judged to have the capacity to become future civic leaders are sponsored by local businesses to be part of a year's training in the life of the town. The experience involves contact with community and business leaders which often proves extremely helpful in launching participants' careers, as well as imbuing them with a tradition of community service.

The Lancaster project set up a parallel educational program for people with disabilities. While retaining (we hope temporarily) a measure of segregation, this effort took the unique step of involving as mentors many current leaders in town who either had disabilities themselves or were particularly dedicated to the situation of people with disabilities, thus in some measure "integrating it in reverse." When I went to the inaugural reception for this project, I found present at the reception many people with disabilities, including the project leader. There were many civic leaders such as the state senator, the high school principal, and a former head of the girl scouts running for political office, but only two professional human services workers — the sponsoring United Cerebral Palsy Association's director and myself.

As a final step, the project gained the guarantee of one place per year in the established Leadership Lancaster group. Thus not only will one person have an opportunity to become part of the leadership of the community each year (think ten in ten years, twenty in twenty years), but every future leader of Lancaster who goes through the program will have done so in the company of a similarly qualified and sponsored person with a disability.

A year or so after the Lancaster project started, we got a call from someone from the state association of volunteer placement offices who had heard of our interests. The association, I was told, held an annual conference of all the people who ran local offices throughout the state that matched volunteers with nonprofit places that needed help. I was asked to give a presentation about the contribution that people with disabilities could make as volunteers.

Sure, I replied. I'd be happy to come — but on one condition: I didn't want to speak. I'd rather help arrange a panel of people with disabilities with a long history of volunteering. This was agreed. The conference, it turned out, was held in Lancaster.

On the conference day we all arrived, headed by Bill Rinaldi, who served as the panel's moderator. Bill is the elected Clerk of Judicial Records of Lackawanna County, and a well-known political figure there. He is also the member of the Council who thought up the citizen participation category. Bill, who has muscular dystrophy and whose movement is limited basically to one hand, arrived in his hydraulic-lift van with his usual entourage of an attendant and four family members to help. He took his place at the front table along with four local Lancaster people with disabilities. Each spoke eloquently about the considerable volunteer contributions they had made to their towns. Some pointed out that they had started volunteering to get some job experience, because discrimination had closed the doors to employment when they were starting out. They were, by any standards, an unusually civic-minded group.

The response from the audience was, to us, totally unexpected. They were tremendously excited. It turned out that in many sessions up to this closing one they had been struggling with their common problem of a lack of volunteers. One coordinator stood up. "It's tremendously hard to recruit volunteers any more," she started out. "All of the traditional sources of people who have the time and inclination to volunteer are gone. There are hardly any housewives anymore — they're all working. And elderly people buy a Winnebago nowadays and go to Arizona for the winter. But here are a whole group of people that we have overlooked!"

Bill took that moment to conclude by announcing that we had grants to give out to any volunteer offices that wanted to try to place people with disabilities as volunteers in their communities. Two of us who were staff members for the Council, sitting in the back, gave out information to people who were interested.

Subsequently, some of the offices represented at the conference applied for citizen participation grants, and we selected two to fund. Volunteer offices in two other cities now have special projects to recruit and support people with disabilities in volunteer jobs. For us, this also represented the first time we had been able to fund ordinary community enterprises instead of human service agencies or voluntary associations focused on the needs of people with disabilities.[6]

The Special Case of Self Advocacy. The formation and operation of *self-advocacy associations* of people with mental retardation is a well-known and important activity. Such associations have been the medium for much growth in independence and freedom for members. In Pennsylvania, the Council has long supported an association of this type called **Speaking for Ourselves**. This group applied for a citizen participation grant. In this, their focus necessarily had to be not so much on self-growth and self-maintenance activities as upon external involvements. They consulted with park rangers at Independence Mall National Park on ways to make the park more welcoming to people with disabilities, and pursued similar activities with other community settings.

One of the things the self-advocacy organization has done quite effectively is to recruit a number of "advisors" without disabilities who help local chapters. This led to an imaginative experiment in forming the kind of relationships seen in citizen advocacy. At one of their retreats, members role-played asking somebody without a disability to be their "partners" in some way. How did you, as a person with mental retardation, ask someone to be your "partner?" Members then asked an advisor of their choice to be a "partner," and secured agreement from them. There were enough advisors to serve as partners for up to three or four members, individually.

It must be clear that this was merely an exercise in "asking." One was not really out asking ordinary citizens. Yet in this exercise another member of the Council, Julian, who had spent eighteen years in the notorious Pennhurst State School and now had his own apartment, asked an advisor named Eric to be his partner. In the months following, they started spending some time together. Eric learned how preoccupied Julian was about all of his lost years at Pennhurst — and about his deep fear that somehow he would be taken back. "It's all empty now. It's closed," Eric tried to persuade him, but it was hard to convince him that it was really true. So one day Eric picked up Julian and they drove to Pennhurst. They walked around the empty buildings. Everything was indeed closed up; all the lights were out. Julian could see it. Pennhurst was dead. Then they went out to dinner.

Sometime later Eric committed suicide. Nobody had even realized that he was depressed. It was a great shock; a great tragedy. Two days after his death the self-advocacy coordinator received an unexpected call from Eric's bereaved wife. She wanted to know if Julian was doing all right. She was worried about his having lost his friend. Thus even in an apparently casual experiment a significant bond was formed, albeit tragically lost. Is there more potential for such relationships to be forged within the work of self-advocacy groups? Is this a potential next focus, after the necessarily inward-directed formation stage of such groups has passed?

Final Comments. There is much to be learned yet from the citizen participation project experiments. Can they be sustained over time? Will one kind work better than another? What will happen to the impulse of the project and the future evolution of the project leaders, many of whom have disabilities? We do not yet know. It is significant, I think, that one of the most evolved projects, that described by Sharon Gretz, seems to have left as one of its legacies some committed leaders who have evolved in their thinking to the point that they have also become interested in citizen advocacy.

Life-Sharing and Cooperative Housing

Citizen advocacy and citizen participation help to bring people with disabilities into freely given relationships in their communities. But the primary setting for relationships is the home. As discussed in Chapter 2, the living situations of very many people with disabilities dependent upon professional services lack the true sense of home. Wolfensberger commented upon this situation in 1975 in relation to the mental health field, in a paper in which he introduced the term "life-sharing".

> "Keep in mind that, by definition, we are dealing with deeply wounded people who are rejected, conflicted, fractured in their human relationships, feeling unworthy, and so on. And just as they need freely given, unbought sharing of relationships to prove that there is something worthwhile, something lovable and acceptable in them, just then we minimize the likelihood that this sharing will occur; we move them in with people who, no matter what their motivations, are paid to relate, and so it is a 'boughten' helping relationship.
>
> Now the bought relationship can perhaps be just as genuine as the one freely given. But somewhere along the line the wounded person must have the world testing to prove the reality of the relationship. He must have someone who accepts him, who sees something worthwhile in him and loves him without that doubt that the helper is doing it because he is paid to do it, that it is his profession. No, the helper must be seen as doing it because there is something in the devalued person that brings forth acceptance, or at least a genuine perception of great value. 'By golly, it's within me; I'm worthwhile.' We violate this world-building principle most profoundly.
>
> Finally, one of the critical things in helping wounded people is generous life-sharing, accepting and sharing love and oneself. Our service personnel do not genuinely share or even encourage sharing. The sharing response is, in fact, trained out of them in their socialization into the mental health profession." (1975b, pp. 106-7)

This concept of life-sharing can emerge from a relationship brought together through citizen advocacy. Statistics from the Georgia Advocacy Office show that citizen advocates often do find or provide homes for those they are in a relationship with. We felt the need, however, to explicitly address the situation of the home, of living together, and of living together without pay. We developed a specific category for life-sharing, which we termed "cooperative housing."

There were a number of sources to look to for experience in this area. Pennsylvania contained communities of both the L'Arche and Camphill movements, although they were generally little-known in the state. L'Arche, started by Jean Vanier in France, had a community in Erie. Although they looked superficially like a series of group homes, they actually comprised a very dynamic Christian community of people with disabilities and those who felt called to share their lives with them. Camphill, inspired by the work of Rudolf Steiner and started by Dr. Karl Koenig in Scotland, had a children's school community and an agricultural village for adults. Both L'Arche and Camphill embraced, although they described it differently, a common belief that people with and without disabilities must live together as Wolfensberger has described. Both were members of established international movements. In both, one might find modern expressions of the ancient city of Gheel in Belgium, where people with mental disorders and other disabilities had been taken into the homes of the populace from the time of its origin as a shrine to which people came seeking a cure for mental disorder.[7]

At about the same time that the Council began its "life-sharing" category, a founder of Camphill in North America proclaimed that it was time to "lift the veil" surrounding Camphill. The influence of the quiet presence of Camphill within Pennsylvania upon the emergence of the kind of "new world view" settings that we have been discussing cannot be overestimated.

In addition, we had heard of the experiences of David Wetherow and Nicola Shaefer in Winnipeg setting up housing cooperatives in which a person with a disability was a member, starting with Nicola's daughter Catherine. We asked David Wetherow to talk at a workshop for people interested in learning about his approach.

Finally, we issued a request for proposals. In it, we invited proposals which would initiate and support arrangements in which people with and without disabilities would live together.[8] We specifically excluded proposals which required paid staff to care for someone. After proposal review, we selected three for funding. Two planned to match people with disabilities with others to share a home. One proposed starting a cooperative, somewhat similar to the Winnipeg model.

To date, the main thing we have learned from these projects is what the principal difficulties of the undertaking are. One "matching" project matched many people who now have homes, but seemed to lack a firm idea of the principles behind the Council's category. Matches seemed to vary between excellent ones and ones that were not thoroughly prepared, or did not last. Were this a citizen advocacy program, a standard evaluation by a skilled team would have been able to establish precisely to what degree the underlying principles and established practices were being expressed. In this area, no such careful way to look at a project yet existed to determine this.

A second matching project started very carefully by convening a local group to examine the possibilities for promoting life-sharing in their town. They followed word-of-mouth introductions from one person to another, searching out and collecting individuals and families currently practicing or interested in life-sharing. As they went, they constructed a relationship map of the people they found, drawing them together into a network. When the network was developed they began to make matches of people to live together, and to support their relationships. One of the things they discovered was that the whole economic sphere of living together required very much more thought. What were various fair ways for people of different earning capacities to share expenses? What was the role of public funding that a person with a disability brought to the setting? How did you avoid situations in which people with a "call" to share their lives could, without intending to, become economically dependent upon the income received by people with disabilities? These pointed directions for future work.

The third project worked to develop a housing cooperative around one specific person with multiple needs who had not been successful in conventional services. This group not only worked to bring together this woman, her daughter, her boyfriend, and others, but to do this work in a particularly economically distressed part of Philadelphia. After much work, the group located a house and made ready to go ahead, but could not gain the financing to make it work. Sadly, although the Council supported the project, federal spending regulations prohibited the use of our funds for purchase of the house or for major rehabilitation. Since the project began, the leadership of the sponsoring agency also changed. Finally, the group admitted defeat and turned back the final year of the grant. Again the key role of economics had become apparent.

Based upon these experiences, the Council refined the request for proposals, arranged for study of the economic issues, and announced the availability of funding for a new three-year trial series of projects. As of this writing, proposals are being solicited.

Although individuals with disabilities have found good and supportive homes through these projects, the complex economic and other issues that the involvement of housing itself brings into the relationship equation requires much more experience and thought before its viability will be known outside of organized movements. After the next cycle of grants the usefulness of this approach will be clearer.

Life-Sharing Safeguards

Once we had begun supporting the creation of settings for life-sharing, it quickly became apparent that we had also assumed a responsibility for seeing that the quality of these settings was somehow adequately maintained. First, it was hard to really grasp what the subtle qualities of life were like for people in disparate places, as one could do in citizen advocacy. Second, there was no guarantee that conditions in these new "life-sharing" settings would not deteriorate; in fact, it was predictable that they occasionally would.

This raised a dilemma. The only kind of safeguards with which most people were familiar were the conventional ones of licensing, regulation, and accreditation. These were foreign to the life-sharing concept, and would unquestionably formalize and injure these informal settings. On the other hand, government could not simply turn its back on a potential risk to vulnerable people. Aside from the moral obligations, once something bad happened in an unregulated setting (an inevitability in *any* setting) government would *have* to respond, and it would respond in a conventional way.

To help resolve this dilemma, the Council called for the creation of a project to develop an alternative approach to assure the well-being of people with disabilities in life-sharing settings. Using the Citizen Advocacy Program Evaluation (CAPE) approach as a starting point (O'Brien and Wolfensberger, 1978), this effort set out to explore the factors which lead to healthy life-sharing situations. In the process of exploration, the safeguards project also began to serve as the center of a network of life-sharing communities in the Northeast. Entering, as of this writing, its third year, this project may hold the promise of a third option for those who are concerned about maintaining the safety of unconventional settings. Chapter Ten explores the conceptual basis for the life-sharing safeguards project in detail.

Adoption

Until fairly recently it was inconceivable to ask someone to adopt a child with a severe mental or physical disability. Indeed, such adoptions were sometimes legally prohibited by law, a vestige of the eugenics movement. Viewed in terms of Kuhn's theory, there was universal belief that no one would adopt such a child, that it was simply inconceivable. Prior to 1956 the child welfare literature contained no references at all to special-needs adoption. Adoption workers, guided by this "known" fact, therefore never attempted such adoptions, and these children languished in institutions or foster care. Yet demonstrations scattered around the country in recent years, coupled with other social and public policy changes, including economic pressure on states, had violated the dominant expectation that such adoptions were impossible (Stone, 1982).[9]

The Council therefore set out to demonstrate the possibility of successful special-needs adoption within the state. We believed that the shift in expectation already underway could be speeded. Impetus for the changes in adoption practice and systems could then be applied, based upon the fact that the "impossible" was undeniably do-able within the state itself.

The success of this work has exceeded even the best hopes for it. As of this writing, seventy-nine children have been adopted; thirty-nine through one project alone. Children have been adopted who require constant physical care, who have mental retardation severe enough to require the greatest subtlety of perception to perceive growth and learning, or who even have terminal illnesses which are supposed to soon take their lives. What families can successfully be asked to do has been found to be far more than ever supposed.

Special-needs adoption is a highly complex thing to do well. Unlike citizen advocacy and citizen participation, adoption involves many technical elements in a process whose elements come within the province of law, of child welfare agencies, and other complicated human services systems. Like them, however, they share an orientation towards becoming expert at "asking." Citizen advocacy practice, as noted earlier, contains the concept of "sharpening the question." How does one ask someone on behalf of another firmly, clearly, without minimizing what one is asking the other to do? Similarly, adoption projects have found that a clear understanding of the whole situation by the prospective adoptive parents is all-important. One must not minimize what one is asking for if one wants the correct people to be called forth to caring.

I have often thought of the world of the old and new world views about caring as being two lands separated by a river. On the near ground, where I stand, is the world of professional human services. On the far shore is the world of community, of mediating structures, of ordinary lives. It is the preoccupation of those interested in the new approach to try to get people whose lives have been totally bound by the world of services across that river. Most of the projects that do this are based on the far shore. Rooted in ordinary communities, the specialized approaches of citizen advocacy or citizen participation send out a little boat to the world of services and bring one person back. Adoption reminds us that this work can be promoted from the near side of the river as well. Settings which perform special-needs adoption, as a highly technical task, must reside in the professional world of human services. They must be, for instance, licensed adoption agencies or be closely associated with one. Yet from this port, ships may set out for the far shore as well. These adoption agencies, in my imagination, place a small child in a boat sent across the river to the world where the adoptive family lives; a world of instant relatives and neighbors, and the rich matrix of mediating structures in which healthy families are embedded.

As projects evolve and talk to each other, new and unexpected approaches may be discovered. Thus we found that one adoption project and one citizen advocacy office began to collaborate. For the adoption agency, citizen advocacy seems to represent both a fertile source of couples called to adopt, and a unique way of helping support the new families. For the citizen advocacy office, the adoption agency makes available the needed professional knowledge of how to actually bring an adoption about. Based upon this discovery, the Council decided to make funding available for a new collaborative project of this nature. If it is successful, it might represent an arrangement in which ports on both sides of the river work together to shuttle children over to the far side. It seems possible that the eventual solution to the combination of technical housing knowledge and the community work apparently required to make life-sharing projects successful may lie in a similar collaborative solution.

Family Support

The first mediating structure of society is the family. Therefore any work in improving the situation of people with disabilities in society must begin with support for the families of children with disabilities. Often conventional thinking has concentrated upon the supposed pathological elements of such families, and provided external services only.[10] For this reason the Council initiated a category to support families in the ways that families themselves defined, and in ways that were comfortable to them. A number of grants were awarded to groups that proposed various ways of accomplishing this goal consistent with the Council's principles. Most involved advisory groups of parents who decided how the money available to families should be spent. Funds in various forms went directly to families for ongoing support, for special expenses, or for appropriate services.

As with adoption, there is an extensive literature rapidly developing about the practice of family support, a literature unnecessary to summarize here. The essence of true family support practice is simply this: to explicitly value the decision-making power of families. Since values are not merely words, but are actions, family support truly expressed means that government gives money directly to families rather than to professionals in service agencies who will decide what they need.

This shift in orientation, it has turned out, has not been an easy one. In early planning meetings of highly dedicated activists, the degree to which cash should be directly given to families was hotly and repeatedly debated. Often opposition to going "too far" was greatest from some parents themselves! (Similarly, I have seen people with physical disabilities argue against giving full control of their public funds to people with disabilities themselves.) To be sure, there is a valid concern here. Many people with disabilities and their families, and families and people in general, do have difficulty handling their money appropriately. Sometimes this is severe: some projects serve families beset by so many financial, legal, drug, and other problems that the child with a disability is literally the least of their worries. For such families, decision-making assistance is essential.

But these "special-case" families really covered an underlying queasiness at taking a full "leap" to a completely new world view in which families and not professionals were in charge. It presumed that professional decision-making for such families was actually working right now. I used to ask planning groups, "How good a record of decision-making do *social workers* have for families?" Almost everyone could agree that the record of professionals working with the usual preparation, in the kinds of environments, with the amount of turnover, and with the kinds of caseloads typical in almost all settings almost couldn't be worse. Yet it was still difficult to fully trust families because "the money might be spent wrong." This seemed a matter of paradigm rather than practicality. As funded projects have gained experience, comfort with this practice has increased.

Passing control directly into the hands of families increases the potential that mediating systems in which families are embedded may be strengthened rather than diminished. There is some anecdotal evidence from funded projects to indicate that this may have happened. One parent, for example, called me to say that she and a group of other parents needed funds for a "respite facility" for their children. We had no funds for the construction of buildings, I replied. But what, I queried, was the basic need that they had? What if we were able to just give them some money? Could they get what they required without the necessity of erecting a building? It took a while for the parent to even begin to understand what I was talking about, so inconceivable was such an idea to someone who had been raised to think of family supports entirely in terms of agency services external to the home. What might such a parent, or group of parents do if they were able to pay a grandmother, or a neighborhood teenager, to help out? In a Seattle study summarized by Perske (1987; Moore, et al., 1982) sixteen families were given $200 a month for six months to pay relatives, friends, and neighbors for help. As Perske reported: "With this money, the families managed to recruit 84 persons who helped with in-home training, respite care, babysitting, transportation, mending clothes, and the building of special equipment. Six months later, when the payments ceased, 64% of the helpers continued their duties as volunteers."

Although results from the Pennsylvania projects are still in an early stage, evaluation findings will show whether effects similar to this study have been seen. If they are, it may be that one of the most important effects of the projects is in stimulating the natural supports potentially surrounding families.

Supported Work

"Next to family," E. F. Schumacher wrote, "it is work and the relationships established at work that are the true foundations of society." It is this aspect of the developing practice of supported work which makes it of primary interest. The practice itself is quite straightforward. One places a person with a disability on a real job and supports him or her at that job, instead of employing them at a segregated sheltered workshop. As in adoption and family support, the emerging literature is vast, and need not be repeated here. As the Council's largest funding category, projects in supported work have gained hundreds of people real jobs, have nurtured the development of many project leaders and job coaches and, in demonstrating another anomalous practice, have helped to stimulate a shift in the way that employment services are approached. All of this has been concretely helpful to Pennsylvanians with disabilities.

The most important and enduring effect of such projects may well be, however, the supposed "side effect" of the development of relationships between new workers with disabilities and their co-workers. In this aspect, supported work might be seen as a way of de-professionalizing assisted employment sufficiently for the service boundary between labeled person and unlabeled person to disappear. That is why it is so important for the person assisting, the "job coach," to be a worker already embedded in the workplace's culture. It is through relationships with such people that the labeled person may join in lunch, or be invited out for a beer at the end of the week. Again, as one can learn from citizen advocacy, physical integration alone may not bring this about; introductions have to be made and support provided in the right way, until the "matchmaker" can fade from the scene leaving a person connected in the natural setting.

This connection may not only address loneliness and feelings of low self-worth (the co-worker, unlike the workshop supervisor, is not paid to be with him or her) but may ultimately be an essential source of protection to the person at risk. In *The Altruistic Personality*, one notes that many Jewish people who came to "rescuers" for help against the Nazis knew them through a work connection. And I always recall that it was the parents of Lucy Hackney, the Council's past Chairperson, who bailed Rosa Parks out of jail when she refused to move to the back of the bus and set off the Montgomery bus boycott, one of the key events of the civil rights struggle. Ms. Parks was their seamstress.

In a culture in which paid work is almost exclusively the criterion for social value, the question of supported work must be dealt with carefully. While pursuing these roles for people with all of our energy, we must remember that it may not be the money itself, or even the job itself, that is essential. There are many different kinds of income, as I can reflect in the advantages and disadvantages of my own current work. As Diane and Philip Ferguson (1986) have cautioned, an exclusive focus upon paid work for all people can tend to reinforce our culture's valuation of competitiveness and productivity. What then about those persons with disabilities who cannot work? There are those for whom this must be said. Are they then without value? As crucial as supported employment is, one must not lose sight of its role as a "reconnector" of excluded persons into ordinary life, as a way of asking co-workers in a culturally normative way to become involved in such a person's life. In this, supported work carries out the same vision as the other categories listed and helps one to understand why many different approaches to including people in community life are required.

State Park Accessibility

Brief mention should also be made of the ways in which the improved environmental accessibility can serve the purpose of reconnecting people in their communities. The Council focused in one category upon Pennsylvania's state parks. Small grants were made available to parks around the state to improve accessibility. This developed simply because of one explorer — a state park superintendent named Bob Peppel who was a past member of the Council, who had a disability, and who had a genius for accessibility. For years we had heard from Bob about his work to make his park accessible but one day, in a swing around the state, I finally made it to the remote area where his park was located. What I found was astonishing.

Not only had Bob Peppel made the park physically accessible, he had made it inviting to people with disabilities. There was a special fishing dock for wheelchairs (in front of which his men might just happen to stock the lake). There were camping areas with electrical outlets hidden behind a tree-stump, in case you had to plug in a respirator. There were raised sandboxes for children in wheelchairs, and swimming docks specially designed to avoid getting wheelchairs wet, so they wouldn't rust. There were sun shelters for people on photosensitive medications. All of this was integrated so artfully into the setting that you literally could not see it unless you were specifically looking for it.

But beyond physical invitation, Bob had figured out how to build an orientation to people with disabilities into the human culture of the park. To be sure that the concession stand near the summer camp for children with disabilities was properly responsive to them, he encouraged a couple who had a child with a disability to submit a bid to run it, and they were successful in winning the contract. He got local service groups and the Disabled American Veterans to build ramps and to help people. Slowly, over the twenty years that he has been there, people with disabilities and their families have started to come, and to come with others, and to meet others there. The presence of people with disabilities has become part of the essential identity of the park without anybody noting it or remarking upon it.

As I was leaving, Bob told me a final story. Each year, he held a winter carnival. His men cleared the snow on the lake and each weekend of the carnival there was ice-skating. A man who loved the park, Bob said, made it a practice for years to come out every carnival weekend and give away hot chocolate. It was not unusual for him to give out 6000 cups in a weekend. Then the man died. "Ah, it's really a shame," Bob said he thought. "He's really going to be missed." But the next year his family continued it on their own. And they made a donation in his memory to improve wheelchair access in the park. Eventually, when the family sold their local business, the new owners took on and continued the tradition at the park.

Working closely with Bob and the Office of State Parks, the Council initiated small ($5000) grants to state parks to see if they would recreate in their own ways what Bob had done.[11]

Education and Leadership Development

"Ideas have consequences," wrote I.M. Weaver. In the projects described above, we can witness the consequences of the light of one such idea lived out through the creation of a spectrum of settings. Any such work, as I noted in the opening chapter, however, consists not in practice alone. It must involve the steady interactive evolution of both theory and practice. It therefore seemed necessary to also initiate some activity which would serve as a focus for the theoretical and reflective aspects of the larger process of social change which we hoped to support. This activity was the foundation of a small organization called the Commonwealth Institute.

In the most immediate sense, the Institute has served to bring in knowledge to inspire and show the way for work in specific categories that the Council has undertaken. Thus the Institute held workshops on citizen advocacy, brought in John McKnight to talk about ideas behind citizen participation, and held sessions on life sharing and cooperative housing. Importing leading thinkers from around the country helped to break down the insularity which seemed to exist in the state when we began this work, typical of the parochialism which besets so many states. It is hard in many places to imagine that anything of real interest lies beyond one's borders.

The roots of the establishment of the Institute, however, ran much deeper than immediate and practical help. Derived from the educational work of Wolf Wolfensberger, it took its form from the original "Training Institute for Human Service Planning, Leadership, and Change Agentry" which he established at Syracuse University. Assistance was particularly gained from a similar project established by Michael Kendrick, a student of Wolfensberger, in western Massachusetts.

Merely to discuss Wolfensberger's school of educational work, much less the entire sphere of related educational activity, would require a book of its own; thus the briefest summary must suffice here. Basically, Wolfensberger had developed the principle of normalization as an intellectually rigorous basis for thinking and practice in human services, especially in the field of mental retardation. These principles were taught widely through an interrelated series of training workshops, chief among them being Normalization, Social Role Valorization, PASS, and PASSING.[12] Thorough understanding of these principles often served as a "seed thought" from which other thought and action could be derived. Such training, Wolfensberger noted, was arduous and demanding, and was intended to be. This was because, in his words: "...the training was intended to (a) spread the word about normalization, (b) elicit strong commitments to seeing it implemented, and (c) identify and develop leaders who could and would promote its incorporation into human service development and practice."

Wolfensberger had decided that the single greatest requirement to bring about the kind of radical changes that normalization and social role valorization called for was the development of "well-trained, competent, and highly ideologized leaders." He set out, through educational workshops, to consciously promote leadership development. Although there was and is unceasing controversy about aspects of his educational work, its long-term effect in nurturing the development of committed and tenacious leaders is clear. Many of us who comprised the change-oriented leadership in Pennsylvania were products of Wolfensberger's educational work. There was a feeling that such formative advantages as we had enjoyed needed to be made available to the next generation as well.

The impact of these educational workshops (particularly the "core event" PASS) became particularly clear to me in a conversation with John McKnight. McKnight, who has participated in and observed many different social movements, noticed something curious about developmental disabilities. Usually, he said, when he asked activists in a field how they got into it, he heard a hundred different stories. When he first started meeting people in this movement in various parts of the country and put this question to them, however, most of them started to reply in the same way. "Well, I went to a PASS workshop in 1976..." they would begin. So he started thinking, "What is this PASS workshop business, anyway?"

The Commonwealth Institute has based its educational work on two distinctly different models. The primary one was developed by Wolfensberger, with the explicit intent of helping to nurture the development of leaders throughout the state through regular workshops. In contrast to this approach, however, some explorations into very different educational styles are also being made, these deriving from the work of the late Myles Horton at the Highlander Center and others, with John O'Brien constituting the principal practitioner of this educational method in the developmental disabilities field. In this approach, the didactic educational method of Wolfensberger is seen as limiting, with its three overhead projectors operating in tandem, workshop attendance prerequisites, and standardized, approved content. People, rather, are encouraged to work through and find truth through reflection upon their own joint experience. It brings to mind Henry Schaefer-Simmern's consideration of the word "education" as holding "its original meaning as 'leading out' and not as 'stuffing in.'" A leading exponent of Wolfensberger's method, in contrast, once proclaimed "You can change values as easily as you can change a carburetor." Although not without its stresses on personalities, these contrasting approaches in fact constitute a fertile polarity in approach. The existence of these poles continues to produce a rich tension in educational work stimulating a great deal of individual growth and development in its own right.

Through its varied trials of different kinds of educational work, the Commonwealth Institute has contributed an essential element to the process of conceptual revolution. Through it, the careful examination of theory can be added to the testing of that theory against the hard rock of social practice. In the richest of situations, leaders emerging through the creation of "new world view" settings find a place to work out and refine their ideas, and to follow the intellectual paths of others who have worked out such theories, such as social role valorization, to distant limits calling one intellectually forward. Or potential leaders in conventional settings, suddenly hearing new ideas resonating with his or her own, may come forward and initiate a project following their own visions.

Through this process a small cadre of young leaders has begun to grow and a state-wide network to develop, a network which crosses the boundaries of Council, Institute, and projects. Around such involvements one can now occasionally come into a tavern or a retreat house around the state and find a group of people excitedly debating the merits of the thinking of Wolfensberger as compared to O'Brien, or the relevance of McKnight, or Horton, or Paulo Freire. In all of this, individual stories about the lives of people with disabilities with which all are engaged are retold. These ideas, this reflective activity, is the true practice of philosophy. If, as Oliver Sacks said, it is when the ideas of philosophers touch the lives of the common man that history is made, then the work of education such as the Institute pursues may contribute to the historical unfolding of a new conceptual revolution in an important way. In one of the Council's projects, or in the back of the room at an Institute event, may be a young future Martin Luther King, Jr. of our field. If so, he will only be recognized years from now; maybe a decade, maybe more. It is in such slow ways that social change is nurtured.

Some Final Comments

Here the chapter on various expressions of the new social concept is concluded. It ends, of course, at an artificial point of evolution; the point where I sit down at the computer to describe it. The oldest of the projects described is still very young. One must wait to see what they will become, and what cumulative effect this scattering of anomalies about the state and this investment in leadership may yield. New experiments, as I write, are on the drawing table: funding categories for projects to nurture friendship between children with and without disabilities, for projects to draw together information and support networks of parents, for projects to develop "support circles," and for more and better employment projects. It will take at least eighteen months from the first idea at a Council meeting to the funding of an actual project; three years beyond that for the project to try the idea in practice. After that, yet another cycle of theory and practice will begin, as the slow process of revolution in thought and practice continues to evolve.

Many of the grants given will result in the creation of a new social setting. Each such setting will come into the world as bright-eyed and convinced of its own immortality as any young child. Yet history tells us that all settings are born into the world containing the seeds of their own dissolution, even if projects and funders alike cling to the myth that each new form will remedy the failures of the old without letting down the people it exists to serve. In addition, settings arising in this historical age to demonstrate an experiment in community face the additional hazard of a regulatory environment which may in itself prove lethal. For this reason, it is necessary to not only think about how new settings can be created, but the companion issue of how people and the communities in which they live may be best safeguarded. Thus in the next chapter we take up the question "What really keeps people with disabilities safe in society?"

Endnotes

1.   I might say that the atoms of a planet are held together by molecular forces, but as recent physics informs us, you can not say that an "atom" is matter and that a force affects this matter, as once one could. There is no saying exactly where the atom ends and the force — or the planet — begins. The same could be said of society. Does the individual exist apart from the social forces of which he or she is a part, and which binds his or her total being into the larger body of his or her society and culture?

2.   Social role valorization and normalization are, for those not acquainted with them, highly developed social theories which have been enormously influential in shaping positive approaches in the developmental disabilities field. This is discussed later in this chapter. Readers are referred to the literature on this subject, most notably Wolfensberger (1983b) and (1972).

3.   Thomas Keneally's *Schindler's List* (1983) is a particularly stirring account of one outstanding "rescuer."

4.   For an excellent essay on this subject, see McCord & Marshall "Missing the Mark: Normalization as Technology" (1987).

5. Citizen advocacy is described by Wolfensberger and Zauhua (1973) and recently by O'Brien (1987b). The latter, *Learning From Citizen Advocacy*, is particularly recommended reading for any "asking" practice.

6. To date, neither of these volunteer office efforts has achieved real success. One lost its leader through illness at an early crucial stage of development. The other, however, has seemed to suffer from both the unfortunate tendency of volunteer-oriented efforts to professionalize the "matching" activity, and the failure to grasp that it is essential that volunteering be approached as an opportunity for a mutual exchange and not as a service to one party only. This will be pursued in another round of grants to see what results can be achieved.

7. The Camphill movement has been frequently criticized for violating the principle of normalization and for not pursuing integration specifically in their operation of contiguous communities, which are thus seen as constituting an obsolete service form. I think this misses an important point. Camphill has maintained a cultural belief in non-paid living together during a period in the field in which the environment has been almost completely antithetical to this. One might claim, in fact, that Camphill has served society by preserving some ancient values, much as certain orchardists maintain the seed-stock of old varieties of apples no longer grown commercially. For the preservation of values in an environment not supportive of them, contiguous communities sometimes serve a necessary purpose; witness the role of monasteries in preserving classical learning during the "dark ages" of Europe.

8. The official document also served to introduce the term "life-sharing" into the language of state policy. Following this publication, the use of this term as a legitimized concept spread widely.

9. A recent revision of the concentration on family pathology is contained in an article by Wikler, et al., (1983) who called for a new program of research to substantiate "new perceptions of these families, in which they are seen not as the odd few who somehow survive a calamity but as successful family systems whose strength has been augmented by raising a child with developmental disabilities."

10. Stone's thesis on adoption contains an interesting analysis of adoption as an indicator of important shifts in belief about people with disabilities.

11. A brief description of the orientation of these grants is described in the Appendix: Rules for Funding Social Change.

12. *Program Analysis of Service Systems*, and *Program Analysis of Service Systems' Implementation of Normalization Goals: A Method of Evaluating the Quality of Human Services According to the Principle of Normalization.*

CHAPTER 10

What Really Keeps People with Disabilities Safe in Society?

"Beware of thinking of systems so perfect that nobody will
have to be good."

— Gandhi

Perhaps Joanie Davis was not destined to end her life in an institution after all. She had been taken to the Willowbrook State School for the Mentally Retarded as an infant, and there she had spent all of her young life. Willowbrook — after the exposé, a name synonymous with horror and neglect. Where Geraldo Rivera had taken his television cameras and shown all, except for the stench, on the evening news. Where Governor Hugh Carey, living up to a campaign promise, could be seen in a television scene I still remember, brushing the flies from the face of a child in a crib. Where no one ever left. Yet here Joanie was with her suitcase and ever-present smile, moving into a nice house on an ordinary street in a small upstate New York city. She, who never had control of her own life, who had been moved from ward to ward and finally to a "family care" home, was moving in with us.

Joanie got to move because of a large and complex lawsuit against the state. Spurred by the Willowbrook exposé and other changes, a shift in social policy was phasing down the institutions and making the creation of group homes possible. We had started a group home, and we were welcoming Joanie into it. We said to her, as we did to all new people in those early days, that this was her home and would be as long as she wanted it to be. The board of directors sent her a plant for her room. They were the first flowers that she had ever received. She was, as far as we were concerned, finally home. Another in a series of battered institutional veterans had been taken into our shelter and attention.

Some people adapt their basic natures to extremely adverse conditions by becoming withdrawn, or aggressive. Some, like Joanie, become especially friendly and likable, cultivating the affection of those in charge. It was easy to try to help her. We took her to one of the physicians in town that we trusted to get a complete look at her physical condition. It was clear that Joanie needed serious attention. Tiny, about four-foot-ten, Joanie walked with a stiff jerky shuffle that made her seem like her leg joints were fused. She had chronic high blood pressure and was on a lot of medication to control it. Most apparent of all, Joanie had a terribly unsightly skin condition that caused her skin to flake off in a kind of fish-scale pattern. We got her the best of attention, and it helped a little. People tended to be put off by her skin condition, but Joanie was so lovable and outgoing that she soon overcame most people's reluctance.

Joanie did well over the years, progressing more and more. I heard, long after I had left the agency, that she was now living in an apartment with a roommate. She no longer needed the supervision and assistance of the group home. She and her roommate cooked their own meals with periodic help. She went to work every day at the sheltered workshop, and went to activities all over town. She grew to know her neighbors, and became accepted in the neighborhood. It was a long way from Willowbrook.

Almost ten years after I had met Joanie, I was back in town teaching a workshop in group home management at the university. Some of the present-day staff of my old agency took the course. During a break, one of them told me an upsetting story. She had been the support person for Joanie in her apartment, taking her shopping, helping her with her money, and being on call for emergencies. And Joanie had had an emergency. She started to have kidney failure.

After testing, it turned out that all of those years of having untreated high blood pressure at Willowbrook had done ineradicable damage. She was losing kidney function, and would die if she did not get dialysis treatments regularly. There was yet no dialysis unit in town. But instead of arranging transportation to this medical center, or arranging for her to be temporarily hospitalized or cared for in that city and then come home, the state office charged with the welfare of former inhabitants of Willowbrook made a significant decision. They ordered Joanie's transfer to the nearest large state institution for the mentally retarded. There Joanie, once a regular neighbor in a normal neighborhood, was put into a bed on a ward for people with the most severe disabilities. After so many years out, she was back as an institutional resident, and very ill. My promise of a permanent home had been an empty one. It was the promise of a person who was no longer there.

The young staff member who told me this story was upset. She had thought that it was terribly wrong to put Joanie back in an institution, to send her away. State institutions were not where you or I would go for medical treatment. This had to be heartbreaking for Joanie, she worried. She tried to get the agency where she worked to tell the state no. But she had found no support. Instead she had been told by the director of residential services that her advocacy was "threatening to get in the way" of her work and, if it continued, that it would be reflected in her next performance appraisal.

Her story prompted me to break my rule about meddling in my old agency's affairs, for Joanie's sake. I had limited success at the necessary cost of good will. But it made me think deeply about the question of what was supposed to keep people safe in our mental retardation service systems, and in our world. For I had heard very many stories like Joanie's. This one was particularly compelling, however, for Joanie was living under the protection of one of the most sophisticated systems of safeguards of any person with the label of mental retardation in America. She lived in a residential service with internal procedures for assuring the welfare of its clientele. The residential agency was monitored by the quality assurance division of the state office of mental retardation with particularistic rigor. For example, if their reviewers found that a resident's bedroom did not have a chair, then a signed waiver that he or she did not want a chair had to be maintained on file in the residence office.

Joanie also had a case manager with the local office of the state office of mental retardation. Because she was a past inhabitant of Willowbrook, this office was required to keep her under specific scrutiny and report her progress to a central office charged with overseeing members of her legal "class." She lived in the state with the most powerful independent oversight agency in the United States, the Quality of Care Commission for the Mentally Disabled. She was served by four separate service organizations. Yet when Joanie was "disappeared" from her new home community, when this woman without family or real friends was taken back to the institution, the only person who raised her voice in protest was the person who had the closest personal relationship with her. Under the most complex monitoring system available, the greatest wrong had been perpetrated upon Joanie Davis. Advocacy efforts and systems had gotten her physically out of Willowbrook and into a network of community services. But beyond that, the system for keeping Joanie Davis safe had not kept her safe at all. How could the system have failed?

How We Came to Put Our Faith in Conventional Regulatory Safeguards

A good social historian could trace how social concern for disadvantaged people developed to the point that it was generally considered the proper role of government to be concerned about their plight. This is too long and complex an issue to explore here. It happened (and with advances and regressions continues to happen) and it was, and is, a proper and good thing.

The world is full of people who are ready to do harm to their neighbor. If you do not rigorously inspect milk quality, unscrupulous producers will thin it with water and pass it on full of bacteria. If you don't inspect industries, some of them will pump the water and air full of toxic effluents. If you do not rigorously monitor people who take care of others in such places as nursing homes, boarding homes, or other settings, some people will abuse those in their care, starve them, and steal their money. It is simply unrealistic to pretend this does not happen, for reading any newspaper shows that it happens with great frequency even with stringent licensing, monitoring, and inspection.

Each expansion of government oversight over a particular area of social life has occurred in response to scandal or outcry. American government is almost always reactive to public sentiment and when bad milk, fouled streams, or abuse of elderly or mentally retarded persons is sufficiently brought to public notice, governmental action is possible. This has usually taken the form of licensing. To control the quality of milk you license the producers and inspect them regularly. If they cheat or fail, you take away their licenses and they go out of business. Although it is more complicated than this, this basic approach actually works very well. When is the last time you read in the paper about watered milk? Yet before government regulation, this was quite frequent. There are many things that can be effectively maintained at a quality level by using this sort of tool.[1]

Since this was the tool that we knew how to use, we reached for it automatically when we came to address quality in the lives of people at risk in society. It started as a maintenance of quality standards in social programs. When the outcry against abuse and neglect of people in such programs began, we knew, without thinking, what to do. The basic approach has remained unchanged since that time.

In my generation the nursing home scandals of the early 1970s were the first clear example of this dynamic in action. Bruce Vladeck, in his excellent book *Unloving Care* (1980), makes an incisive analysis of the wrongs and the changes implemented to right them. He also provides a clear view of a situation in which the full weight of traditional regulation was applied and in which, although significant gains were made in some areas and at great cost, it largely didn't work. Nursing homes, despite their expense, are among the most stringently regulated social programs in the United States, and they are still mostly miserable places to live.

In the field of mental retardation we have followed the usual cycle of scandal and regulation to attempt to protect the lives of such people. There is no question that this has done a great deal of good. I have seen the transformation of many living conditions in the last twenty years. Many earnest workers in our field pressed for ever-increasing quality control standards in the belief that the one way to assure the quality of people's lives was to go about it as if this problem were spoiled milk. It has worked, up to a point. But two problems remain. First, we are starting to notice that the sheer weight of our regulatory control itself is starting to interfere with real care. Secondly, the Joanies whom we are concerned about are losing everything important to them in the highly regulated environments that we have created.

The Down-side of Traditional Regulatory Safeguards

I: The Magic of Thinking That People Are Now Safe

The negative side of our traditional approach to safeguarding the quality of people's lives through regulatory control could be thought of as having several aspects. The first is Joanie's lesson: it doesn't really keep people as safe as we think that it does. There is ample evidence of this; incidents such as Joanie's are far from scattered events. Just recently it was reported in a Philadelphia newspaper that nineteen children who had been under the specific supervision of the city's department of human services because there was clear evidence of imminent risk of parental abuse had died in the past fifteen months (Goldman and Myers, 1988). Despite the highest alert level in the system, they ended up dying at the hands of their own families.

Paralleling New York State's suit over Willowbrook has been Pennsylvania's suit to close Pennhurst State School. Watched from all over the country, efforts under Pennhurst far exceeded those under Willowbrook. Oversight, licensing, monitoring, and regulation were authorized to new limits. Temple University was hired to conduct a comprehensive, long-term assessment of the condition of the individuals moved from the institution to group homes. The state special management office had enormous (and frequently resented) authority over provider agencies. Yet evidence of low quality and even abusive conditions in the new services accumulated steadily, to the point that the state Association for Retarded Citizens, who had brought the original suit to close Pennhurst, went back into court to bring charges of contempt.

In all, it seems likely that we who rely upon regulatory control are frequently guilty of what can only be called magical thinking. We think that by creating regulations, or by passing a law, or by requiring certification, or by implementing some other complex quality assurance system, that we will in fact assure quality. If we think hard enough we can believe that it will work. And it may well work, for a little while. But over the long term, the magic starts to fade. General Motors, after all, has one of the most sophisticated quality control systems one can probably find, but I still wouldn't buy a car made on a Monday.

II: The Weight of an Effort Become Empty.

In May of 1987 Clarence Sundram, chairman of New York State's Quality of Care Commission for the Mentally Disabled, gave what many people must have thought was a highly unusual address at his annual conference. He called it "Regulation — Have We All Gone Mad?"

In his address, Sundram noted that regulatory control didn't seem to be accomplishing what it had been set in place to do, and that it had perverse effects as well which must be seriously considered. To start, Sundram observed the effect of converting state-funded community residences in New York to federal Medicaid funding. These residential programs, after conversion, became considerably more expensive to operate, primarily because of the increased level of clinical staffing required by federal regulations. Sundram's commission looked at the conversions and found that:

> "...as we visited a number of homes, we were struck by the absence of any evident benefit to the residents from this increase in staff. It turned out that much of this newly found clinical staff time was consumed in preparing detailed treatment plans with long-term goals and short-term objectives, performing a variety of assessments, and filling the client's records with a battery of tests and scores and indicators. Many of these procedures and processes were made necessary by Medicaid regulations. In essence, what this sounds like is that we went into the Medicaid program to get more money to hire more clinical staff to fill out the forms that the Medicaid program requires." (p.6)

There have been observers who have pointed out this kind of thing before, of course. Back before New York got into Medicaid conversions, a number of us were warning about this. One residential administrator, Guy Caruso, brought a soapbox to a state conference, climbed up on it in the atrium of the very hotel in which Sundram's speech was delivered ten years later, and handed out leaflets showing why the state shouldn't pursue Medicaid funding. What was significant in Sundram's case was who was speaking.

The Commission on the Quality of Care was probably the most advanced and effective traditional project to safeguard people labeled developmentally disabled or mentally ill in the United States, and perhaps in the world. The Commission's careful investigatory reports had spurred the state Office of Mental Retardation and Developmental Disabilities and the Office of Mental Health to expand regulatory control significantly. The investigation of a scalding in a group home, for instance, might conclude with a recommendation that the state require temperature regulators in all such settings in the future. Requirements with the aim of safeguarding people's lives were thus gradually and steadily built in by the same basic process that led to the Medicaid regulations noted above. When a problem occurs, write a regulation designed to prevent its reoccurrence.

Here was the leader and architect of the best of the safeguard programs realizing — and even more courageously confessing — that it wasn't working particularly well, and that the vast weight of the regulatory control was a problem in itself. Referring to the work of Harvard's Christopher Argyris, he observed that "both the regulator and the regulated know that the underlying problem is not being addressed but rather that elaborate games are being constructed." Had these efforts become merely, as Sundram termed it elsewhere, a "regulatory ballet?"

One might claim that one could somehow make this "regulatory ballet" really work effectively if one had enough absolute authority over the regulated. But is this true?

In 1985 an interesting bit of research was undertaken by Richard Fiene of Pennsylvania's Department of Public Welfare. Fiene looked at the performance of county Children and Youth agencies charged with getting permanent homes for children who are in their legal custody. He ran a simple correlation between the number of children placed by each agency and the agency's compliance with state regulations, plotting the two factors on a graph. The line of the graph plotting number of placements did a curious thing. Although it started out going up, at high regulatory compliance levels it turned back down again. Fiene discovered, in other words, that there appeared to be a curvilinear relationship between regulatory compliance and outcomes. While placements correlated with compliance with regulations up to a point, after that point they actually diminished. In his words, "substantial compliance with state regulations had a greater impact on the number of children leaving placement than did full compliance."

There seems to be growing evidence that we have put our faith in an approach to safeguards that is not producing the intended outcomes. Indeed, the cure itself is being found to have many unfortunate side effects.

III The Deleterious Effect of Regulatory Control

> "The healthy society, like the healthy body, is not the one that has taken the most medicine."
>
> — Robert K. Greenleaf

Believing that constantly increasing levels of regulation will keep the social environment of vulnerable people safe and healthy is like believing that constantly increasing doses of antibiotics will keep a sick child healthy. It only deals with the symptoms. By misdirecting our attention from deeper causes, it can unwittingly do long-term harm to the fabric of human relationships through which the life of mankind really works.

Anecdotal evidence that our "caring systems" in the mental retardation field are suffocating under the weight of regulatory paperwork is widespread. One has only to talk to any worker in any setting in the field to hear story after story of how caring is being displaced by compliance activities which were originally installed by "system advocates" to improve care. Sundram, again, is worth quoting:

> "The assumption is that, through the elaborate oversight structure we have created and through the requirements for documentation we can assure quality — the motto could be: 'In God we trust; everyone else documents.
>
> In the human services field, our best asset, our most valuable resource, is the people who are drawn to this work. This is a noble, indeed a sacred calling. Thousands of people enter this field out of a desire to invest themselves in improving the human condition. We need to make it possible to use this vast reservoir of caring, this desire to help the less fortunate, to produce programs of excellence, to infuse the power of new ideas into enriching the quality of life for people with mental disabilities.
>
> When we regulate not wisely, but too much, we stifle initiative without replacing it with something of a higher value. ...We breed an attitude of compliance with regulation rather than reinforcing the sense of mission that draws so many people into this field. And too often, satisfying auditors and regulators *becomes* the mission rather than caring for the human beings the system was created to serve." [2]
>
> "...over time, the priority for paperwork can have a by-product of eroding initiative and breeding apathy, with mindless tasks that try to measure the immeasurable or the irrelevant, while tasks which nourish and enrich the human spirit go neglected." (p.7)

In seizing upon the deterioration of the spirit of service, Sundram has pointed out the main toxic effect of increased regulatory control. Once we wipe out spirit we have killed off the heart of the entire enterprise. Heavily controlled bureaucratic systems (and regulation is but one expression of centralized control) differ markedly from social movements and personal caring relationships. Idealistic and caring people are drawn to moral enterprises and to people and need. They tend to be driven away by bureaucratic machinery.

The consequences of the conversion of social movement to bureaucracy are clearly observable in the field of community residences in the past ten or fifteen years. Most of the idealistic young colleagues of mine who started group homes in the mid-seventies have left the field, finding it increasingly incompatible with vision, creativity, and caring.

One of my friends remains at work despite the rising tide of regulation. A few years ago, he helped to set a person up in a little apartment. Life for this man flourished. He became known and accepted in the neighborhood, and became a fixture at the corner market. His life, after many years of bloodless warehousing or programming, began to mean something in a social context. Eventually the inspector from the state office of mental retardation came for a routine certification visit. He inspected the man's apartment and found it substantially in compliance, except for one problem. The back stairway door, the required "second egress" in the code, was too short. People could bang their heads running out if there were a fire. This was serious; the apartment would have to be decertified. The man would have to move.

Move? My friend didn't know what to think. But he had worked for the state office himself. He knew a few of the tricks. He tried a weak, ironic joke. He pointed out that in fact this person would never bump his head — he was only 5'5". "Why don't you just give me a waiver of regulations," he asked, "a waiver for short people?"

A creative bureaucrat found a solution. The agency's operating certificate was "limited to only [allow] occupancy by clients who are 5'5" tall or shorter." The man is still there. How long will my friend stay? My guess is not forever, for every such event probably erodes his ability to maintain commitment to his work.

Sarason's *The Creation of Settings and the Future Societies* examines the process by which "settings" such as human service agencies deteriorate. He found that death usually seems to come in the same way; things go sour and the zeal runs out of the enterprise. In normal settings it might just die. (In marriage, the smallest of settings, people often get divorced at this point.) Human service agencies, pumped up with external resources, just keep going, alive to surface appearance but dead inside. I can name numerous agencies whose sense of mission has expired but whose cadavers still litter the landscape, processing clientele from input to output. It is just possible that through regulatory and other kinds of control we are unconsciously doing this to the entire mental retardation caring system.

Understanding Current Evidence of Decline in Caring Enterprises

Evidence of this phenomenon may be found everywhere in modern western society. Medicine, with its technology and bureaucracy, is the most frequently used example. But community residences, again, offer a good example of this process in the developmental disabilities field. Certainly many gains have been made in serving people in community programs over the years. People with much more challenging needs are being served now, for instance, than were ever served when this work began. Against this, however, there is increasing evidence that caring has deteriorated as formalization has progressed. While thus far this is largely anecdotal, some limited research has begun to confirm in formal language what most workers in the field already know. If a breakdown in caring has progressed this far, then less apparent aspects of a process of deterioration must be at work as well. Symptoms of community system dysfunction discussed in Chapter 5, such as psychotropic drug overuse, high staff turnover, and social isolation may illustrate this breakdown.

It is said in the field of child abuse that a primary correlate of abuse is lack of "connectedness" of the family with others. It is said in the field of corrections that a primary correlate of recidivism is lack of connectedness with family and friends and community. What then is the vulnerability to abuse of people in socially isolated community residences? Does not each layer of well-intentioned regulatory control, each regular upstairs apartment with a state waiver for 5'5" people applied to it, pull a piece of real estate out of the neighborhood and into the province of bureaucratic administration? Does not each inspection, each certificate, unconsciously brick the wall between neighbor and "client" a tiny bit higher? What is at the root of these developments?

Clarence Sundram's speech reveals the dominance of professionalization in thinking about service system problems. Despite his insight about regulation, what was his language? We must "use this vast reservoir of caring." We must "produce programs of excellence." Does this not display our fundamental error? For if caring can be produced, if it indeed is a *product*, then the quality of this product can be regulated. If caring is a resource to be used, then the process of helping care to arise into the world is a process of production, in which economic and mechanical laws are primary. From such beliefs the eventual development of regulatory control is inevitable, for it proceeds logically from the same conception of the activity. That is why quality assurance programs in human service settings are so evocative of industrial quality-control programs; the former were patterned directly upon the latter. We believed that we were dealing in both cases with "products."

We must realize, as John McKnight has pointed out, that we are confusing two very separate approaches to human endeavor. We might think of these approaches as tools. The one, professionalistic and hierarchical, works well to produce automobiles. The other, informal, relationship-based, and community-oriented, is good at caring. Somehow along the way we have gotten the two muddled. We have found ourselves with the wrong tool in our hands. Thinking all problems to be nails, we strenuously hammer away at caring as things get steadily worse.

The Progressive Expansion of the Regulatory Tide.

One cannot explore the history of regulation here in any but the most shorthand form. Yet most of the regulatory authority in the developmental disabilities field has developed within the last fifteen or twenty years, within the memory of most of my colleagues. We have seen most of this happen, and have participated in its development.

Each service setting, history shows us, establishes itself with the expectation that the new beneficial service itself will help, rescue, or protect vulnerable people. Often these services arise as reform movements in reaction to older services which deteriorated once the early fervor of enthusiasm had passed.[3] Each new movement to start a new service begins with the same belief that the deterioration which injured the vulnerable people in previous settings will not occur in its current replacement.

The history of service settings can, from one perspective, be viewed as a succession of services which have fallen to a false faith in their own invulnerability, layered like the cities of Troy. (Unlike Troy, however, they are mostly still inhabited.) It is in reaction to this recurring failure of services to protect people over the long term that regulatory safeguards have arisen.

One can view the most recent origins of this impulse through the history of the Willard Asylum for the Chronically Insane in New York State, which became internationally known after its founding in 1869 for visionary, humane care of people with chronic mental disorders. From the work of literally freeing people shipped to them in cages, it was only a few years before the administration found itself unable to slow the growth of abuse of patients by once dedicated attendants. As a safeguard they engaged a "gentleman of good character" to walk the wards to exert a "wholesome restraining influence" upon the staff through his presence. Perhaps one gentleman from the world outside the asylum walls was not enough, for soon the directors escalated to asking the legislature to pass a state law making the abuse of mental patients a misdemeanor. Notices of the new law were to be posted in the attendant's very bedrooms.

Study of the history of such early efforts reveals very clearly the pattern of social reform: abuse, followed by scandal in the press, followed by public outcry, followed by efforts at reform such as increased control measures. One can follow the origin and expansion of regulatory safeguards up to the present, including the establishment of a succession of oversight commissions which themselves eventually fell to the same dynamic seen in service enterprises. Mr. Sundram's current Commission on the Quality of Care for the Mentally Disabled can be traced from these roots, which may add some perspective to his recent disconcerting findings (Schwartz, 1983).

One can observe the beginnings of the regulatory control of state institutions as early as the close of the last century. This effort is still continuing through the efforts of many states to achieve ACDD (Accreditation Council on Developmental Disabilities) certification for their mental retardation institutions. The expansion of regulation to new "less restrictive" settings immediately follows the establishment of each new form. The mostly futile struggle to regulate the quality of care in nursing homes has been documented. Scandals and subsequent efforts to effectively regulate personal-care boarding homes can be observed in press reports in most states.

Fulfilling historical expectations, the crisis over quality has recently spread to community residences. As abuse and neglect are increasingly detected here, we see the pattern of increased monitoring and regulation extended as advocates and government officials attempt to protect the people dependent upon these newest deteriorating services.

Why Regulatory Control Always Expands

Regulatory control always expands. This expansion is driven by two factors: the innate inclination of bureaucratic systems to expand control, and the periodic cycles of scandal and response to incidents. There is no more eloquent description of this process than that made by Alexis de Tocqueville in 1835:

"...it is in the nature of all governments to seek constantly to enlarge their sphere of action; hence it is almost impossible that such a government should not ultimately succeed, because it acts with a fixed principle and a constant will upon men whose position, ideas, and desires are constantly changing.

It frequently happens that the members of the community promote the influence of the central power without intending to. Democratic eras are periods of experiment, innovation, and adventure. There is always a multitude of men engaged in difficult or novel undertakings, which they follow by themselves without shackling themselves to their fellows. Such persons will admit, as a general principle, that the public authority ought not to interfere in private concerns; but, by an exception to that rule, each of them craves its assistance in the particular concern on which he is engaged and seeks to draw upon the influence of the government for his own benefit, although he would restrict it on all other occasions. If a large number of men applies this particular exemption to a great variety of different purposes, *the sphere of the central power extends itself imperceptibly in all directions, although everyone wishes it to be circumscribed.*

Thus a democratic government increases its power simply by the fact of its permanence. Time is on its side; every incident befriends it, the passions of individuals unconsciously promote it; and it may be asserted that the older a democratic community is, the more centralized will its government become." (pp311-13; emphasis mine)

If de Tocqueville observed this accurately, then it may be correct to say that, one hundred and fifty years after his observation, these same dynamics may be found in our current quandary over the expansion of regulatory safeguards. We might draw several lessons from this for our particular situation:

1. Governmental control and hence regulation over settings in which people with disabilities are found will always expand over time, even if individual governmental officials at particular times desire to limit it.

2. Each incident or scandal, or pattern of incidents, is likely to precipitate an expansion of regulatory control as a method of trying to keep whatever bad thing that happened from happening again.

3. If you find the current "edge" of regulatory control and find those settings or practices which are currently just ahead of the "tide," you can predict that regulatory control will soon extend to these settings or practices as well, unless some significant other factor to

the contrary intervenes. This expansion is likely to be precipitated by an incident of some type.

4. The "passions of individuals," most potently expressed through voluntary advocacy associations, will unwittingly prompt the expansion of governmental regulatory control through attempts to protect those whom they represent.

5. The expansion of control will, by formalizing and increasing paperwork and related practices, increase the weight under which formalized caregivers must operate, at the cost of individual and organizational vitality.

6. The professionalization of relationships with people with disabilities under these dynamics will be increased. The authority of bureaucracies will increase, and the power of citizens will conversely diminish.

7. These dynamics are largely unconscious, and thus are promoted and carried out by people of good will in an attempt to improve circumstances for people with disabilities in society.

Current Evidence for Expansion

Evidence of expansion of control is on the increase. For a month or two while I was thinking about this phenomenon, I noted interesting examples that I encountered. Examples which seemed particularly absurd but logical extensions of regulatory direction were good indications of the regulatory trend. A few were:

•   In a northeastern state, someone choked to death on a gift of food brought into a group home. In reaction, the state office of mental retardation promulgated regulations on bringing food into houses.

•   In a midwestern state, group home residents must have a prescription from a doctor to use cough drops or Vaseline. Physicians think that this is ridiculous and won't write prescriptions. Residents cannot therefore legally obtain them.

•   Again in that state a group home was fined $500 because a staff member, following a change in a doctor's instructions, wrote "give in PM" on a prescription bottle instead of taking it back to the pharmacist for official relabeling.

- In Pennsylvania, staff members of a day program were barred by their employer from taking friends who were clients of the agency's group homes to their own homes to dinner, or to church with them on weekends, because of federal labor laws prohibiting such unpaid association.

- In Pennsylvania a foster home was deemed out of compliance with regulations, which might result in moving the two foster children elsewhere, because there were children of opposite sexes sharing a room when one was over a certain age. The children involved were a teenage mother and her infant son.

The effect of regulations on a program on the edge of the regulatory "tide" can be observed with particular clarity in the case of a "Family Living" program started in Pennsylvania recently. Under this program families are found who wish to care for a person with mental retardation. Governmental planners were delighted to find "real families" for people outside the traditional service system of group homes and shift staffing. It was soon realized, however, that the new program fell under existing community service regulations. This meant that inspectors had to go into families' homes, which caused considerable resentment among them. Enforcement of the regulations could mean such things as installing hot water temperature boosters to prevent the spread of hepatitis, then putting in temperature regulators to guard against scalding.

Since the applicability of regulations designed for group homes and influenced by Medicaid and institutional controls was clearly problematic, advocates, service providers, and government staff all recommended that a special, "watered down" version of the regulations be developed for this application. Yet, if our earlier observations are correct, we can expect that the reduction of regulations in this case will be temporary, despite the reasonable aspirations of all involved. Once the regulatory structure for the Family Living Program is in place as a control tool, expansion of control is predictable and inevitable.

What Holds Promise for Better Assuring the Safety of People than the Traditional Regulatory Approaches?

In Chapter 8 I cited John McKnight's conceptualization of action on behalf of people with disabilities as deriving from one of three approaches, the first of which he termed the "therapeutic vision." The therapeutic vision was once the dominant one in the field of mental retardation, when "professionals knew best" and professionals ran the institutions. The therapeutic vision was what doctors saw when they advised new parents of infants with mental retardation not to even bring their children home from the hospital. Regulatory control is compatible with the therapeutic vision, but is inherently compromised. Good examples are the quality assurance departments of state mental hospitals, whose primary job is to prepare the institution for quality control surveys by therapeutic provider associations. These do, of course, have an important role in certain areas of physical medicine.

The therapeutic vision in the field of mental retardation was considerably displaced after a prolonged (and ongoing) struggle by what McKnight terms the "advocacy vision." It was not meaningless that an early goal of the New York State Association for Retarded Citizens in the 1950s was to replace medical directors of state mental retardation institutions with nonmedical ones (Lerner, 1972). The real energy behind regulatory control has come from the advocacy movement, in its necessary urge to protect vulnerable people from terrible things happening to them. It is at the behest of such groups and their political pressure that government agencies have vastly extended regulatory requirements.

Just as the therapeutic vision was found disappointing in its ability to ensure decent lives for vulnerable people, so the advocacy vision, used exclusively, is now starting to show its limits. For those of us who have worked hard to erect a "protective wall" of vigorous systems advocacy around vulnerable people, this failure is very painful to see. Predictably, there is much resistance to acknowledging it. We are uncertain, for our vision promised that things for people with mental retardation would be very much better by now than they have proven to be. The evident decline of the community residential systems for which we advocated so tirelessly against the old institutional therapeutic vision has struck us hard, for this was to be the promise of freedom and quality of life for our people. To combat this decline we have reached for the same tool we utilized to try to improve institutional life. To hear that this safeguard approach is inadequate is disconcerting and is unlikely to be accepted.

This lack of acceptance can be understood as an example of the kind of resistance described by Kuhn to new paradigms. Thus, while vulnerability increases, we see escalating activity to introduce more and more powerful and complicated traditional safeguards such as laws, regulations, monitoring, and like measures. These could be pictured through Kuhn's metaphor of paradigms as more intricate moves on an existing chessboard of understanding, without questioning the rules of the game. In this case, the rules themselves may be in decline.

One might say that, as in a garden, the growth of the new crop must involve the decay and composting of the old. It is only through the unhappy decay of our old tools for assuring quality that we have been brought to the point of considering in our bewilderment the central question which is now offered to us: what really keeps people safe in society if regulatory safeguards do not?

We might begin by examining what keeps *un*labeled people safe in this world? I start with two beliefs:

1. There is no real guarantee of safety in this world. In a practical, immediate sense, we are all unsafe. The only way to try to escape danger is to build a prison around ourselves. Some people, in this hazardous world, choose one way or another to do just that. True communities have always known this truth. Systems — whether advocacy, therapeutic, or regulatory — do not. As McKnight eloquently writes:

> "The surest indication of the experience of community is the explicit common knowledge of tragedy, death, and suffering. The managed, ordered, technical vision embodied in professional and institutional systems leaves no space for tragedy; they are basically methods of production. Indeed, they are designed to deny the central dilemmas of life." (1977b, p.58)

While society must especially protect vulnerable people, it must avoid the delusion that ultimate protection is achievable. To believe so is to cast ourselves as gods, and sets us on the path of building a monument of protection, a Tower of Babel, which expresses only our hubris in the face of the ultimate mystery of life. It can lead us only to inhuman environments, whether the walls surrounding them are visible or invisible.

Bob Perske wrote of this long ago in his essay about "The Dignity of Risk and the Mentally Retarded." Of course this has been inappropriately drafted to serve as an excuse for instances of neglect, as when a person with mental retardation was placed in an apartment on a dangerous street with inadequate supervision against the wishes of his parents. When he was quickly killed in traffic, the agency claimed "dignity of risk" as their excuse. But to acknowledge the reality that we are all ultimately unsafe is most explicitly *not* to abandon vulnerable people, although such a statement could of course be readily perverted to such ends. It is merely to acknowledge that excessive protection costs the person being protected his or her ultimate human-ity.

2. The Only Real Protections for a Person are Other People. In the example with which I started this chapter, I told about how Joanie had been failed by all systemic safeguards. Her hope of protection was at last revealed to be one single person. This person, unfortunately, was not free to advocate for her because she was responsible to the service system as well. The lesson of such incidents is that the protector of a vulnerable person, if such a protector is to arise, is always another person or group of persons.

This is, after all, clearly the case with me and everyone I know who does not have the label of "client." I am fortunate to have a family and friends. It is they whom I count on, and they count upon me. This is how the world works, and how it has always worked. In the case of vulnerable persons, however, we have forgotten this idea, driven by our vision of formal advocacy. Somehow we gained the belief that what is a safeguard for us is not a safeguard for people with disabili-ties. In doing so we have created two classes of people: citizens and clients. To the latter, to paraphrase McKnight, we have offered only a service for consolation, while we ourselves are consoled and sup-ported by friends, family, and community.

Wolf Wolfensberger, in his work on citizen advocacy, has exam-ined this question in great detail and holds that personal relationships must be the foundation of any approach to advocacy and protection. In a well-known passage, he writes:

> "There are many people, especially wounded and handicapped people, who now do not have viable, relatively unconditional one-to-one sup-portive relationships. If people are no longer willing to engage in those kinds of relationships, laws can be passed, unlimited funds can be allocated — and still, nothing will work."
>
> "...if individual citizens, *on a personal basis,* do not bind the wounds of the sick, do not give bread to the hungry, do not console the broken-hearted and visit the imprisoned, do not liberate the captives of oppres-sion and do not bury the dead, then nothing will work." (1977, p.66)

There are people, Wolfensberger has pointed out, who believe that informal relationships are very fragile and untrustworthy. All of us, from our own personal experience, know that this can be so. We have all been abandoned to some degree in an hour of need by family, friends, community. Yet community is also very strong. We can, from our own experience, cite at least as much evidence for that. Our error in the developmental disabilities field is not in thinking that safeguards based upon personal and community relationships offer less than total security, but in believing that there is something better.

Possible Biological Parallels to Social Safeguards

It is commonly accepted nowadays that human society harbors an innate inclination to devalue those who are different or less able. There is certainly no lack of evidence for this conclusion. Is there as well some counter to this tendency in human nature? Is it possible that some degree of innate resistance in society to neglecting the weak exists alongside our propensity to abuse?[4]

Rumination on such a question leads me back to patterns of biological and ecological thinking from my early education in psychobiology. One, of course, is always at risk of attempting to draw too broad an analogy between what are very diverse phenomena. Yet it may be worthwhile to speculate on whether similar questions have been encountered in biological and perhaps medical fields to see whether any parallels exist.

Our emphasis in the advocacy vision of regulatory safeguards has been to try to prevent, to "stamp out," as it were, injurious things from happening to people at risk. In medicine, injurious agents are often germs; in gardening they are similarly plant diseases. In each of these fields there is now an intellectual community moving the emphasis of thinking from noxious agent to environmental factors of resistance. These discoveries have arisen, perhaps provocatively, at the same time in history as the one which finds us in our own current dilemma in our field. It may thus be worthwhile to look at each in turn.

Second Thoughts on the Germ Theory

The famed microbiologist Rene Dubos wrote a great deal of work which helped to raise thinking in medicine and biology to a new level. Microbiologists—and Dubos was a brilliant one—classically searched out and identified the causes of diseases, like the tubercle bacillus. Then they tried to find a substance that would kill the virulent agent or perhaps ward it off. In this way they discovered, for instance, sulfa drugs or antibiotics. Though miracles had been attained through this vision of how the world works — what might be termed a paradigm — after some time its predictive and useful power declined. Dubos was early in noticing this. It was a great breakthrough to discover the tubercle bacillus, which caused tuberculosis, for instance. According to the prevailing conception, all that one had to do was to go after this "germ." But this eventually didn't fit with the finding, long known, that most people carried the bacillus in a dormant state but didn't get the disease. They didn't, that is, until other factors changed.

As early as 1955 Dubos wrote in an article called "Second Thoughts on the Germ Theory" that "During the first phase of the germ theory the property of virulence was regarded as lying solely within the microbes themselves. Now virulence is coming to be thought of as ecological." In physiology, he noted that the disturbance of equilibrium could in fact precipitate the appearance of disease, infectious agents remaining constant. Although microbes were clearly responsible, was there not possibly a zone of influence where "the presence of the microbe is the prerequisite but not the determinant of disease, a situation in which the fact of infection is less decisive in shaping the course of events than the physiological climate of the invaded body?" "What is needed," Dubos concluded, "is some understanding of the agencies responsible for natural resistance to infection, *and of the factors that interfere with the operation of those agencies*" (emphasis mine).

Is such a concept useful in our own work? One thinks of troublesome instances. No matter how hard we try, even in the controlled environment of an institution, to eliminate "bad and abusive" staff it has consistently failed, even when one goes so far as to resort to undercover police officers. Is the problem an "infection," we might say, of "bad staff?"

Jerome Miller, who was famous for closing Massachusetts's youth detention institutions, mentioned a story once about how he came to decide to close the institutions rather than to reform them. He had come to Massachusetts initially with only institutional reform in mind. As a first step he hired a few of the brightest, most socially committed sixties activists that he could find at Harvard and introduced them into one of the institutions. "In two months," he reflected with amazement, "they were all fascists."

If the microbiological analogy holds, then we could ask: "What in the environment precipitated dormant abusive impulses to virulence in these Harvard activists?" Another, and perhaps more important, question would be: "Why, if the propensity for abuse is contained within us all (as has been demonstrated convincingly by various psychological studies), does abuse not occur even more often than it already does?" Dubos notes that the problem in microbiology is not merely "How do some microbes cause disease?" but rather "Why are not all microbes capable of causing disease?" If our problem is not "bad" people but rather dormant propensities for abuse becoming virulent, then are there, in Dubos's terms, factors that *interfere* with the operation of such tendencies? If we were to look with the eyes of an ecologist, or perhaps a cultural anthropologist, at settings in which abuse rarely occurs, might we discover such factors operating within them? We will examine this question a little further on. A second question which might be considered is whether or not the use of regulatory control is in some ways analogous to the use of anti-microbials (such as antibiotics) without reference to the environment — physiological or social — in which the infection or abuse occurs.

Organic Agriculture

"The study of plant and animal life in their mutual interconnections, and in their relation to the earth, serve ...to lead us to a better understanding of 'dynamic' relationships."

"The fundamental aspect of this method of thinking is that it permits one to see an organic relationship, a functional coordination between various factors, which leads us finally to recognize the formation of a unit, whether biological, agricultural, social, or artistic."
— Ehrenfried Pfeiffer

At the same time in recent history in which medicine embraced the germ theory and discovered antibiotics, agriculture discovered pesticides and what has been termed "chemical agriculture." The eradication of many diseases arose together with "the green revolution." The immediate and concrete results in both medicine and agriculture seemed initially impressive.

If one looks into the field of agriculture currently, however, one can find a growing minority that believes the thinking upon which modern chemical agriculture is based is deeply in error. Such persons, who might be termed "organic" gardeners or farmers, hold that the use of pesticides and related substances represents only a very short-term solution to problems such as insect damage and plant disease. Instead of introducing external chemical interventions, they are more interested in learning how to increase the natural resistance of plants and animals. Rather than looking at the problem of an insect infestation, for example, as something to be solved by applying the correct toxin, such farmers tend to see their farms as living organisms or biological units.

The connection of the thinking of organic gardeners with that of Dubos about medicine seems important and striking. For both have made a similar change in their approaches to the problems in their respective fields. Each has moved from a rather simple theory based upon toxic agents and external interventions to a view decidedly ecological in character. Both seem to be concerned with the concept of equilibrium.

In organic gardening practitioners start from a belief that the natural equilibrium of biological forces in the ecology is foremost. They believe that external agents such as pesticides and fertilizers are not only harmful to humans, but that they also sap the natural resistance of plants and animals by disturbing the complex balance of the biosphere. Chemical agriculture, they say, can be seen as successful only if viewed from a very short time perspective. In mere decades since the introduction of certain pesticides, they note, a constant escalation of toxins has been underway as insects have lost vulnerability to each. (One can see the same phenomenon in medicine with resistant forms of certain sexually transmitted diseases and other infections.)

Organic gardening is a way of thinking about growing food that had to be rediscovered by pioneers of this field who were disenchanted with the direction that modern agriculture was taking. Some of the beginnings involved the study of agricultural methods of societies where "modern" methods had not penetrated. How did they keep worms from potatoes? How did they keep plants and animals healthy?

The organic gardening field seems characterized by constant and ongoing experimentation and sharing of information of this sort. This kind of flower planted next to tomatoes keeps this kind of insect away; painting the trunks of the apple trees with mud at this time of year keeps bark-borers away. The mixing and decomposition of composts which will grow the most vigorous and resistant plants seems central to their work. The results of such farming practices are often impressive.

An additional striking difference from conventional farming practices is what I can only call a certain acceptance of disease. In the grape farming community in which I live part of the time, the appearance of insect damage or disease brings an immediate response of the proper chemical spray until it is eradicated. Organic farmers, on the other hand, seem to approach such problems differently. While they would argue that their healthy plants have fewer disease problems than those of their neighbors, and they take vigorous steps to fight infection, they seem to accept that a certain small portion of the tomatoes will get blossom-end rot in a wet year. While this probably could be absolutely prevented by a liberal application of fungicide, organic farmers seem too preoccupied with balance, with the equilibrium of the whole farm as an organism, to risk sacrificing its health for the benefit of treating a symptom. They seem to believe that once one reaches for external technology as a way of treating symptoms, one embarks upon a downward spiral that demands increasingly escalating interventions and ends only with disabling the internal organic balance of the farm itself.

The analogy to the social sphere runs the risk of being overdrawn. Yet the idea that communities of humans as well as plants or animals have an inherent degree of resistant equilibrium is not a new idea. While ecologists were discovering that the spray that killed the bugs that ate the corn was weakening the corn's ability to resist the bugs on its own, psychologists and sociologists were finding that new formal services such as institutions weakened community tendencies to accept responsibility for and respond to the needs of its members. Seymour Sarason observed this over a decade ago. He noted that the development of such services tended to paradoxically erode the natural inclination and ability of communities to respond to each other's needs. One built an institution for people with mental retardation or a community mental health center in a town, and the town tended to lose its capacity to deal with human needs once they had been defined as professional problems. The community no longer saw such problems in their province. John McKnight's "John Deere and the Bereavement Counselor" draws the parallel between modern farming practices and modern practices of one professional human service discipline particularly poetically:

> "The [bereavement] counselor's new tool will cut through the social fabric, throwing aside kinship, care, neighborly obligations and community ways of coming together and going on. Like John Deere's plow, the tools of bereavement counseling will create a desert where a community once flourished." (1985, p.19)

There is one place where one can observe the commonality or unity in the phenomena of natural resistance as seen in agriculture and in society in the same setting. In certain types of intentional communities of the Camphill movement, which I will discuss in more detail later, one finds organic farming practices, an extraordinarily nurturing environment for people with disabilities, and a culture in which neglect or abuse is extremely rare, even in the case of challenging people who had received abuse in previous settings. As one investigates further, one finds these phenomena, along with certain beliefs about medicine similar to Dubos's, are perceived as an organic unity among members of such communities.

In Search of Natural Resistance

An analysis of history often shows that many phenomena which seemed disparate while they were occurring show unified relevance from the perspective of time. In such perspective they tended to emerge as differentiated manifestations of a single thought or a change in conception or world view. Although the reader may wonder if I have gone rather far afield from the matter of safeguards and regulations by delving into biological issues, the exercise has value. For it may be possible that we are observing similar changes in all areas of human effort due to fundamental changes in human conceptions.

If this is so, then it may be valuable to pursue an ecological investigation of what keeps people safe in society, in emulation of discoveries in the more concrete biological sciences. From this perspective, we might discover that the pattern of thought which makes the conventional farmer reach for his spray can when he sees insect damage may be similar to that which causes us to reach for regulatory control when we see people being hurt. Are regulations our DDT, or our liberally prescribed antibiotics? The positive results of each are often immediate and satisfying. Yet it is over the long term rather than the short term that the drawbacks of each tend to appear.

If we are to take an ecological view, then it makes sense to think about and identify what the mechanisms of resistance in the social sphere might be. If we can gain some idea of these mechanisms, perhaps we, like a good physician who keeps us well, or an organic farmer who keeps his or her farm healthy, can find ways to recognize similar activities in our quest to learn how to keep vulnerable people safe.

Relevance to Regulation

When we look at human ecology, we are immediately brought to the concepts of mediating structures and associational life discussed earlier. If there are personal relationships through which vulnerable people are protected they will be found solely as part of such associational groups, for relationships are always in reference to a family, a club, a group of friends. Relationships are not in the domain of the state, or within the vision of an individualistic advocacy. That is why the concept of citizen advocacy always seems so hard to explain in formal advocacy or government meetings, and so easy in the diner. If, in addition, there is a natural resistance to neglect and abuse to be found in society, or stated positively, a natural propensity for caring, we know from the experience of our daily lives that it is to be found in the associational life of the community and not in the structures of governmental control.

From this perspective one can use the concept of mediating structures to look at the expanding tide of regulation. Seen in this way, settings still outside the sphere of regulatory control may still express the theme of pluralism. Many of these structures contain the capacity to develop different pluralistic "psychological communities" for those who inhabit them.

Our current public policy, by not recognizing the importance of maintaining and respecting a healthy plurality of mediating structures, works to reduce the creative tensions which diversity creates. It imposes unitary solutions to bring conditions into uniformity. As tools of management megastructure, such solutions create environments which natural associational communities find increasingly inhospitable for growth and development. As Berger and Neuhaus write:

> "A strong argument can be made that the dynamics of modernity, operating through the megastructures and especially through the modern state, are like a great leviathan or steamroller, inexorably destroying every obstacle that gets in the way of creating mass society." (p.44)

The tide of regulatory control can be seen as one expression of this larger tendency. As the tide expands, we can expect diversity to perish as we favor more and more a unitary management model. Yet such small groups, and particularly the voluntary associations, as Berger and Neuhaus point out, serve as laboratories for innovation within social services, precisely due to their lack of bureaucratic controls. As more and more settings are brought within the sphere of unitary regulatory control, we can expect the creative tension which such anomalies bring to diminish.

The dynamics driving governmental expansion previously noted by de Tocqueville are echoed by Berger and Neuhaus, who point out that in current times increases in regulation and credentialing are closely linked with the trend toward professionalization of services, and the growth in power of professionals, at the expense of power of the citizenry.[5] An especially clear example of this dynamic was brought to my attention in a bill before Pennsylvania's legislature that would require the services of professional nutritionists in a wide variety of settings. Such a bill seems clearly driven by a professional association's attempts to increase its power. It shows the dynamic of expansion of regulatory control into spheres of everyday life by finally going so far as attempting to, in the words of an opponent of the bill, "monopolize and professionalize an otherwise unregulated and unlicensed area of life, namely, eating" (David *A.* Schwartz, 1988).

The idea of a mediating structure or associational group thus gives us a useful tool for thinking about how people thrive in communities, and what factors may act to keep people safe within the social context of "the little platoon" in which we all actually conduct our lives. Perhaps one might find in the mediating structure an analogy to certain physiological processes which keep the body in equilibrium, healthy, and resistant to disease. If so, what might happen if such natural mechanisms are suppressed and displaced? Or perhaps, in our ruminations for an ecological parallel to gardening, the mediating structure represents the ecological community of the garden or the farm, upon whose balance the flourishing of each plant and animal is dependent.

If safety is to be found in the relationship embedded in the mediating structure, is there an "ecological" approach to determining the health of communities and, by derivation, the safety of those vulnerable members within it? Are there certain characteristics by which we might recognize a community in which a vulnerable person is likely to be safe as against one in which safety is unlikely? If one could learn to recognize such factors, could one consciously foster and protect them from the opposing forces of unitary regulatory direction? It is such questions that we have been considering in Pennsylvania, and which have led us to an experiment to determine whether such an approach can work.

Searching for an Approach to Safeguards Which Recognizes the Importance of Personal Relationships and Mediating Structures

Those who work to protect the welfare of people with disabilities are experts in failed or failing communities. We are accustomed to the fact that abuse and neglect will occur unless we stringently forbid it, and probably even if we do.

We frequently overlook the fact that communities exist in which abuse and neglect of vulnerable people is notably infrequent, and in which such people are even especially valued and protected. Large communities known for protecting all of their members include various settlements of Hutterites and Amish, the former being well known in mental retardation literature for their living witness in earlier years that institutional care of people with mental retardation was unnecessary.

The field of mental retardation has within it two international networks of intentional communities whose social mission specifically involves living in community with people with disabilities: the Camphill and L'Arche movements. While there are a number of differences in the two movements, there seem to be many fundamental similarities. Particularly notable for our purposes is the fact that neglect and abuse are rare in both types of community, and they are far safer than most comparable professional service agencies. This fact is well known to the many parents who seek them out after experiences with conventional service providers.

Few of us in this field have become knowledgeable about such "healthy" communities which are not deteriorating or failing. Yet if we were to assume the role of "naturalists" on a search for what keeps people safe, we would have to study success rather than failure, healthy communities rather than deteriorating ones. This search would soon lead us to Camphill and L'Arche, where we could begin to try to discover why people seem so particularly safe in these environments.

Many of my own observations have been at a Camphill agricultural village in Pennsylvania. On my first visit, I was struck (as most visitors are) by the evident richness of the lives of those people with mental retardation living there. It seemed like a real working agricultural community, in which differentiation between disabled and nondisabled members could not be reliably made at any distance. The residents of Camphill Village were clearly thriving. My assumption, as mentioned earlier, was that deterioration and abuse would occur over time in every setting unless there were some significant factors to the contrary. Since deterioration was not present, such factors clearly existed. Yet the kinds of familiar safeguards one is culturally conditioned to look for in a "care" setting, such as regulations, rules, and written procedures, were virtually absent. The "real" safeguards were apparently invisible to superficial scrutiny.

My initial observations convinced me that the question of safety was the kind of thing noted by Rene Dubos earlier, when he spoke of searching for "the agencies responsible for natural resistance to infection, and of the factors that interfere with the operation of those agencies." Discovering the agencies responsible for natural resistance led one immediately to an ecological investigation of the community as a whole. I could not begin to discover the factors at Camphill, I decided, until I knew why they farmed the way they did, why they lived as they did, why they celebrated religious services in a particular way.

A number of factors began to emerge as identifiable elements of the Camphill community which are clearly related to the question of natural safeguards embedded in the daily life of the community.

Some of these seem to be:

1. A shared system of religious belief leading to a common world view in which all people, including those with disabilities, are believed to have inherent and equal human value regardless of apparent differences in ability or productivity;

2. A consequent reluctance to differentiate those with disabilities from those without them by name, title, living situation, dress, economic status, or privilege;

3. A practice by members without disabilities of doing almost everything (work, cook, travel, worship) together with members with disabilities;

4. The existence for all members of a wide range of freely given unpaid relationships with many people inside the community and, to a lesser extent, outside it;

5. The apparent perception, by members with disabilities, that members of the community had numerous "responsible" roles (such as housefather, farmer, or board president) but a relative lack of any perception of people as having "power" roles (such as director, boss, case manager, etc.);

6. The rejection of the proposal that they are a utopian community;

7. The correction of individual minor examples of potentially negative events for members with disabilities through cultural and interpersonal means, such as a long difficult talk ("That's not how we do things here"), or group meetings or discussions aimed at increasing understanding;

8. Value placed on the importance of personal growth for all members of the community;

9. A belief that the encroachment of formal safeguard procedures such as licensing would threaten and erode the cultural values and processes which make living at Camphill appealing.[6]

Identifying Factors Applicable to All Communities

Study of one particular community such as Camphill can help one to begin to see factors of natural ecological resistance in the social sphere.

The above list is merely a superficial impression of these factors; much deeper delving into this matter is required. The question, however, is not whether identified factors apply to one Camphill community, but to all communities in which people with disabilities are known to thrive. A second step, therefore, might be to compare these identified factors with life at L'Arche communities. Do these same factors seem to characterize daily life there? From my own limited experience with L'Arche, this appears to be the case. A third step could be to compare these factors with those found in the life of "traditional" community agencies known for exemplary service to people with disabilities.

What I am describing is a process of learning how to see what really keeps people safe in communities. Such factors as I have mentioned are merely a sketch, a suggestion of the direction we might take if we really wanted to investigate the question of what could be counted upon to keep people with disabilities safe in society. What would happen, for instance, if one invited a real cross-section of people from healthy community enterprises outside the formal human service system to identify together the factors they believed they shared? Perhaps one might begin to develop a fairly refined list of factors to help one see what is, by its very nature, hard to see and under the surface, unlike file notes or medication schedules.

What one would surely find through such a process is that the factors which serve to keep a community formed around people with disabilities functioning safely and well would be identical to those one would find in any sound community in the larger world.

A Proposed Process to Discern Whether a Community is Safe

Drawing upon the concept of the encroaching "regulatory tide" offered earlier, one could say that two tasks are called for along the edge of this tide at this particular moment. The first is holding back expansion. This tide is now at the very edge of the organized human services world and upon the doorstep of community. Camphill is a community on the "border." It looks like human services from the perspective of human services. If governmental regulation is to apply to communities such as this, whether or not they receive funding from a regulating governmental body, then the authority of government has passed its usual border and assumed a responsibility to use conventional regulatory safeguards for all labeled people based upon the existence of the label alone. From here we can predict the fairly rapid extension of such controls into any situation in which such labeled people live, since the situations past this point are only demarcated by shadings of degree. One might use McKnight's terms to say that these intentional communities appear one way from the therapeutic or advocacy vision side, and another way from the community vision side. The task is thus preserving community from the onrushing water. The final dike now eroding is the receipt of government funds. This will apparently no longer be sufficient to hold the sea back.

A second task concerns the prevention of abuse in communities. For communities are extremely likely to abuse and neglect people, contrary to any recent infatuation with a romantic image of community in the developmental disabilities field. Camphill is, after all, a very unusual and complex international culture, and even it is far from immune to the influences of deterioration and decay which affect all works of man. How much more vulnerable to decay, then, are the many other situations which we wish to preserve in the community sphere: cooperative housing or life-sharing situations, people simply sharing homes, adoptive families? One has the responsibility, in trying to hold off conventional safeguards, to be realistic about the inevitability of abuse and neglect arising here, and of taking steps to help safeguard vulnerable people in more appropriate and successful ways.

To pursue this responsibility, the Council commissioned an effort termed the Life-sharing Safeguards Project. Based on the success of the Citizen Advocacy Program Evaluation (CAPE) in supporting the proper development and operation of citizen advocacy offices, the project was initiated to develop an analogy to CAPE which would be applicable in informal settings in which people with and without disabilities lived together. These include the "life-sharing" anomalies sponsored by the Council and other settings of a similar nature which are not yet subject to regulation.

The "evaluation" process now in development has been examining a wide variety of informal settings to attempt to identify the "invisible" or hard-to-see factors which act as natural safeguards or perhaps serve as indicators of their presence. A peer review, participatory process rather than a traditional evaluation, it may ask such questions about the situation of a vulnerable person as:

- Does he or she have any freely given relationships with others outside their home?
- Does he or she belong to any community groups or associations?
- How many people in the neighborhood or town know him or her and might notice if something was wrong and take action?
- Who assists with the person's finances?

- Does the person have the same living conditions as those he or she lives with?

As this line of inquiry is followed, it is anticipated that we will be able to construct a process which not only looks at the natural human ecology of resistance, but which raises the attention of members of communities to those aspects of their functioning most closely correlated with health. If this works as conceived, it may prove to be a way to address the issue of safeguarding the welfare of vulnerable people in a way that is not intrusive to natural settings and which may even strengthen their development. It may also help to buy a "space" for such natural settings by offering those in government a way out of their current dilemma in which the choice is either to regulate traditionally or to ignore the community settings beyond the current edge of the regulatory tide until something bad happens there and they are forced to step in.

Romanticizing Community

" As we position ourselves to conceivably entrust the lives of millions of people to a life in 'community,' it is useful to ask if we have truly squared ourselves to a view of 'community' that contains human beings that are less than ideal."

— Michael Kendrick

Throughout this chapter I have emphasized the strengths of communities and the limitations of technological systems for keeping people safe. While there will be considerable resistance to this point of view by many of my colleagues who are deeply invested in regulatory and other systemic reform, there will be some openness to it as well. The appeal of "community" as a valid way to address the situation of people with disabilities has been increasing lately, as we become aware of what our service systems have failed to do, and as we lose faith in this exclusive solution to human need.

As we search for some new source of hope it is not unexpected that the offerings of community will be glorified, just as institutions, group homes, and each successive programmatic conception has been glorified in its own day. This tendency has great hazard for people with disabilities.

It is easy for us to forget that the original institutions were created by deeply committed social visionaries specifically to help vulnerable people who were being neglected or even abused in their own communities. The deficiencies of communities were supposed to be "fixed" by institutions. When this social cure proved worse than the disease, we turned to community services, and the institutions were "bad." Today we have come full circle, with professional services "bad" and "community" the solution. Where we can go most terribly wrong here is in believing community to be the perfect solution. We have always gone wrong with perfect solutions.

"The empowerment of people in neighborhoods," as Berger and Neuhaus write, "is hardly the answer to all our social problems. Neighborhoods empowered to impose their values upon individual behavior and expression can be both coercive and cruel. Government that transcends neighborhoods must intervene to protect elementary human rights." There are evil and abusive people in this world, and there are evil and abusive communities. I agree with Clarence Sundram that for such situations a vigorous enforcement of the law is essential — and not a convoluted, complex law that reads like regulation, but a simple law. The Bill of Rights, for example. Parodoxically, while our field sees a great deal of regulatory activity, we have very weak enforcement of basic laws relating to people's freedom of expression, freedom from imprisonment, or freedom from harm.

In acting to preserve people's rights in communities we must, as Berger and Neuhaus go on to caution, attempt to achieve a balance. In recent years, they point out, "an unbalanced emphasis upon individual rights has seriously eroded the community's power to sustain its democratically determined values in the public sphere." We forget that if caring is really to be done, it must be done by real people in real communities. On the other hand, forgetting the issue of individual rights and abandoning people to an idealized notion of community will do nothing but open vulnerable people to great harm.

The point about community is not that it is the answer to all of our struggles on behalf of people with disabilities, but simply that it is the true reality of how people live. Community, Michael Kendrick says, "is rightfully idealized when it is emphasized as the communal reality that human beings both need and create if left to themselves." If we accept this reality, and its human fallibilities and limitations, then perhaps we can be free to think about how to help communities generate and regenerate themselves to be as strong and healthy and caring for all people as they can become.

It is important, then, that in rediscovering the ancient value of community we have our eyes open. Community is not a programmatic tool to be harnessed, a useful environment to be used. It will not cure affliction and disability, either. As Jack Yates has concluded:

"The problem is not that mental retardation cannot be cured; the problem is that life cannot be cured...We need to remember that community, like the other things we have been tempted to romanticize, cannot be judged by whether it 'fixes' people or situations; like [de-institution-alization] and like associations and like friends, and maybe like life, community is worthwhile for other reasons.

So if community isn't utopia and won't fix people and won't resolve people's situation in life, then what is it good for? To paraphrase McKnight, it's the only uncontrolled space, the only place you can sing together and the only place you can die together, the only place you can never abolish suffering, and the only place you can never abolish joy." (1988)

It is the only place, one might say, still beyond the tide of the compulsive regulatory ritual with which our culture attempts to hold back and deny the anxious realities of evil, suffering, and death. Like a person with an obsessive-compulsive neurosis, our defense system is rigidifying and expanding as it slowly fails, leaving a smaller and smaller circle of free life untouched. The only cure is to really free oneself to face living in this dangerous, scary world.

It is this larger social dynamic which is one of the real reasons behind what happened to Joanie. As I was revising this chapter, I received a telephone call from a friend to tell me that Joanie was dead. It was the Sunday before Columbus Day. She had died of pneumonia, suddenly, at the state institution.

Joanie's health, I was told, had considerably improved with dialysis to the point that a few weeks before her unexpected death she had visited a group home in her old town (not one operated by our old agency) in preparation for moving back to the city and her friends. A local dialysis unit had been started while she had been gone. People said that she was very happy about the prospect of coming back home.

After Joanie's death there was apparently some effort by people in the town to return her body there for burial. But they were informed by the institutional staff that financial obstacles prevented this, and she was quickly interred in the institution graveyard. So she never made it home, even in death. My friend visited with some flowers for the grave, and found it in a neglected area behind a shed beside the interstate. A cheap plastic marker served as a headstone. They had spelled her name wrong.

There are many Joanies in the world, and many of them are at unusual risk of something harmful happening to them. It seems to me that it is our task and opportunity now to try to think clearly about what might hold a realistic hope of keeping them as safe from harm as possible. Regulatory safeguards, it seems clear, will not ultimately offer the protection we once had hoped for. Community may, if we can be content to accept community merely for what it is.

Involving people with disabilities in community life will promise no panacea. "Democracy," Churchill once quipped, "is the worst form of government that there is. Except," he continued after a well-timed pause, "for all of the other ways." So may it be with the fragile safeguards that community has to offer as well. They may be, in the long term, all that we have really had all along.

Endnotes

1.   Hubert Zipperlen has pointed out that the need for government control of milk quality has its real origin in the expansion of societies to the point that consumers of milk no longer know the producers, unlike the situation in small villages.

2.   "On the other hand," Sundram points out elsewhere, "for the dishonest agencies, no amount of regulation is sufficient. What those agencies require is a strong and effective enforcement of the law."

3.   A striking example of this can be observed in the fact that both Dorothea Dix in 1843 and Burton Blatt in 1967, in addresses to the Massachusetts legislature over a century apart, cited the same kind of conditions for people with mental disabilities, despite the erection of a massive service system to address these problems in the intervening period (Blatt, 1970).

4.   Kriegman and Knight (1988), examining this question from a psychobiological and psychoanalytical framework, cite Robert Triver's concept of "reciprocal altruism," which "suggests that there may be a bio-genetic basis for altruistic behavior." In Chapter 9, we briefly looked at evidence of altruism in human societies emerging under the extremely negative conditions of the Holocaust. Yet even more extreme examples exist. What about a situation in which individuals are engaged in the act of killing each other? Kriegman and Knight cite a fascinating example from the trench warfare of early World War I:

> "Much to the consternation of the generals," they write, "the 'disease of cooperation' between the opposing soldiers broke out all along the line. Stationed week after week, and month after month, in the same spot facing the same 'enemy,' the ideal conditions were present for the generation of reciprocal altruism. Soldiers shot to miss. Troops left the trenches and worked at repairing them in full view and within range of enemy soldiers who passively looked on. Christmas was celebrated together. One striking incident occurred when in one area an artillery burst exploded sending both sides diving for cover. After several moments, a brave German soldier called out to the other side and apologized, saying that his side had nothing to do with it: 'It was those damn Prussian artillerymen.' ... Finally the generals solved this thorny problem by ordering random raids (and shooting those who resisted) that broke down the mutual trust and cooperation that had evolved."

While the objection may be raised that such examples are highly unusual, Kriegman and Knight reflect that "human interactions are, in fact, often highly cooperative, and while there may be tension and competitiveness, the destructiveness that supposedly characterizes our species is relatively unseen. Murders are relatively rare within stable living communities and account for very little of human mortality" (1988, p.53).

5.   See also James Fallow's excellent 1985 article on credentialism for a thorough examination of this subject.

6.   In Dubos's terms, one might say that regulation would be considered to be a factor which would operate against the natural resistance to infection.

CHAPTER 11

Hazards in Implementation

"It should be a sobering reminder to us that, when the pioneers in our field undertook this task, despite the greatest good will and thoughtful deliberation, they led to the development of modern institutional settings. In offering enormous benefits, their work led to the loss of everything important to their beneficiaries."

— Burton Blatt

There is always the risk that in the initial enthusiasm over a new concept it will be seized upon as a fail-proof solution. This inevitably turns out to be a serious error. This truth is certainly applicable to the approach outlined in the preceding chapters. Considerable opportunities exist for problems to arise when the ideas behind the concepts discussed here are translated into action. It is therefore important to consider in what ways implementation of this approach can "go off the track," so that one can avoid falling into predictable difficulties. Primary hazards to implementation seem to be of four basic types: falling prey to professionalism, romanticizing the idea of community, indulging in anti-professionalism, and becoming recruited for political ends. As in any other endeavor, good intentions are not enough to ensure success.

Falling Prey to Professionalism

Once a new revolution in practice is adopted, there is no guarantee it will continue. It is common, in fact, for the new approach to be quietly absorbed into the old one. Consider, for example, the curious brief life of "tent treatment" in mental hospitals around the turn of the century.

Mental hospitals had long been infatuated with the importance of fresh air and ventilation for proper treatment.[1] Around the time of the earthquake at the Agnew Asylum reported in Chapter 8, when inmates lived outside and showed such spontaneous improvement, a new interest in fresh air and sunshine as curative treatments arose. This took the form of the development of tent "camps" on the grounds of asylums, into which inmates were placed to reap the healing benefits of sun and air. Originally these camps were small. Life was no doubt very different in these small communities of tents from that within the walls of institutional buildings.

Soon, however, as Caplan (1969) noted in the case of New York State, this began to change. Several changes happened over a very few years. First, one hospital dreamed up the idea of building *revolving* tents that could be turned to face the sun. Then camps were enlarged until they could hold several hundred patients. Tents, however, were a problem to heat and maintain, and had to be replaced frequently. So finally tents were replaced by "wooden pavilions with large windows and sun porches." "Thus," according to Caplan,

> "tent treatment...lost its distinctive features and was...absorbed into the rest of the hospital.
>   ...Staff and equipment shortages would follow; the patients would no longer be able to wander about the lawns because there would be doors and locks. The whole atmosphere of the improvisation, adventure, and group cohesiveness would disappear, as would the concern and pride of the staff and their special attention to individuals..." (p.281)

By the time the concept of tent treatment was established in buildings with designed ventilation which precisely maintained the desired "superabundance" of fresh air and sunshine, the effort was long moribund. It had been pressed into a professionalistic world view in which qualities of ventilation rather than qualities of interpersonal relationships were seen as important. If you look among the abandoned buildings of mental hospitals today, you may find relics of the old pavilions, dried-out skeletons that are all that is left of the original idea.[2]

Tent treatment provides a good illustration of how dependent new settings are upon the larger environment of belief into which they emerge. The vision of living in small communities in tents, obviously beneficial as it was, could not be expected to survive long within the completely different dominant culture of a professional/bureaucratic world view found in total institutions. Erosion of the new settings would be expected to be incremental. Tents would not be turned back into institutional buildings in one obvious step. Rather, they were slowly "improved" until one day there were simply no longer any tents. The end result was the absorption of the new vision into the old. This same phenomenon can be observed in a culture as a whole.

It is important to remember that just because one has been successful in making a shift in approach, it does not mean that the shift is a permanent one. Reversion, as in tent treatment, is typical.

The practice of breast-feeding provides another example, this one within the larger culture. For many years in the United States there was a steady decline in breast-feeding and a replacement of it by bottle-feeding with formula. Formula manufacturers and many doctors discouraged breast-feeding. Formula was seen as "modern" and "scientific," while breast-feeding was seen as "common."[3] As a result, the natural activity of breast-feeding became scarcer and scarcer and the knowledge of how to do it, traditionally passed from mother to daughter, became rare. By the 1950s, it had gotten to the point that two mothers who met at a picnic in a Chicago suburb realized that many women who they knew wanted to breast-feed were not being success-ful, since they were having such a hard time finding out answers to some of the questions they had about various problems that arose. In reaction, they founded a self-help group to promote the practice of breast-feeding known as the La Leche League (La Leche League, 1958). Today, breast-feeding has become a culturally normative prac-tice once again, and much of the credit for the change may well be due to the League's work.[4] By the mid-1980s, prevailing American senti-ment and medical advice seemed to be in favor of natural breast-feeding. The informal unpaid advice of the mothers of the League had helped to change a technological, commercialized practice back to a natural one.

A few months ago, however, I suddenly became aware that this change might not be as permanently established as I thought. I received in my office mail a brochure for a breast-feeding consultant group. This group, I was amazed to read, was composed of nurse "lactation consultants" who conducted workshops across the country "on issues related to the 'lactation consultant practice.'" They offered training to show consultants how to help mothers "achieve [their] individual breastfeeding goals." They even held sessions to "help prepare candidates for the examination offered by the International Board of Lactation Consultant Examiners." !

I have little doubt that these consultants are trying to do some-thing that they consider important and worthwhile. It is possible that individually and over the short term mothers and children may benefit from their paid advice. In only a few years, however, this development shows a full-circle paradigm shift from:

1. breast-feeding being in the province of mothers and grandmoth-ers, to

2. it being in the province of manufacturers and doctors (and changed into a "dosage" form), to

3. it being de-technologized by mothers, to

4. it starting to be re-technologized again, this time apparently by nurses who only want to help it be performed better, using systemic behavioral approaches.

Drift

If you fund the creation of many new projects, you are in a unique position to observe trends and commonalities among them. Often social trends and tendencies which are not observable in individual cases, or which seem only individual characteristics, arrange themselves into a pattern when viewed over a larger sample. This is the case with what I have called a "drift" to professionalism. The nurses didn't decide to shape their mission to help mothers breast-feed better in a cultural vacuum. They didn't come up with concepts like goals, consultant practice, and qualifying examinations as the best way to pursue their campaign on their own. Their approach almost certainly reflected unconscious assumptions of the general culture about how human helping should be pursued.

This phenomenon is easily observable in proposals submitted to our Council. Many of these approach other ordinary functions of life such as becoming part of one's community in the same way that the nurses approach breast-feeding. Its influence over time is observable in the evolution of many individual projects that are funded by us or others. One citizen advocacy office, for example, began to set itself up with sheafs of forms and procedures for intake, reporting, and other practices borrowed from typical human service agencies. Another tried to communicate with advocates by memo rather than meeting them at a diner for coffee. A family support program invented a "family stress index" through which the amount of stress on a family determined fiscal support. An imaginative agency started by referring to those it existed to support as "members" and pioneered ways of recruiting neighborhood bank clerks, landlords, and others to help people with disabilities. Eventually it came to have social workers see "clients" in their offices instead, to the point that a campaign to build more offices had to be launched. In supported work, universities started promoting the necessity of degree programs for job coaches, thus starting down a road in which persons doing such work would be professionals unconnected to the interpersonal culture of the work site.

The fact that the trend toward professionalism can be seen in such diverse settings indicates, one might say, evidence of a current in the river between world views. While many boats may set out for the far shore, a number slowly and without noticing it begin to drift back, still believing they are on their way to a destination different from the place where they set out.

Understanding this tendency toward drift is important. It means that one must seriously recognize the role of professionalism as an unconscious belief system in modern society. Such professionalism, we can see, always tends to displace ordinary community practices. The task of people trying to do this work, then, is not only to rediscover community, but to find ways to counter the tendency to drift towards professionalization. To do otherwise is like setting to sea without consulting the winds and currents. One is likely only to lose one's way.

Fortunately, a variety of approaches have been found which seem to counter drift well. The first of these is being sure that individual settings trying to live out a different world view do not attempt to pursue their work in isolation. In any of the different areas we have tried, it has proven to be essential to help settings develop informal networks which assist them to maintain a group vision in the face of daily misunderstanding from their immediate human service surroundings. Second, the existence of some type of appropriate project-review mechanism seems quite important. Appropriate is a key word, for the review or evaluation must itself be based on an understanding of the new world view. Such an instrument as the Citizen Advocacy Program Evaluation not only detects early signs of drift and brings them to attention when they are easier for projects to correct, but serves as a unifying process for a network maintaining shared values.

Third, the availability of educational and leadership development programs through efforts such as the Commonwealth Institute seems important to help creators of new settings to reflect upon and learn more about the vision they are pursuing as it evolves. Fourth, thinking through funding approaches that will minimize pressure for professionalization by the funder is a consideration. As mentioned earlier, it is sometimes important to structure an intermediary between small informal settings and large bureaucracies like government if the former are not to be overburdened with procedures necessary to do business with the funding source. Finally, there is the ultimate reality that if all else fails, some projects caught inextricably in drift must be de-funded. If you want to garden, as I note in the appendix, you have to be ready to weed.

Thinking of Community as a Perfect and Easily Attained Solution

There are great dangers, as noted in the previous chapter, in romanticizing the idea of community. As the popularity of community approaches grows in the field, this will be an increasingly worrisome hazard. There is every possibility for "community" to become yet another fad in human services to be oversold, fail, and quickly fade.

There is already evidence of projects in various places which assume that by merely rejecting paid human services and injecting people into a community — any community, in any way — that their work is done. Dropping a group of people with disabilities into a local garden club, or the neighborhood barber shop, or assigning them to a potential advocate and just leaving, is guaranteed to fail. In fact, efforts of this kind are exactly what we used to see in deinstitutionalization, in which removing people from a physical institution was seen as enough, without thought or work to arrange community support. This was labeled "dumping" in the deinstitutionalization movement, and deserves the same name here. Dropping seeds on the ground without bothering to till the soil, thinking that things will magically grow without work, is not gardening in either the botanical or the social sphere. Community is not a Garden of Eden; it is merely a garden. Nurturing either gardens or societies to their fullest health and potential are crafts worthy of careful study and energetic and accurate work.

Falling Prey to a Culture of Anti-Professionalism

Despite the awareness of the dangers of professionalism that workers for a community approach must have, this is not a movement merely against professionalism. To understand it as such is both inaccurate and unbalanced. Professionalism is not "bad" and community "good." To conceive of it this way is to imitate Luddites wrecking looms, or Red Guards sending the intelligentsia out to the fields to plant rice with the peasants. Such an approach glorifies folk wisdom rather than understanding its realistic contributions.

Professionalism does have its purposes in human services. There are great benefits offered by many kinds of professions which are essential for the welfare of people with developmental disabilities. Medicine, psychology, physical therapy, speech therapy, and all of their professional cousins have highly important roles to play. The question is one of balance in approach. Because our society is so completely out of balance on the professionalistic side at the moment, one could easily be tempted to fall into the belief that professionalism must be rejected in its entirety. This would be a serious overreaction and a grave error.

Nothing in what I have said should be interpreted as scapegoating professionals. Professionals, too, suffer from the long-term negative effects of the professionalization of fields, even when that process has been most successful. Dissatisfaction of doctors with medicine, for example, is now extremely high. A recent Gallup survey for the American Medical Association found that almost 40 percent of doctors interviewed said they definitely or probably would not enter medical school again if they had the choice to make over, based upon what they now knew about medicine as a career (Altman, 1990). While this is probably due to a number of factors, such as an increased regulatory environment, influence of insurance, and larger changes in society, overprofessionalization has probably made a key contribution to it, and unhappy practitioners and their patients are now paying the price.

Being Drafted into Serving Political Ends.

Social policy exists in a political world. One therefore is not realistic if one fails to understand that policy directions of any type can be drafted into serving political ends unrelated to their original intent. During the Nixon administration, for instance, then Assistant Labor Secretary Daniel Moynihan strongly sought an anti-poverty policy that would favor a guaranteed annual income. The idea of giving cash directly to families, eliminating the "middleman," is of course precisely what I have spoken about earlier in current efforts the Council is pursuing for families with children with disabilities.

As Nicholas Lemann (1989) explains in an analysis of this period, however, this "elimination of the middleman" turned out to be an act with considerable political potential. While at the beginning of the War on Poverty social workers were middle-class whites, he explains, after five years:

> "the world of government workers had ... become the economic basis of the black middle class: it was probably the locus in government of the kind of left-liberals that Moynihan and Nixon considered a threat to the stability of the country. If the government simply gave poor people money — adopted an income strategy instead of a services strategy, as Moynihan put it to Nixon — this would end the period of legitimizing, empowering, and enriching social activists, community organizers, civil rights leaders, and the like. The social workers could hardly complain, because even as the government was cutting them out of the action, it would be passing the most sweeping anti-poverty program in history. They would be neutralized as a moral and political force.
>
> To Nixon this was an attractive notion. He, too, disliked social workers. At the meeting where Moynihan proposed the Family Assistance Plan, when Moynihan said it would eliminate tens of thousands of social workers from the federal payroll, Nixon's eyes lit up." (p.66)

In truth, as Berger and Neuhaus point out, a public policy which recognizes the importance of mediating structures is something which really has no political orientation. They thought it encouraging, in fact, to find it simultaneously accepted and condemned by members of both the political left and right. It could, if one was not careful (and possibly even if one was) be used by either side for the less than high purposes ascribed to Nixon.

One state which I follow, for instance, enthusiastically seized upon some of the ideas proposed by McKnight to start a new project. In this project, they proposed that a position for a community "bridgebuilder" to make connections between people with disabilities and communities be added to the state civil service system. As that person pursued his or her work, a parallel "cost/benefit" evaluation was to be performed to establish how much government money was saved as paid services were replaced by unpaid supports. This venture, taking place as it did at the time of the Reagan administration, in which a thin veneer of "volunteerism" was used to hide a campaign to cut benefits to people with disabilities, seemed frightening in its potential for being recruited to such ends. For the new conception in developmental disabilities to be recruited as yet another method to abandon the poor would be a sad end indeed.

Unrealistic Time Perspectives

One of the eternal fictions afflicting social program development is that suitable programs can be quickly developed and implemented to solve social problems. It used to be believed that you could fund the erection of an institution of one kind or another once and the problem would be taken care of; now we think the same of social programs that use fewer or even no bricks. That this never turns out to be true does not seem to have deterred in the slightest our propensity for believing that it can be done. Work on social concerns always takes a great deal more time and work than most planners expect. This hazard is just as likely to be encountered in the very different kinds of social programs that we have been describing as part of a new conceptual and social revolution as in any conventional program.

These new programs, of course, have an additional difference. Rather than setting up a professionally provided service, they act by nurturing the natural positive tendencies inherent in human communities. Through asking people on an individual basis to care for each other, they attempt to stimulate the development of bonds of reciprocal relationships which form the basis of a healthy society. Rather than injecting or teaching a practice that is different from the way that people normally live, they encourage communities to do what they have always had the capacity to do, and did more strongly before these natural functions began to be displaced. In this they could be said to be merely catalyzing a tendency that exists innately, ready to be called forth.[5]

This catalyzing image has great relevance for the question of funding. To use the term *catalyst* means that you believe that there is some kind of process which can be initiated or accelerated through the introduction of a catalytic agent which itself remains mostly unchanged. In a chemical reaction, if I understand it rightly, a reaction between two substances can take place when a small amount of a third substance is introduced. After that, the reaction should proceed of itself.

The question in catalyzing inherent but latent social tendencies thus seems to me to be: how much catalyst do you need, and for how long? My own hypothesis is that the process of inclusion might well become a natural habit in associational groups if we can just help that habit to become ingrained. To do this, a certain momentum must be established, a certain "ripple effect" started. How long does it take for the necessary momentum to be established? We do not yet know this for sure. It certainly takes more than a year or two. Our organization usually limits funding to three years. This may well be enough; one recalls Saul Alinsky's original belief that you should permit community organizers to work in neighborhoods for only three years. The proof of whether you have accomplished anything, he said, came only after you were gone. From our own experience with this type of work, I am not convinced that three years of funding is frequently enough. Overcoming years of learning that the lives of people with disabilities should be solely in the hands of those professionally qualified will not be easy. Looking for quick results may doom these efforts to failure. Like the question of setting the level of funding neither too high nor too low to properly nurture projects, the duration of support and of effort must be similarly calculated. At this point, underestimating the time that this kind of work will need to be sustained in order to have an impact will remain a significant hazard in a culture intent on speedy results.

Understanding the Life-Cycle of Social Movements

"We applaud the promoters of change, and are horrified with the results of their efforts.."
— David Rothman

"At the beginning of every community," writes Jean Vanier of L'Arche,

"there is a founder who gives it spirit and vision and takes on final responsibility. But as the community takes root, it has to establish a charter which defines its fundamental goals and spirit, and a constitution which specifies how it is governed... A community also needs some external authority which will prevent those who carry responsibility in the future from deviating from the spirit and becoming tyrants who create their own project.

> This guarantor is necessary because human beings are weak and fallible
> and the forces of evil outside and even within a community are such
> that, if there is no external authority, the community will sooner or later
> decline." (1979, p.71)

Vanier's comprehension of the eternal risk of decline for settings is doubtless one reason behind the L'Arche movement's continuing success. I am not sure whether the external authority that he prescribes, however, is an essential safeguard over the dissolution and perversion of a community's original impulse. While this works well for L'Arche, and while the Pennsylvania Council currently serves this ultimate role for our funded projects, it may not be completely compatible with a community approach over the long term.

The founders of the United States faced this question in coming up with the design of a self-balancing system of powers in their new government which would be independent of external authority. The nation's founders knew from their broad experience and their deep knowledge of history that social movements and settings seem to have limited life spans. This is the most important thing that Vanier says above. Without careful thought and well-designed ways of safeguarding the integrity of communities, of whatever type, they tend to go wrong eventually. This "eventually" is, in social welfare settings, often a very brief period of time, frequently only a few years. As Sarason documented in *The Creation of Settings and the Future Societies*, the processes of setting creation and dissolution follow a number of predictable dynamics which can be planned for and countered, but which must be ultimately endured and experienced.

The new conceptual approach which I have been describing in these pages is still in its infancy. As such, most of its early and anomalous settings are in the stage of their existence in which the original visionary founders are still at their centers. As these settings mature and reach later stages of the developmental process, it will become an increasing challenge to maintain their integrity and original vision. As they evolve, they will have increasing questions to ask, questions which are starting to be asked now. What is "life-sharing," precisely, and what is it not? What is "citizen participation?" How does one write a charter of belief and practice for work in such areas, without ossifying the principles which give them life? If one cannot prevent the dissolution and decay of settings, how can one counter the natural dynamics of decay to stave off the inevitable as long as possible? As the life of these early settings proceeds, those whose responsibility it is to guide, nurture, and support them will have to become increasingly knowledgeable about the dynamics of organizational growth, and how to help settings which have run onto one or another of the many reefs that are the obstacles to any growth process.

This is true for the larger conceptual movement as well. How does one help it toward the full expression of the idea which it is bringing into the world, without losing it prematurely or preserving it only through institutionalization? An increasingly evolving "charter" is needed here as well. This book's intent is to make a beginning contribution toward that need, one which will need to be continually evolved and refined as the work proceeds.

Endnotes

1. This, as pointed out by Foucault (1973), had to do with the historical association of mental disorder with leprosy.

2. It is probable that you could even find such pavilions on the same institutional grounds in New York State upon which the institutional group homes mentioned in Chapter Five are being erected. Both, of course, show the same process of professionalization and formalization of an idea having to do with "community," a century apart in time.

3. As is well known, this view was consciously promoted in third world countries by American manufacturers of infant formulae, resulting in malnutrition and probably in resultant mental retardation because mothers watered it down to be able to afford it. It is a particularly good example, also, of the clinicalization of ordinary functions for economic ends.

4. It would, of course, be simplistic to attribute this change entirely to the League, without reference to the emergence of back-to-nature and health movements of the sixties and seventies to which it is related. But the League is most importantly one example of the emergence of the self-help movement in the United States. Alcoholics Anonymous is an even more well-known example of the literally thousands of self-help groups that have arisen in areas considered the province of medical and other professional fields. The emergence of this movement as a phenomenon, Sarason points out, cannot be understood without an awareness of widespread grass-roots dissatisfaction with professionalism (1990).

5. Innate negative and destructive social tendencies are just as possible to elicit, of course.

CHAPTER 12
Relevance and Conclusion

On New Year's Day 1989, I awoke in the home of friends in their little neighborhood a few blocks behind the Capitol in Washington, D.C. It was a beautiful, clear day; we had played music late into the night, and the children were not yet stirring. I picked up a copy of the *Washington Post* at the corner store, and sat down with a cup of tea in the silent house to look at the first day's news. The featured guest editorial had this headline: *"America the Anxious,"* it said; *"Uncertain, Fretful, We're Dithering Into 1989."* The editorialist, named David Osborne, summed up the mood of the country on the dawn of the new year like this:

> "As we enter the last year of the 1980s, we are a society holding its collective breath. We are taking no risks, embracing no heroes, falling in love with no sports teams or celebrities or rock stars. We know we have serious problems. We know we have been profligate. We know we are no longer number one. But we do not know when, or in what form, the other shoe will drop. Nor do we know what to do to minimize the pain. All we can do is wait, anxiously."

These are surely significant words, I thought. But there are always those who believe that the outlook is troubled. What was more significant here was that the *Post*, one of the nation's most influential newspapers, chose to print it, and on this day. But in this city, the nation's nexus for the institutions and social programs of our society, there was undeniable evidence that all was not well. When the architects of laws and social programs went home at night, they had to think about the vast drug epidemic that had taken over their city. They saw the fruits of random violence daily on the evening news; the young black men mowed down in drug killings every night, the little children shot dead in crossfire by automatic weapons as they played on their front steps, the emergency room doctors reporting floods of wounds of types that had not been seen since M.A.S.H. units in Vietnam.

Next to the Osborne editorial was another one by the Assistant Police Chief of the District commenting on the drug crisis. He, a policeman, was pointing out that the traditional reliance on police activity was proving completely insufficient to contain either drugs or drug-related crime. It simply was not working. How reminiscent of our discovery about the failure of regulations to control abuse in human service programs, I thought to myself! You could see again that these trends in society were always linked. Yet in the face of this discovery the President had just appointed a "Drug Czar" to fight a "war on drugs." Clearly a mere agency director, or even a cabinet officer, would not suffice anymore. If we required a war, then we needed a general — or even better, a czar. And so the media would label him as such, and the label would stick.

The phenomenon of AIDS had recently brought a new term into common language: "opportunistic infection." This term represented the finding that, with the failure of immune resistance that AIDS represented, unusual infections of all sorts moved in. Medicine could not fight this particular syndrome traditionally, germ-by-germ, except in a symptomatic, retreating action. The very ability of the body to resist infection by agents commonly in the environment had collapsed. Was not the drug "infection" a similar phenomenon on the level of the social organism? Why did so many people suddenly want to be stoned all of the time?[1]

As we started the new year the Drug Czar, however, was not apparently thinking about things in this way. How do you have a war if there is nothing to fight but one's own lack of strength to resist an invader? So we could see now a program emerging which put even greater emphasis on police enforcement, called for massive expansion of prison capacity, and pointed a warning finger and an implied threat of military action at the South American countries where the evil infectious agents grew from plants in the ground. What would people think of an AIDS doctor who launched a "war on germs" to protect people from the pneumonia that many people with AIDS die of? Reflecting on all of this, it seems to suggest some social version of psychological projection: the more one feels one's internal ability to cope slipping, the more firmly one fixes the problems securely "out there" in order to maintain psychological equilibrium. At the furthest extreme of such projection is paranoia. Meanwhile, of course, the intrapsychic problems do not go away. "The Russians are putting thoughts into my head!" people years ago at the state mental hospital had complained. That was how these poor struggling people had tried to survive with their suffering, at great cost. Is our public policy perspective on the all-too-real drug crisis so very much different, I wonder?

So, for a time, we will have more prisons, more mandatory sentences to incarcerate and isolate this "bad seed" in society against which we must wage war to save ourselves. We shall have more "shock" boot camps to "straighten out" children, more prisons to bring employment to rural areas. We shall live by incarceration.

I remembered that only seven years ago and six blocks away from where I sat that New Year's morning, John McKnight had testified on the subject of families to a congressional subcommittee. In his remarks he predicted the present drug crisis in the ghettos, then yet to emerge.

He told the congressmen that if public policies did not begin to support the life of poor families, if it did not begin to support their ability to build an economy in the neighborhoods where they tried to survive, that the drug economy would take over. Not many years later, his words have come true. Apparently there are not so many young black men as there were in these Washington neighborhoods when McKnight was speaking. So many are in prison; so many are dead. Ten months later, as I write these lines, the fire and ambulance sirens split the Harrisburg night. Inmates in the massively overcrowded prison across the river have rioted, burning much of that institution down, with themselves inside it. "We are caged up here like animals," inmates cried to reporters from their locked, burning building. "They should drop a bomb on it and sterilize the whole thing," a neighbor of the prison told newsmen.

Why should I, as a person concerned with the welfare of people with disabilities, be concerned about prisoners, and people who abuse drugs, and "wars on drugs?" Of course, I am first concerned because these are all human beings, too. But I also remember from my history what one previous "evil seed of society" was, one other group that was supposed to be responsible for all of the crime and social problems we were then experiencing. They were people with mental retardation. We built a vast gulag of institutions to incarcerate them, too. But our problems didn't go away as they were sent away. I also remember from my history of the Holocaust that the Nazis started their killing with prisoners, and mental patients, and people with mental retardation. What is happening now to people who abuse drugs, as Jerry Miller reminds us, could happen to people with disabilities again. Once a society starts needing to see people as less than human, as devoid of worth, as "useless eaters" to use the Nazi term, it is a habit that tends to grow. And I remember that all vulnerable people, all of us vulnerable people, are inextricably linked in this world.

These are serious and disturbing thoughts, and it is not pleasant to think about them. I have preferred in my work and in this book to concentrate on the brighter possibilities for creation and action that are open to us. But we cannot ignore the historical backdrop against which these positive actions are taking place and which give them particular urgency. The increasing dysfunctionality seen in the community service system for people with disabilities, discussed in Chapter 5, is only a manifestation of this larger historical process as reflected in our field. We seem to be observing a social process in which, in Sarason's words, forces of the modern world have "weakened the bonds that keep people together" in a society. We are observing a culture, according to Wolfensberger, in which "every social glue is coming unstuck." Wolfensberger, who grew up in Germany during World War II and survived the bombings, remembers clearly what it was like when a society literally stopped working; when there were no policemen, no hospitals, no firemen, no mail delivered. When he says it can happen here, it is because he has seen what most Americans today cannot even imagine. But if the bonds between citizens weaken beyond a certain point, it is predictable that the institutions of society will eventually cease to operate too.

There are many who, like Wolfensberger, see terminal dissolution in these developments; whose vision seems apocalyptic. They may, of course, be right. But it seems more likely to me that what we are living through is a traumatic historical transition. We may be seeing the beginnings of a kind of repair of the excesses of the industrial revolution; professionalism and formal systems, having proceeded to their furthest, most unbalanced extent, may now be falling to pieces, to be succeeded by a movement toward "regluing" the culture together in a new way. It may be just a particularly extreme swing of the historical pendulum. If this is so, then the little projects that I have talked about in this book may have larger significance as initial attempts to put the world back together again for a new phase of historical evolution in a somewhat corrected direction.

I began this book with the metaphor of sea change, and obviously I am of the suspicion that this difficult time has meaning as a passage to a different historical phase. It should be admitted, however, that in a sea passage there is no guarantee that one's ship will actually reach the far shore. Ships sink; civilizations perish. Whole worlds do, according to Stephen Hawking. One may embark upon the sea, tacking back and forth against the winds in one's progression, but any one tack, taken to its furthest extent, will lead one ultimately onto the rocks. At a critical historical moment like this one, there is enormous momentum pushing us onward, even though the danger of a continued course on this one extended reach is increasingly apparent. Can it be turned in time? It is a question of how far one has gone in one direction, and how much room there is left to turn. Is there enough time left to save the rain forests, or reverse the greenhouse effect, to save the environment of the planet? It is the same problem.

In a philosophical sense, one might say that this change in direction has to do with failure of the mechanistic view of the world based upon Descartes and Newton which has characterized western man's recent thought. In commenting on the crisis in the field of medicine parallel to the crisis in the disability field, Fritjof Capra writes that this is "inextricably linked to a much larger social and cultural crisis" observable in energy, pollution, unemployment, crime, and other areas. He goes on:

> "All of these can be seen as different aspects of one and the same crisis, which derives from the fact that we are trying to apply the concepts of an outdated world view — the mechanistic world view of Cartesian-Newtonian science — to a reality that can no longer be understood in terms of these concepts. We live today in a globally interconnected world, in which biological, psychological, social, and environmental phenomena are all interdependent. To devise this world appropriately we need an ecological perspective, which the Cartesian world view doesn't offer." (1982, pp. viii - ix)

This new perspective, Capra says, is likely to proceed from current theoretical changes in modern physics, the kind of changes, incidentally, that Thomas Kuhn examined in his book cited in Chapter 6. "The conceptual revolution in modern physics," Capra continues later, "foreshadows an imminent revolution in all the sciences and a profound transformation in our world view and values."

Using Capra's conception, we might think of the Cartesian world view, in which nature is seen as a grand machine, as having proceeded in a "wave" through theoretical and applied fields. It was first applied in physics. Eventually it affected the conceptions of physiology and medicine, leaving astonishing advances but also a certain depersonalization in its wake. From medicine, it was passed along such allied fields as psychology, occupational therapy, and other fields related to disability. From these, they became expressed and embodied in the physical and social architecture of our helping institutions and programs. From a philosophical point of view, it would have been theoretically possible to predict that a Cartesian conception of the world would result in the eventual conceptualization of mental retardation and related disabilities as "things" to be repaired by the caring machinery of social institutions. In terms of ideas, it is consistent.

It is not so neat as all of this, of course. No evolutionary process can be contained in such a simplistic theoretical package. Nonetheless, if it is useful to consider this stance for a moment, then we might look at the conceptual revolution in modern physics that Capra refers to. The Cartesian view of the universe has long been abandoned in this advanced theoretical world. One hears instead of Heisenberg, and Hawking, and of the incredibly complex relativity of the phenomena of the universe. No modern physicist thinks of the universe as a grand machine anymore. That is a very old paradigm indeed.

In the disabilities field, the new wave embodying this very different world view, coming toward us from the rarefied theoretical worlds of atomic structure and astronomy and their cousins, has not fully reached us yet. We can see its effects in medicine, especially since the concept of psychosomatic medicine began to counter the prevailing view of bodies as merely complicated machines. It was upon the work of this emerging concept that my father spent his professional life. Now, in the generation of the son, the waves are lapping at the threshold of the disability field and of social institutions. The orderly classification of nineteenth-century institutional inmates and the symmetrical architecture of its edifices were the Cartesian view of the universe reflected unconsciously in that approach to caring. As we have seen, the apparently "different" community service system of today really evolved from that same view of the world. The messy and relativistic world of real community which this book examines is the currently emerging analogy in the developmental disabilities field to the conceptual revolution in physics. It is not enough to say that these two conceptual revolutions are linked; it is the same conceptual revolution, working its slow way through human consciousness and activity.

But we are in a uniquely advanced position in this field, too, because of the presence of people with disabilities. This presence may help to guide us back to considering the question, "What are people *for*, anyway?" Are people valuable only because they can produce, run machines, command the energies of other men and women, build institutions and systems? If so, then according to the apparent values of our culture, people with severe disabilities should not be "worth" anything. It is thus significant and counter to this impression to see the emergence of highly visible and valued roles for such persons in recent books, film, and even television.[2] The rediscovery of Ashley Montagu's *The Elephant Man* in a modern film version, the television biography of "Bill," an individual with mental retardation played by Mickey Rooney, the addition of an actor playing a person with mental retardation to the bright, career-oriented "yuppie" cast of the television series "L.A. Law," and the presence of an actor with Down syndrome in the situation-comedy family of "Life Goes On" — all these suddenly bring to visibility in the media individuals whose life stories seem to stand in stark contrast to the usual objects of our admiration. These are no glamorous billionaires — they are all relatively poor. They probably can't even do fractions. Yet their stories have become quite popular. Why?

This question makes me think of the 1989 film *Rainman*, which is about a person with autism (Dustin Hoffman) and his "normal" brother, played by Tom Cruise. Cruise is aggressive, young and flashy, pursuing his car-importing business with charming dishonesty and bravado. He is living beyond his means and is tight for cash. The opening scenes of the film show expensive sports cars being swung out of the hold of a ship to the dock. One could say that these extravagantly expensive items of consumer technology represent Cruise's view of what is important in life; his values, if you will. Through the death of his wealthy father, Cruise discovers that he has an unknown brother, Raymond, who lives in a private institution. The institution has been left all of the money. Cruise sets out to kidnap Raymond to barter his ransom for his inheritance, and they set off across the country back to Cruises's Los Angeles.

All this is mere background for their journey across the country; it is the journey the film is about. Raymond will not fly. He will not even ride in a car on interstate highways. He refuses to go out when it is raining. The two cross the country in the old way, in an antique car, on the old two-lane roads. Cruise is completely frustrated at the wasted time; his brother is autistically constant and unmovable. But the journey takes a very long time and gradually, a bit at a time, Cruise begins to slow down, something you can see that he has never done before. He begins to truly love his brother, to want to take him home to live with him. Ultimately, the money becomes less important — what he wants is his brother.

Novels and films are about a change, a transformation of a protagonist through events. From this perspective, it is Cruise who is the protagonist of *Rainman*, for it is he who is transformed; Raymond remains pretty much the same. Cruise's life, however, will never be the same. The two brothers' journey across the country could, indeed, serve as a metaphor for the process of social transformation we have been talking about. Forced away from the fastest, quickest, most-efficient ways of getting from here to there, Cruise is shackled to the softening and gentling presence of someone who will not go fast, will not be efficient, will not even be fixed or cured by all the technology that the culture can muster. Yet Raymond's quiet presence eventually leads Cruise to a re-evaluation of his direction. It is not impossible that the presence of people with severe disabilities may, at this particular point in time, be serving a similar role in our larger culture, highly "inconvenient" but perhaps not without importance in other, more subtle ways.

What is it that Edouard Seguin, one of the great founders of the mental retardation field, said just a little over a century ago?

> "God has scattered among us...rare as the possessors of genius...[people with mental retardation, with blindness, with deafness,] in order to bind the rich to the needy, the talented to the incapable, all men to each other, by a tie of indissolvable solidarity."

"To bind all men to each other." It is just that, we are discovering, that we are lacking in the world. That is what community is about, the bonds between individuals. Perhaps that is why people in the communities of L'Arche and Camphill see people with disabilities not so much as individuals to be served, but as people whose presence is necessary to help them together to attain community, a community which has special meaning for them. Perhaps this is, as Vanier and Wolfensberger say, partly due to the affectivity of many people with mental retardation, who, lacking the ability for the cognitive concerns which so preoccupy our culture, tend to live lives more focused upon personal relationships. Perhaps, as McKnight thinks, it is the very needs which people with disabilities bring to communities which call forth collectivities of people to *do* something. Families and communities, as I have discussed, no longer have much of anything to do; all of their functions have been commodified. If there is one thing that is known about communities, it is that they must have something to *do*, some work larger than themselves to bring them together. Caring for my elderly grandmother was, I recall, a great labor for my mother and aunts and uncles, but there are cousins I no longer see since grandma died and we don't have to get together to fix her roof. Her need is not there to bring us together anymore. The facts that the Amish near me have incredibly strong families and communities and that they do all of the demanding work on their farms by hand, without modern power equipment, are not unrelated, as well. In Amish life you still need families, or you literally cannot survive. They work hard to keep it that way.

In calling community together a number of conditions may be necessary. It is necessary to have work which community must exist to perform. It may even be necessary, under current conditions, to have vulnerable people who may serve in some ways as "seeds" to mobilize community formation and maintenance. I am not sure, however, that these things are enough. In each successful community that I have seen, there is another element as well.

Living together is dauntingly hard work. When you get a group of people together, the irritation of their daily friction against one another tends to act as a centrifugal force, pushing people further and further from each other. Gradually, bonds become so attenuated and individual emotional territoriality so extreme that the community collapses. My generation lived through this social process in the commune movement of the seventies. Thousands of communes, formal and informal, were founded out of the great hunger for community experience rising up in so many of us. In only a few years

unavoidable, natural shrinking-down of existence, made both bearable and untreatable because not realizable — not directly realizable. How could one know that one had shrunk, if one's frame of reference had itself shrunk? One had to be reminded of the great world one had "forgotten" — and then, only then, could one expand and be cured."
— Oliver Sacks

"For the handicapped person who had felt abandoned, there is only one reality that will bring him back to life: an authentic, tender and faithful relationship. He must discover that he is loved and important to someone. Only then will his confusion turn into peace. And to love is not to do something for someone; it is to be with him. It is to rejoice in his presence; it is to give him confidence in the value of his being."
— Jean Vanier

Once, when I was young, I met a man who had been in a federal prison, and he told me a story about a Christmas day that he had many years before. As I am writing this it is Christmas Day today, and I am thinking about what he told me.

He was living, he said, in a dark cellblock four stories below ground. There were thirty-two cells in the block, but they had been abandoned from use except for him and one other person who were there under special guard. Once a day they were allowed out of their cell for one hour. During this hour they could sometimes speak with some other men through a crack in a wall. Once a week their occupation was to clean all thirty-two unused toilets.

He had been living underground like this for many months, not seeing the light of day or knowing for certain whether it was day or night, when Christmas arrived. And on this day he received some good news. He had written to his senator and other people some months before in an attempt to be allowed to attend Christmas Mass. The good news he had waited for, not knowing whether he would even receive a response at all, was that he could go. He was fastened into handcuffs and leg-chains (even though this was the heart of a maximum security prison) and shuffled under close guard up the five flights of stairs to the prison chapel. He attended Mass, received Communion, and started back down to "the hole." As he went around a corner of the metal staircase he saw a small window.

Mild winter sunlight — the first he had seen that year — was streaming in the small aperture in the thick wall. He slowed as he was being taken past to look out.

He looked out for a brief moment on a deserted winter scene. There was the river, running past, and the fields, and the woods off in the distance. But his attention was suddenly caught by two off-duty soldiers assigned to the prison, far from their homes, shooting baskets in the parking lot on this mild Christmas Day at about eleven o'clock in the morning. He had just time to see the two men leaping in the air for a minute, and then the guard tugged him away and back down to his underground cell.

Life had been miserable but tolerable to that point, he told me. He was unhappy but mostly dead inside. He had tolerated the months in the hole up until then, and had six more months to go. Those next six months, he told me, were incredible anguish. He paced, he created trouble; he could not bear it. The glance out the window at free men had made his own incarceration impossible to bear. The one moment at the dusty window had ripped the scar tissue from his buried and unbearable human feelings.

Coming back to life can be an extremely painful experience, as anyone who has successfully come back to encountering life from the retreat of a mental disorder can readily attest. People reach for growth and freedom as a plant stored in a basement will reach toward a cobwebbed high cellar window. But for us the situation is an ambivalent one. For we can live in the basement only so long as we never look out of the window.

For anyone who feels the force of social rejection, an adaptation must be made to ongoing pain. Continuing to feel such pain acutely is not an option that the design of the body, thankfully, permits. Adaptation is usually made.

Most people with disabilities and their parents start out naturally "reaching out" for help, assistance, and reassurance. The rejection with which this "asking" is frequently greeted is often so repeatedly disheartening they stop asking altogether. Such persons reach a "steady state" of living with rejection, dulling their feeling life and dimming their expectations in ways necessary to adapt to living in the sub-ground dwelling which seems their lot. All of us, of course, do this in some way in our lives. People who have been severely rejected frequently become so encapsulated in this steady state that they become almost unreachable, rejecting pre-emptively anyone who approaches with the promise of something better.

An "asker," like a citizen advocacy coordinator, "ups the ante" in these situations by proposing new, higher expectations for the devalued person's life. It is such an "asker's" intent, by doing so, to "crack the steady state" in which the individual has become bound. By entering such a person's life and doing this, and by asking new people to become involved with the encapsulated person, he or she opens up terrible new possibilities for acute rejection and pain. *It is the asker's deepest ethical responsibility to absorb any new rejection on behalf of the handicapped person.* This means that any new rejection which is risked by reaching out is risked by the "asker" alone and that any new rejection which is precipitated is felt by the "asker" alone. The asker might go out day after day representing the person with a disability and be rejected nine times before the tenth accepts and an introduction is actually made. This rejection (and rejection always feels bad, even if you are only the "agent" of the person being rejected) is never passed on to the person involved.

Once a "match" is made, the door is opened to healing in the way that Vanier, in the quote at the start of this section, points out. An actual mitigation of the rejection felt by the person with a disability can occur, to some degree, although this is far from saying that one's essential existential wounds can be fully healed by another. One has a faithful and loving relationship, and through that one relationship the door is almost always opened to others. That one relationship has "cracked the steady state."

And even if rejection is not reduced significantly, such a relationship can leaven or moderate the experience of it. My father-in-law died two weeks ago after years of sickness and months of great pain and fear and despair. Yet he died at home in his own bed surrounded by his wife and all seven children, who had flown in from all over the country to be with him. Being surrounded by his family did not probably objectively reduce his pain or his fear of dying. Yet it did moderate the experience in important ways in providing a context for the suffering and the passing out of this life to take place. One has only to imagine what his dying would have been like alone in a cold nursing home to capture the essential difference brought in by the sharing of anguish in the social and religious context of meaning.

Finally, and most importantly, this sharing of the experience of rejection by others around the rejected person frequently makes important changes in the "helping" person's entire world view. This process brings the experience not only into his or her life, but re-embeds it through a thousand tiny channels into the life of the larger society. It is the kind of work the "asker" does that resonates with William James's statement about working in "the cracks of the world" rather than upon "big and important" things. For when one wonders how the larger social attitude toward people with disabilities has been and can continue to be changed, one focuses not necessarily on new laws or programs or regulations (as important a role as they may have to play in their proper place) but upon the thousands of relationships which exist and may continue, if we work rightly, to form in the culture. Through the sharing of this experience streaming softly through a thousand cracks, the cumulative effect of tiny capillary action may move the stones themselves.

Thus the difficult work of the "asker" continues, always in hidden and unglamorous ways, trying to find that "tender and faithful relationship" that must, somewhere, exist for the person he or she is thinking about. In this process the asker must be prepared to face rejection, and to protect the rejected person until the risk — and it always, no matter how carefully the stage is set remains a risk, seems proper to take. Until that relationship is potentially waiting on the other side, until the asker's hand is on the prison-door key and the key is sliding into the lock, he or she takes care to keep some cardboard over that small window. Once the door is open, the introduction is made and the asker fades away on some pretext, to hold his or her breath and hope. Then the asker starts asking for someone new.

Society

> "There are some thoughts that a man thinks, and there are others that a God puts into his heart."
>
> — Attributed in mythology
> to the Goddess Athena

Not long ago we had a meeting of all ten of the little organizations who are being funded under our "citizen participation" grants. They were a lovely group: all just regular folks, not "advocates," or professionals, who knew and loved their towns. A number of them were people with disabilities.

Being summoned to a meeting in Harrisburg was probably a big event for many of these folks. This was their funder; the Governor's Council. Should they dress for a business meeting? Should they be prepared to quote outcome statistics? They probably wondered. But we didn't seem interested in statistics. We asked them to talk about what they were doing. As they talked, Beth Mount, our facilitator for the day, made drawings in colored magic markers of what each project was doing on newsprint on the wall.

Frank and Gene, with the oldest and most successful project, set the tone. Frank, a retired businessman, serves as the life-long "community organizer" of the town Sharon Gretz described in Chapter Two. When somebody first said the town's name, Frank chimed in automatically "the garden spot of America." He did it several times. You could see that it was a very old joke with him that he used with people. I was there once, and what I know is what Frank knows: there are not really many gardens in his town. It is a little factory town where the factory is pretty much closed down. Unemployment got so high that Frank started a food bank to feed hundreds of his neighbors four years ago. "I was wondering what to do with my life next, then," Frank had related, showing me the basement food storage. "I was praying for God to show me what to do. Then I was down in my basement, one day, and all of a sudden a great heat came over me like a rush. My skin was like it was burning, and I started to tremble. Then I knew all of a sudden in my heart what I had to do. The plant was phasing down, and there were going to be a lot of people hungry. I had to start a food bank. I had to feed those people."

Frank was the person that Sharon was automatically sent to by the mayor when she got our grant to try to introduce people with disabilities into the real life of the town. Frank knew just how to do it; he just did it in the same way that he included everybody else. He brought people into the food bank, and the Bible study group, and the YMCA fund drive, and the city celebration, and all of the other things that he had his fingers into — which was most things in town — at the moment.

Gene spoke next. Formally dressed like Frank in a good suit, his pin-striped, Gene looked like a successful corporate salesman of some kind, which it turned out was precisely what he once was. Then he fell on some hard times, and as things would have it, ended up at the food bank talking to Frank. Gene, the successfully dressed businessman, looked at the group and started unexpectedly talking about his great love for Frank; how what motivated him was how much he loved him and admired what he did for the town, how much he brought out in the people around him, how much Christian love he had in his heart. How he knew how to draw people in and get people to pitch in and care for each other.

Gene talked about how he had come to know people with disabilities through the grant project, and how he had realized that the business of acceptance and integration was all wrong; that what was really true was that these people contained, like everyone else, great attributes that were needed. Albert, for instance was the one person to bring up how bossy people were getting in the tension before the food bank opened for the week, giving Frank an excuse to bring up the topic of working together and harmony at the pre-opening prayer meeting. Albert was the one who spotted the air leak where all the heat was going because the weatherstripping was missing under the door; he was the only person sitting down low enough, in his wheelchair, to see it. "Everybody is rushing around these days," Gene went on, growing impassioned. "Nobody has any time to see anything. But these people have spent a thousand hours sitting and watching for every hour you or I have spent. They *see* things!"

For the rest of the day, as people told what they were doing with their little grants in their communities, Beth was kept busy making drawings about all of the ways people were discovering to do essentially the same thing. A neatly dressed young man in a wheelchair told about their leadership seminars to get people in disabilities introduced into business and public life, and how the "Leadership Lancaster" group, in which the future leaders of the community were developed, now always had one person with a disability sponsored by the Chamber of Commerce. Two volunteer centers contributed their efforts to match what people with disabilities had to offer with volunteer jobs that needed doing in their communities. When one group noted that the accessibility of volunteer sites was a problem, the person from the other group showed how they had put together a volunteer "accessibility team" who, when such a problem arose, took contributed materials and just went out and made the place accessible! Good grief!, I thought. While advocacy groups meet again and again to pursue accessibility strategy, while legislation and "system advocacy" is plotted (all useful things to do, in their own way), while places like Developmental Disabilities Councils fund needs surveys for hundreds of thousands of dollars, these folks are too unsophisticated to know the problem is so complex. They just go out and do it.

As group after group talked during the day, I pictured what was going on in their towns in the energy around them. I thought of the scores of people whom these leaders represented who were no longer sitting someplace watching but who were out somewhere doing important things. They had friends, they were visible, and they were adding, as Gene had so eloquently expressed it, to the life of their towns. Beth led us on in exploration: what were all of the project's similarities? She listed them in green magic marker. Everybody liked to tell stories. They couldn't say no when people asked for help. They were enthusiastic. The list went on. Next to it sat another list, ready and headed in the color red. It said: "What are our differences?" Somehow we never got to that, although differences there certainly were. It just never came up in conversation. Differences didn't seem important.

Finally Mark Friedman, a veteran companion of hundreds and hundreds of advocacy meetings, of planning meetings, of government meetings over the years, a person like me a little weary of the constant battles and bickering, rose to go. "I just want to say before I have to leave," he said, kind of wonderingly, "that this is the only completely positive meeting I have been to in a lot of years."

I thought, looking around the room, that this whole roomful of effort, ten grantees, probably added up to only $125,000. In a grant-making organization like ours, this was the size of many single grants.

After dropping off people at the airport I went home and got my bicycle, riding out along the park by the river, past the new island ballpark, and up to the bluff overlooking my little city and the river, where I go to think. It is my favorite view. From up there the broad river, dotted with islands, flows down from the cut in the mountains. Sometimes there is fog, and it looks like a Japanese painting. Across the river the buildings of the city nestle tightly around the dome of the Capitol. It reminded me of the Duomo in Florence as seen from the hills above the city. Each is a city that has some identity, some compactness, some feeling of human scale, although the walls of Florence were ancient brick and those of my city, freeways. I thought of the people whom I had met today, and imagined ten little cities like my own in which this tiny ferment of imagination and growth was taking place quietly within them.

After six or seven years of difficult work this, then, was something to show. These projects and their cousins whom they had not yet met: the five citizen advocacy offices, linking up people in their towns from Philadelphia to Beaver; the three cooperative housing ventures, connecting people with and without disabilities together to share homes, instead of having one of them go into nursing homes, or group homes, or intermediate care facilities, or maybe even the street. I thought of the project to discern the natural safeguards of healthy communities, as an alternative to regulatory control of the safety of people with disabilities. I thought of the seventy children with disabilities who had been adopted, of the hundreds of people who had found real jobs, of the scores beginning to be connected for the first time with one other person and with their communities. I thought of all of the leaders who were growing and emerging in these projects, who were finding through them the same media to take the measure of their powers that my own projects — certainly including this current one — had offered to me. Leaders — leaders with disabilities, now — were growing; the next generation of people to be city selectmen, or mayors, or the wise old lady on the block, or the mother who knew how to help the family next door with a child in trouble. The person with a disability, someday, to take my current job. It was all happening; it was all underway. Even if all of the funding disappeared tomorrow, even if all of the projects disappeared back into the primordial soup from which such associational entities are constantly emerging and disappearing, something had happened in the lives of people. If we could keep the support and the protection and the encouragement going, it would just keep growing and multiplying even more, and each project would have another six months, or a year, or maybe even three, to grow and create and thrive and try to change the world.

Perhaps the world itself was having a bit of a change of heart, reflected in part in the changes being slowly wrought by the "askers"

I had seen. What was it that Laurens van der Post had to say about how change takes place?

> "For that was how all real change began; a change of position in some lone, inexperienced and suffering heart...not in great collective resolutions and movements and consensus of established opinion. Only one heart had to find its own true position and travel on from there and all the rest would follow, for no matter how isolated the *one* felt himself to be, in the deeps of life all were united and no one could move accurately without ultimately moving with it; just as no star could make a change of course without all the others keeping station with it." [1974, p.304]

Was this the meaning, the reason, for continuing with such challenging and difficult work?

Continuing

> "...the Utopian dreams of social justice...are, in spite of their impracticality and non-adaptation to present environmental conditions, analogous to the saint's belief in an existent kingdom of heaven. They help to break the edge of the general reign of hardness, and are slow leavens of a better order."
>
> — William James

Anything good in society that you seem to be doing, the activist Byron Kennard once stated, is not your doing. It is society itself which is trying to bring the change about. You are only clearing away the obstacles to such a change taking place. Clearing away obstacles is a good role. One is part of a brotherhood of "small is beautiful" — the organic gardeners, the solar energy people, the environmentalists, the Franks and the Genes and the grandmothers and the organizers of babysitting cooperatives — the thousands of people pursuing roles of which this work in the disability field is merely kin in a trend of much larger significance. It is nice to have such a seemingly good and useful role in the world. As the world of technological man races headlong towards the abyss, it is good to see that countertrends within the onrushing forces exist, are growing, are spreading. It is that, there is no doubt, which will save us, if anything does this time. And even if it doesn't, these ideas and efforts must be seeds for some future, someday. Thoughts and ideas do not die, even with people, even with the land.

The true significance of any work like this cannot really be known at the time that it is being pursued. Those involved in the social unfolding of what they believe to be a conceptual revolution have no proof that such a conceptual revolution really will in fact occur. History is littered with thousands of false starts. You can always be wrong. There is always risk. It is like any other art: you have only your reason and your intuition. You learn to trust in them and try not to worry too much about the outcome, knowing that it is most important to simply keep your action true.

"The goal of social action," as Sarason once pointed out, "is not to produce once-and-for-all solutions in the scientific sense but to stir the waters of change, hoping and sometimes praying that more good than harm will follow..." The theory and action which I have written about in these pages represent a stirring of tendencies in the developmental disabilities field and in the world at large, both of which seem poised on the edge of great change. There is much to be worried about, but much to be hopeful for. Will a conceptual revolution in the way that we think about human beings with needs take place? Will our social approaches re-vision themselves in such a way that people with disabilities will truly thrive? Are we right or are we wrong? Continuing our efforts with full heart, we can only hope that we are right.

I have spoken of our current world in the metaphor of a river: professional services on the near side where I pursue my daily work, community on the far side in the free space where people may flourish. We are crossing that river. A few small boats at a time, perhaps, but the far shore is no longer a *terra incognita* to us. That our passage is a metaphorical one makes it no less challenging a journey. In this journey, many of us may have to rethink our own conventional roles in support of the people whom it is our calling to help.

There is a Zen koan, one of those "unanswerable" meditational questions like "What is the sound of one hand clapping," in this somewhere. It addresses, somehow, a bit of the personal dilemma I have felt in all of this, along with some of my friends and colleagues in similar roles. I have been working, writing, about the far side of the river, the side of community. Yet my work has taken place not there but here, on the near side of the river, the bureaucratic side. The contrast has been great and often uncomfortable, but one can learn a lot from such a rich dilemma.

The koan is this:

"What are you doing on the wrong side of the river?"

Perhaps this book is a meditation on that question.

Endnotes

1.   As this book was going to press, I learned from Christian Marzahn of his interesting historical thesis that all societies form "drug cultures" around the use of drugs. These drug cultures, he believes, act in some ways as self-limiting mechanisms on drug use. One example is the set of implicit social expectations

which moderate alcohol intake at cocktail parties. One is to drink, but one is not to become drunk.

Suppression of "drug cultures" by governmental campaigns may thus actually reduce social resistance by eliminating natural social mechanisms of resistance. This may be a parallel example of the dynamics of social vulnerability discussed in Chapter 10.

2. In the professional literature, which is slower to respond, one can take the publication of an article by Wolfensberger in the journal *Mental Retardation* entitled "Common Assets of Mentally Retarded Persons" (1988) as a similarly significant event.

3. Readers are urged to read Sarason's full article, "And What is the Public Interest?" (1986).

Rules for Funding Social Change for People with Disabilities

David B. Schwartz & Mark Friedman

Over the past six or so years the Pennsylvania Developmental Disabilities Planning Council has given out grants for a total of about fifteen million dollars. As participants in that process, the two of us have had an unusual opportunity to see what projects work and don't work, and maybe even why. Based upon this experience we offer the following observations or "Rules for Funding Social Change."

Rule 1: Leadership is Everything

A small proportion of all grants really result in an outstanding success; a positive change in the lives of people with disabilities. Projects which truly bring about social change share one thing in common: they have an unusually talented project leader. The importance of other factors is minor in comparison.

One of the Council's most successful grants supported an effort to pass an attendant care law through grass-roots organizing. This small advocacy effort stimulated the creation of millions of dollars in new state-funded services. The staff leader of the project was a talented organizer named Bob Garrett. From this success the Council realized that funding a grass-roots effort to organize for change was more effective than funding model service projects to demonstrate that the change was feasible. We called our new discovery "the Bob Garrett model." We tried to replicate it on a bigger scale with a larger issue. It didn't work.

Corollary A: There Are No Models, Only People, or "The Bob Garrett Model Fallacy"

Our new replicated model, we discovered with some embarrassment upon its failure, had a serious flaw. *It was this: to make the Bob Garrett model work, you had to have Bob Garrett.* Or, if not Bob Garrett himself, then you needed somebody equal to Bob Garrett in skill. In which case it's not the Bob Garrett model anymore, but the whoever-it-is model which, because it can't be replicated by anybody else anywhere else, is no longer a model either.

Although we fund a lot of alleged "models," we have noticed that in the case of true models (stellar projects causing social change), there is an unconscious transfer in the way that we begin to think of and speak of the project. Rather than calling it the "Rehabilitation Institute's STAR Project" we start referring to the project by the leader's name, as in "Susan Maczka's Project," "Sharon Gretz's Project," "Jim Vagnoni's Project," etc. Often in fact we have to think for a minute to recall the project's original name.

Corollary B: Since There Are No Models, You Can't Replicate One

If Rule #1 and Corollary A hold, then the really pertinent question to consider in deciding whether to make a grant is whether a talented or potentially talented leader is involved in it. Since we are giving out taxpayers' money through a vast and arcane bureaucracy, however, it is necessary to conduct the approval ritual of RFP (Request for Proposals) issuance, proposal writing, and scoring in absolutely proper (and even in meticulous) fashion. This is important because: (1) it is the only way you will be permitted to do it, (2) it protects against the corruption that will inevitably creep into the giving out of public money over the long term without such safeguards, and (3) it gives you reasons (like scores) to explain to unsuccessful applicants why they didn't get any money from you, and who find therein a reassuringly fair (and it is) process.

In addition, (4) if one is going about funding social projects that are likely to be perceived as "soft" by some people, it is essential that your procedures are exemplary, even in comparison to those of organizations dealing in "hard/measurable outcome" projects. The organization with which we are involved, for instance, has developed some of the most rigorous and careful grant selection procedures for social services in state government. Neither the Council Executive Director nor the Chairperson, for example, ever participates in proposal selection meetings, reads the proposals before they are selected by the impartial committee, or even goes into the meeting rooms. Complex scoring checklists are completed. Numerous other safeguards ensure that proposers who are turned down find the process fair, even if the decision was not to their liking.

One should not, however, confuse properly carried out selection rituals with what common sense and experience tells you actually predicts grant performance. That is something else entirely. It requires leadership, and conditions for its support.

Corollary C: Leadership Development Is Everything

If the most essential element of social change is leadership, then for more and better social change you need more and better leaders. Leaders, to the best of anyone's knowledge, are not replicated, trained, or even developed. Potential leaders are arising all of the time in society, but few seem to develop to maturity. Often socialization in traditional service settings seems to seriously impede their development.

There are a number of known educational approaches which seem to nurture leaders or, stated another way, approaches which leaders tend to be drawn to and thrive upon. Teachers who help leaders develop themselves are one key element in nurturing effective leadership. A second key element is a project. Leaders, being activists, learn best on the job. Part of a conscious approach to nurturing leadership is therefore having meaningful projects for developing leaders to develop through. These projects can be quite small in financial terms. Giving out grants to leaders and potential leaders thus not only "gets the job done" (Corollaries A & B) but "feeds the source" from which change comes (Corollary C).

Rule 2: The Real Action
Is Where Everyone Thinks It Isn't
(Friedman's Rule)

Attention of Developmental Disabilities Councils, advocates, and other funders is often focused on big, important projects that cost a lot of money. These usually express an attempt at "systems change," frequently through the traditional "study - model project - evaluation - replication" model. There are always many people and organizations eager to pursue such grants. They are the highly visible grant projects that councils undertake.

Real change, however, is more likely to be found around small informal projects developed by a visionary leader on the margins of established practice. Such projects focus on the situation of specific people and families: project leaders can always describe the effect of the project by its effect on individuals by name.

Large project grants for system change or service development are what people understand. This is where most attention is thus focused. The real action, however, is with the small projects that receive less attention.

The Inverse Effect Corollary

The impact of a grant is thus frequently inversely proportional to its size. Since large expensive projects tend to draw a lot of attention, they rarely can be expected to challenge currently prevailing conceptions by doing anything which might promise to change things too radically. Big projects, as well, invariably involve "experts," in the presence of whom ordinary people (including members of a funding Council) tend to grow shy and reluctant to ask questions that might seem unsophisticated and uninformed, like "What have you done with our million dollars, here, anyway?"

Rule 3: Successful Social Change Efforts Enlist Allies in the Cause

Leaders of successful efforts involve others in their projects. Bob Peppel, Superintendent of Chapman Dam State Park, enlisted the support of local VFWs, service clubs, and others over the years in his campaign to make his park accessible. Local groups even contributed money and labor. They not only donated the money to build an accessible fishing dock and picnic area and built it as a work project, but they come out periodically to help people fish, clean their fish and grill it out for them when groups come from the VA hospital. Traditional "service development" grant projects that do not enlist others expire, usually without a lasting impression, when the external grant runs out. They have provided everything to the community themselves, and have failed to build the capacity of local groups.

Rule 4: Systems Don't Change: People Do

Real change involves direct personal contact between people with disabilities and those without them. This change may take place for both an infant with a handicap and her adoptive parents, a worker with a disability and an employer, a person at risk and a citizen advocate, etc. Each change in the experience of two or more people changes their attitudes, their lives or, one might say, their "biographies." A saying attributed to Jerome Miller goes "change enough biographies and you will change a system."

This is the opposite of the way that we usually think. It is a "trickle-up" theory of social change rather than a "trickle-down" one. It is a perspective which is less interested in "systems change" than world change.

Rule 5: John McKnight Was Right

John McKnight says that if you ask people in communities to care for people with disabilities they generally will. He has outlined some rules for asking. We add to them the following:

Corollary A: Asking Will Be Most Successful If It Is Done
When the Person Being Asked Is On His or Her "Home Ground."

If you walk up to a person on the street and ask them to be involved in the life a person with a disability, they will shy away. Yet when Speaking for Ourselves, a self-advocacy group, met with the park rangers of the Independence Mall National Park to suggest ways of making the park more accessible to people with handicaps, the rangers welcomed it. Since part of doing a good job as a ranger involves soliciting suggestions from the public, seeking and receiving public opinion on park usage was a familiar and comfortable role for them. It's what rangers *do*, and people with disabilities were just helping them to do their jobs better.

When we wrote an RFP to make state parks more accessible, we thus included a requirement that the park superintendent wishing to apply for money consult with any person who uses a wheelchair regarding the proposed work to be done on the park. They had to put the name and telephone number of this person on their application forms. Aside from rooting the park accessibility work to the actual needs of people with disabilities, this structured one way for a person with a disability to meet a park superintendent while the latter was in a comfortable role. We imagined a superintendent coming home and saying "Martha — You know anybody that uses a wheelchair? How about at the church? I *need* one to be able to get this grant." Our office received a lot of calls asking for names of people who use wheelchairs from park superintendents all over the state.

A year later the state parks department, acting on their own, surprised us by announcing their new policy of requiring every state park to have a local advisory committee — mandating that at least one member had to be a person with a disability.

Corollary B: Some People Will Reject
People With Disabilities When Asked

Perhaps you thought that the world was populated exclusively with people eager to come to the aid of their fellow man, or woman? Rejection, of course, will occur frequently. The "asker" must be prepared to encounter this. Such rejection is the asker's responsibility, and is not to be passed on to the person he or she is asking on behalf of. If they had not been injured by rejection in the past, they would still be asking on their own. As an asker, you will share in a small taste of this experience.

Rule 6: Social Visionaries Can't (Or Won't) Add

If you give funds to a really dynamic leader of social change, be prepared for the paperwork to be late. Social activists are rarely interested in paperwork, while those interested in paperwork are seldom interested in social action. Occasionally you will have the good fortune to encounter someone who can lead a visionary project and balance the books too. But generally, when you get in the business of funding small activist projects, be ready also to give them lots of help filling out the forms. That's not what they went to school (or wherever) to learn how to do.

If you want to reach real community activists and groups, you often need an intermediary to "detoxify" your money. If the little neighborhood group really learns how to fill out and add up all of the bureaucratic forms that come with your funding, they will turn into a little bit of a bureaucracy just in the process of talking with you. A good local human service organization with vision and a tolerance for community "messiness" can often translate and prevent your bureaucratic procedures from spreading to others.

Rule 7: To Regenerate Community, a Certain Minimal Level of Community Must Already Exist

Regeneration efforts work through involving and connecting people to help community grow and flourish. This is obviously easier to do when some level of community exists. It is easier to grow a garden on rich country soil than in an abandoned lot in the South Bronx. For this reason some people incorrectly believe that regeneration or "connection" projects work only in rural areas and not in cities. This misses the point. A rural town which has deteriorated and is no longer a real community may be much more challenging a place to help connect people with disabilities than an urban neighborhood that still is one. If a community has so deteriorated that no "feel" of community still remains, it may be for all practical purposes impossible to start a successful project in that area.

One key exception should, however, be noted. Nobody would try to grow a garden on a topsoil-stripped, broken-glass strewn, vacant lot — except somebody who lived on that block and called it their home. Every once in a while you will read a human interest story in the paper about some genius with a green thumb who has grown a bountiful garden where everybody agreed it couldn't be done. It is the same with community regeneration. Don't dismiss what a charismatic community leader might do against all odds. If you meet one of these, fund him or her. Forget about soil testing.

Rule 8: Those Who Fund Social Activists are "Patrons of the Arts"

Seymour Sarason once called the creators of new settings "artists of the social fabric." Their canvas is like the ever-flowing surface of a river: constantly changing, and gone in an instant.

Social activists, like artists, need patrons to supply money for materials so they don't have to paint houses to feed themselves. Behind every leader of social change living on rice and beans and working out of some storefront are some funders finding them money. As an industrialist supporter of Gandhi is once supposed to have said, "It takes a lot of money to keep Gandhi poor."

Rule 9: The Quality of an RFP is Inversely Proportional to the Time Spent in Reviewing and Revising It Before It Is Issued (Knowlton's Rule)

The more people who review a Request for Proposals in the system, and the more revisions and amendments are made by various offices, the more watered-down the original idea will become. If the document is thoroughly revised by all of the offices remotely concerned, you can be sure that the RFP will be sufficiently compromised so that it is assured that nothing will happen when the grant is finally given out.

Rule 10: The Iannuzzi Rule of Project Comprehensibility

Jerome Iannuzzi is a member of the Council who represents a self-advocacy group. He is a man of considerable common sense. If you can't explain your proposed RFP idea to Jerome so that he can reliably explain it to somebody else, the idea is not worth doing.

Rule 11: Gardening Entails Weeding

If you are going to "plant a lot of seeds" for social change, some of those seeds (grant projects) will expire, not come up right, or otherwise not grow correctly. Plants or projects that can't hold themselves up can't be propped up forever. If you take on the responsibility of planting seeds, you have to have the willingness to do the unpleasant job of weeding, and you have to pull the plug on unsuccessful grantees. Although you may wish to be kind in artificially keeping alive an association or effort which is not thriving or drawing natural or local support, you may be maintaining an obstacle to action which natural social processes might replace if it were not for you.

There are also lots of infections out there in the world and it is always possible that one of your little projects may catch a lethal bug. We invited a proposal from a poetry group for a project to help people with disabilities write poetry, for instance, that came in with a provision for "pre- and post-" attitude testing to demonstrate the efficacy of the intervention. ("But we put it in for you," they protested, when we called. "I know," we replied. "Take it out. Send us a book of poetry.") Or a community "bridgebuilder" may come down with a stubborn case of social work-itis and have to be quarantined. In gardening, weeding is not optional.

Rule 12: Need Surveys are Misdirected Attention

Need surveys, as John McKnight once said, are "inventories of emptiness — you count up enough emptiness and you can trade it in on a program." They measure the deficiencies of communities rather than their capacities. Not only are they usually the wrong way to start thinking about what needs to be done, but they are extremely expensive if done "right," and outdated as soon as you do anything about what you have measured, anyway.

You don't need need surveys to figure out what to do; real needs, as Wolfensberger once noted, "are crying to heaven!" There are some people, however, he goes on to say, who will only be convinced by numbers to allocate resources. In these cases, he advises, use "junk data" — rough, easily collected evidence of what you are concerned about (385 people with disabilities in our county are unemployed) which lacks the elegance of "proper" research but which usually works for the purpose just as well.

Rule 13: Evaluation is Simpler Than You May Have Been Told

To find out if a project is having an impact: 1) go and see it; (2) if there are simple measurable outcomes which can be determined by questions (how many children have been adopted, or how many people employed, and in what kinds of jobs, at what pay) find out what they are; or (3) hire a knowledgeable evaluator to go out after the project is over to see what happened.

Learn the questions to be asked. If you don't know the questions, keep asking until you do. If you can't get simple answers to your questions, something is seriously wrong.

If the outcomes for the project are hard to determine, ask the people themselves what they accomplished. Probe their answers. Bear in mind that what is accomplished and worthwhile is sometimes different from what you started out to do. Remember that when you have a really successful project, the people doing it will think that it's no big deal and will wonder why *you* do.

On university campuses, astute grounds superintendents know that if you want to put the sidewalks between new buildings in the right place, you should wait and see where people wear paths in the grass. Then put the sidewalks there. If you put them where you think they should go, you will probably put them in the wrong place. Thus it's usually better to sow seeds and then go and see what has come up than to build in a quantitative "outcome evaluation" from the start with lots of forms for projects to fill out.

If, on the other hand, you really think that you need a good "outcome evaluation" for your grants, hire a big consulting firm or research institute. They probably need to buy a new computer anyway.[1]

Rule 14: Keep Expectations Reasonable

As projects experience success, funders' expectations can increase to the point that everyone may someday decide that grantees are falling short of expectations, even though expectations were supposed to be limited to begin with. Expectations must be managed or they will become unmanageable. If citizen advocacy works, after all, why isn't there an advocate by now for five hundred people, or a thousand, or for everybody who used to live at Pennhurst State School?

Rule 15: You Have to Accept a Glacial Sense of Time in Order Not to Lose Heart. (Pierce's Law)

If you need to see immediate results, you're in the wrong line of work.

Rule 16: Keep Yourself Honest

Finding and staying honest is, finally, the hardest thing to do of all. To ensure frequent encounters with honesty in this work, it is absolutely essential to have one or more friends who are unafraid to ask you hard questions and who confront you with bitter truths that you would really rather not see. You are unlikely to hear such truths from, for instance, your grantees, nice truthful people though they may be.

By way of illustration: I was drifting off to sleep in a little room at a convent retreat center a few years ago when the door opened and three of my closest friends and most fearless critics walked in and all plopped themselves on the bed. After pausing to admire my red flannel pajamas, they announced: "O.K., David. This is your evaluation. You've been in Pennsylvania three years. Your organization has spent millions of dollars. Now, tell us. What have you accomplished for people with disabilities with all that time and money?"

It had finally happened. An accounting was due. They waited. Thinking carefully, I tentatively gave my answer.

"Let's see. A hundred and ten people have gotten supported jobs. Probably half of those, maybe, are good ones?"

The evaluation team nodded. Good. Acceptable.

"Adoption. Fifty-five children with disabilities in new homes?"

Slowly: three considered nods.

"Oh, and citizen advocacy. Thirty-five new relationships. How about that?"

Yes, that was good. Now, was that it?

I thought for a moment. "Well, I guess so, to speak of."

"That's it ?"

A nod.

"How much money?"

I told them. It seemed like a lot.

There was a silence.

The evaluators, my three friends, looked at each other. Finally they nodded together. Acceptable. They were satisfied. The evaluation had been passed. Try another year. Keep on working. They filed out, flipping the lights back off on the way out, leaving me to reflect upon reality in the darkness of my convent cell. As the last of them grasped the doorknob, he tossed off a final comment over his shoulder. "Oh, "he said, "but don't get a big head about it."

Then the door clicked shut.

Endnotes

1.   Fortunately, there are some notable exceptions to this. There are many cases in which carefully designed evaluative studies are extremely useful and sometimes essential, and when one needs one, a good researcher is invaluable. What is important is to decide precisely when you need this level of evaluative sophistication to find out something significant. Like most powerful techniques, this is best if not overused.

References

Altman, L.K. (1990, February 10). Changes in Medicine Bring Pain to Healing Profession. *New York Times*.

Balfour, E.B. (1943). *The Living Soil: Evidence of the Importance to Human Health of Soil Vitality, with Special Reference to National Planning*. London: Faber & Faber.

Berger, P.L. and Neuhaus, R.J. (1977). *To Empower People: The Role of Mediating Structures in Public Policy*. Washington DC: American Enterprise Institute.

Blatt, B. (1966). *Christmas in Purgatory: A Photographic Essay on Mental Retardation*. Boston: Allyn & Bacon.

Blatt, B. (1970). *Exodus From Pandemonium: Human Abuse and a Reformation of Public Policy*. Boston: Allyn and Bacon.

Blatt, B. (1987). *The Conquest of Mental Retardation*. Austin: PRO-ED.

Blatt, B. (1981). *In and Out of Mental Retardation: Essays on Educability, Disability, and Human Policy*. Baltimore: University Park Press.

Boggs, E.M. (1972). Federal Legislation 1966-1971. in Wortis, J. (Ed.) *Mental Retardation, an Annual Review*, vol.iv.. New York: Grune & Stratton.

Boggs, E.M. (1977). State Developmental Disabilities Planning Councils: Are They Worth Their Keep? *State Government*, 50(4), 238-245.

Boggs, E.M. (1990). Personal communication.

Broad, W.J. (1989, May 30). At Conference On Cold Fusion, The Verdict is Negative. *New York Times*.

Buck, J.A. and Sprague, R.L. (1989). Psychotropic Medication of Mentally Retarded Residents in Community Long-Term Care Facilities. *American Journal on Mental Retardation*, 93(6), 618-623.

Caplan, R.B. (1969). *Psychiatry and the Community in Nineteenth-Century America: The Recurring Concern with the Environment in the Prevention and Treatment of Mental Illness*. New York: Basic Books.

Capra, F. (1982). "Forword" in Dossey, L. *Space, Time, and Medicine*. Boulder: Shambhala.

Center for Urban Affairs and Policy Research and Department of Rehabilitation Services, State of Illinois. (1988). *Getting Connected: How to Find Out About Groups and Organizations in Your Neighborhood*. Evanston, IL: Center for Urban Affairs and Policy Research, Northwestern University.

Conroy, J., & Feinstein, C. (1988). *The Philadelphia Community Residence Service System: Indicators of Quality*. Unpublished report, Temple University, Philadelphia.

Cowen, E.L. (1982). Help is Where You Find It: Four Informal Helping Groups. *American Psychologist*, 37(4), 385-395.

Department of Human Services, Office of Human Development Services, Developmental Disabilities Program. (1984, March 27). Final Rule. *Federal Register*, 49(60).

Deutsch, A. (1949). *The Mentally Ill in America: A History of Their Care and Treatment from Colonial Times* (2nd ed.). New York: Columbia University Press.

Dubos, R.J. (1955). Second Thoughts on the Germ Theory. *Scientific American*, 192(5), 31-35.

Dyson, F. (1979). *Disturbing the Universe*. New York: Harper and Row.

Edwards, G., & Snyder, D.P. (1988, Spring). An Assessment: Have Things Changed? Families and the Future: Sustaining the Social Base of Our Economic Enterprise. *National Council of Family Relations Newsletter*.

Fallows, J. (1985, December). The Case Against Credentialism. *Atlantic*, 49-67.

Ferguson, D.,& Ferguson, P. (1988). The New Victors: A Progressive Policy Analysis of Work Reform for People With Very Severe Handicaps. *Mental Retardation*, 24(6), 331-338.

Fiene, R. (1985, Spring). Measuring the Effectiveness of Regulations. *New England Journal of Human Services*.

Foucault, M. (1973). *Madness and Civilization: A History of Insanity in the Age of Reason*. New York: Vintage.

Furey, E.M., & Haber, M. (1989). Protecting Adults With Mental Retardation: A Model Statute. *Mental Retardation*, 27(3), 135-140.

Goldenberg, I.I. (1971). *Build Me a Mountain: Youth, Poverty, and the Creation of New Settings*. Cambridge, MA: MIT Press.

Goldman, H., & Meyers, D. (1988, June 23). Search for DHS Boss Began Months Ago. *The Philadelphia Inquirer*, 3B.

Gowdey, C.W., Zarfas, D.E., & Phipps, S. (1987). Audit of Psychoactive Drug Prescriptions in Group Homes. *Mental Retardation*, 25(6), 331-334.

Graney, B. (1979). Hervey Backus Wilbur and the Evolution of Policies Toward Mentally Retarded People. Doctoral dissertation, Syracuse University, Syracuse, NY.

Groce, N.E. (1985). *Everybody Here Spoke Sign Language: Hereditary Deafness on Martha's Vineyard*. Cambridge, MA: Harvard University Press.

Hawken, Paul. (1989, Jan-Feb). Entrepreneurs: The Real Cultural Revolutionaries. *Utne Reader*.

Illich, Ivan. (1976). *Medical Nemesis: The Expropriation of Health*. New York: Random House.

July Almanac. (1989, July). *Atlantic.*

Kallenback, D. and Lyons, A. (1989). *Government Spending for the Poor in Cook County, Illinois: Can We Do Better?* Evanston, IL: Center for Urban Affairs and Policy Studies, Northwestern University.

Kendrick, M. (1988). Romantization of Community. Unpublished manuscript.

Keneally, T. (1983). *Schindler's List.* New York: Penguin.

Kennard, B. (1982). *Nothing Can be Done, Everything is Possible.* Andover, MA: Brick House.

Kharasch, R.N. (1973). *The Institutional Imperative: How to Understand the United States and Other Bulky Objects.* New York: Charterhouse.

Kolbert, E. (1989, June 8). Who Wants New Prisons? In New York, All of Upstate. *New York Times.*

Kriegman, D. and Knight, C. (1988). Social Evolution, Psychoanalysis, and Human Nature. *Social Policy*, 19(2), 49-55.

Kuhn, T.S. (1962). *The Structure of Scientific Revolutions.* Chicago: University of Chicago Press.

La Leche League. (1963). *The Womanly Art of Breastfeeding* (revised). Franklin Park, IL: La Leche League.

Lemann, N. (1989, January). The Unfinished War. *Atlantic*, 263(1), 52-68.

Lerner, H.J. (1972). *New York Association for Retarded Children and New York State Government, 1948-1968.* New York: New York State Association for Retarded Children.

McCord, W.T. (1982). From Theory to Reality: Obstacles to the Implementation of the Normalization Principle in Human Services. *Mental Retardation*, 20(6), 247-253.

McCord, W.T., & Marshall, W. (1987). Missing the Mark: Normalization as Technology. In Schwartz, D.B., McKnight, J., and Kendrick, M. (Eds.). *A Story That I Heard: A Compendium of Stories, Essays and Poetry About People With Disabilities and American Life.* Harrisburg, PA: Pennsylvania Developmental Disabilities Planning Council.

McKnight, J. (1977). The Professional Service Business. *Social Policy*, 8(3).

McKnight, J. (1985). John Deere and the Bereavement Counselor. *Institutions, Etc.*, 8(2), 17-23.

McKnight, J. (1987). Regenerating Community. *Social Policy*, 17(3), 54-58.

McKnight, J. (1989, Jan-Feb). Why "Servanthood" is Bad. *The Other Side*, 38-41.

McNally, R.J. (1988). Neuroleptic Malignant Syndrome in a Man With Mental Retardation. *Mental Retardation*, 26(6), 385-386.

Molella, A.P. (1989, Spring/Summer). America's Golden Age: An Interview with Thomas P. Hughes. *American Heritage Invention & Technology*, 22.

Nowell, N., Baker, D., & Conroy, J. (1989). *The Provision of Community Medical Care in Philadelphia and Northeastern Pennsylvania for People Who Live in Community Living Arrangements and With Their Families*. Philadelphia: Report to the Pew Charitable Trusts.

O'Brien, J., & Wolfensberger, W. (1978). *CAPE: Citizen Advocacy Program Evaluation*. Toronto: National Institute on Mental Retardation.

O'Brien, J. (1987). Embracing Ignorance, Error, and Fallibility: Competencies for Leadership of Effective Services. In Taylor, S. J., et al., *Community Integration for People with Severe Disabilities*. New York: Teacher's College Press.

O'Brien, J. (1987). *Learning from Citizen Advocacy Programs*. Atlanta: Georgia Advocacy Office.

Oldenburg, R. (1989). *The Great Good Place: Cafes, Coffee Shops, Community Centers, Beauty Parlors, General Stores, Bars, Hangouts, and How They Get You Through the Day*. New York: Paragon.

Oliner, S.P., & Oliner, P.M. (1988). *The Altruistic Personality: Rescuers of Jews in Nazi Europe*. New York: Free Press.

Pennsylvania Association of Resources for the Retarded. (1988). Recruitment and Retention Crisis in Community Mental Health and Mental Retardation Programs. *Privately Speaking*, 7(1).

People First of California. (1984). *Surviving In the System: Mental Retardation and the Retarding Environment*. Sacramento: California State Council on Developmental Disabilities.

Perske, R. (1972). The Dignity of Risk and the Mentally Retarded. *Mental Retardation*, 10(1).

Perske, R. (1980). *New Life in the Neighborhood*. Nashville: Abingdon.

Perske, R., & Perske, M. (1988). *Circles of Friends: People With Disabilities and Their Friends Enrich the Lives of One Another*. Nashville: Abingdon.

Perske, R. (1987). Attitudes, Acceptance, and Awareness: The Changing View Toward Persons with Down Syndrome. In Pueschel, et al., *New Perspectives on Down Syndrome*. Baltimore: Brookes.

Pfeiffer, E. (1942, Spring). Money, and Working for the Sake of Work; an Aspect of Rudolf Steiner's Social Impulse. *The Forerunner*.

Pietzner, C. (1983). *Who Was Kaspar Hauser?* Edinburgh: Floris Books.

Sacks, O. (1986, March 27). *Mysteries of the Deaf*. New York Review of Books.

Sacks, O. (1988). The Divine Curse. *Life*, 94.

Sarason, S.B. (1959). *Psychological Problems in Mental Deficiency*, (3rd ed.). New York: Harper.

Sarason, S.B. (1972). *The Creation of Settings and the Future Societies*. San Francisco: Jossey-Bass. Reprinted Cambridge, MA: Brookline, 1988.

Sarason, S.B. (1977). *The Psychological Sense of Community: Prospects for a Community Psychology*. San Francisco: Jossey-Bass. Reprinted Cambridge, MA: Brookline, 1988.

Sarason, S.B., & Doris, J. (1979). *Educational Handicap, Public Policy, and Social History: A Broadened Perspective on Mental Retardation*. New York: Free Press.

Sarason, S.B. (1985). *Caring and Compassion in Clinical Practice*. San Francisco: Jossey-Bass.

Sarason, S.B. (1986). And What Is the Public Interest? *American Psychologist*, 41(8), 899-905.

Sarason, S.B. (1988). *The Making of An American Psychologist: An Autobiography*. San Francisco: Jossey-Bass.

Sarason, S.B. (1990). Personal Communication.

Schaefer-Simmern, H. (1948). *The Unfolding of Artistic Activity*. Berkeley, CA: University of California Press.

Schumacher, E.F. (1973). *Small Is Beautiful: Economics as if People Mattered*. New York: Perennial.

Schwartz, D.A. (1988, May 10). Letter to Senator Riebman.

Schwartz, D.B. (1983). Quality Assurance in the Asylum. *Quality of Care, New York State Commission on the Quality of Care for the Mentally Disabled*, 6.

Schwartz, D.B., House, R.B., Caruso, G., Adams, N., & Goodwin, W. (1983). *Community Residence Management Simulation*. Ithaca, NY: Cornell University, New York State School of Industrial and Labor Relations, Human Services Administration Program.

Schwartz, D.B. (1988, May/June). What I Saw at the National Conference. *Disability Rag*.

Senate of Pennsylvania. Senate Bill #842, Session of 1987, General Assembly of Pennsylvania.

Sheerenberger, R.C. (1987). *A History of Mental Retardation: A Quarter Century of Promise*. Baltimore: Brookes.

Smull, M.W. (1989). Crisis in the Community. Unpublished report, National Association of State Mental Retardation Program Directors.

Spect, D., & Nagy, M. (1986). *Social Supports Research Project: Report of Findings*. Holyoke, MA: Western Mass. Training Consortium.

232   **Crossing the River**

Spitz, R.A. (1946). Hospitalism: A Follow-up Report on Investigation. *Psychoanalytic Study of the Child*, 2, 113-117.

Stedman, D.J. (1975). The State Planning Council on Mental Retardation. *Mental Retardation*, 23(3).

Stone, E.S. (1982). The Adoption of Handicapped Children: An Exploratory Study. Doctoral dissertation, Yale University, New Haven, CT. (University Microfilms No. 8221755).

Sullivan, W.M. (1982). *Reconstructing Public Philosophy*. Berkley: University of California Press.

Sundram, C.J. (1987, September). Regulation — Have We All Gone Mad? *Quality of Care, New York State Commission of the Quality of Care for the Mentally Disabled*, 6.

Szasz, T. (1978, March 16). Why Do We Fear the Retarded? *Newsday*.

Taylor, S. (1988, May). Some Lessons Learned. *TASH Newsletter, The Association for Persons with Severe Handicaps*, 5.

Taylor, S. (1988). Caught in the Continuum: A Critical Analysis of the Principle of the Least Restrictive Environment. *Journal of the Association for Persons with Severe Handicaps*, 13(1), 41-53.

de Tocqueville, A. (1973). *Democracy in America*. (Translated by Henry Reeve, revised by Francis Bowen, edited by Phillips Bradey.) New York: Alfred Knopf, (1945).

Turnbull, H.R. III, & Brunk, G.L. (1990). Quality of Life and Public Philosophy. In Schalock, R.L. (Ed.), *Quality of Life: Perspective and Issues*. Washington: American Association on Mental Retardation.

US Congress. Public Law 91-517: Developmental Disabilities Services and Facilities Construction Amendments of 1970.

US Congress. Public Law 100-146: The Developmental Disabilities Assistance and Bill of Rights Act Amendments of 1987.

US Congress. (1985). Emerging Trends in Mental Health Care for Adolescents: Hearing Before the Select Committee on Children, Youth, and Families. Washington: US Government Printing Office.

Van der Post, Laurens. (1974). *A Far Off Place*. New York: Harcourt Brace Jovanovich.

Vanier, J. (1979). *Community and Growth: Our Pilgrimage Together*. Toronto: Griffin House.

Vladeck, B. (1980). *Unloving Care: The Nursing Home Tragedy*. New York: Basic Books.

Wieck, C. (1990). Personal communication.

Wikler, L., Wasow, M., and Hatfield, E. (1983). Seeking Strengths in Families of Developmentally Disabled Children. *Social Work*, 28(4), 313-315.

Wolfensberger, W. (1969). Twenty Predictions About the Future of Residential Services in Mental Retardation. *Mental Retardation*, 7(6), 51-54.

Wolfensberger, W., & Menolascino, F. (1970). Reflections on Recent Mental Retardation Developments in Nebraska. I: A New Plan, & II: Implementation to Date. *Mental Retardation*, 8(6), 20-28.

Wolfensberger, W. (1972). *The Principle of Normalization in Human Services*. Toronto: National Institute on Mental Retardation.

Wolfensberger, W., & Zauha, H. (Eds.). (1973). *Citizen Advocacy and Protective Services for the Impaired and Handicapped*. Toronto: National Institute on Mental Retardation.

Wolfensberger, W., & Glenn, L. (1975). *PASS 3*. Toronto: National Institute on Mental Retardation.

Wolfensberger, W. (1975b). Values in the Field of Mental Health as They Bear on Policies of Research and Inhibit Adaptive Human-Service Strategies. In Schoolar, J.C. and Gaitz, C.M. (Eds.). *Research and the Psychiatric Patient*. New York: Brunner/Mazel.

Wolfensberger, W. (1975c). *The Origin and Nature of Our Institutional Models*. Syracuse: Human Policy Press.

Wolfensberger, W. (1977). *A Multi-Component Advocacy/Protection Schema*. Toronto: Canadian Association for the Mentally Retarded.

Wolfensberger, W., & Thomas, S. (1983). *PASSING*. Toronto: National Institute on Mental Retardation.

Wolfensberger, W. (1983b). Social Role Valorization: A Proposed New Term for the Principle of Normalization. *Mental Retardation*, 21, 234-239.

Wolfensberger, W. (1983c). A Brief Reflection on Where We Stand and Where We Are Going in Human Services. *Institutions, Etc.*, 6(3), 20-23.

Wolfensberger, W. (1988). Common Assets of Mentally Retarded People That Are Not Commonly Acknowledged. *Mental Retardation*, 26(2), 63-70.

Wolfensberger, W. (1989). Self-Injurious Behavior, Behavioristic Responses, and Social Role Valorization: A Reply to Mulick and Kedesdy. *Mental Retardation*, 27(3), 181-184.

Wolfensberger, W. (1990). Personal communication.

Woodson, R.L. (1981). *A Summons to Life: Mediating Structures and the Prevention of Youth Crime*. Cambridge: Ballinger.

Yates, J. (1988). The Fallible Community. Unpublished manuscript.

Index